Guide to
Living
Abroad

The Daily Telegraph

Guide to Living Abroad

TWELFTH
EDITION

Michael Furnell
&
Philip Jones

**KOGAN
PAGE**

First published in 1986 entitled *Living and Retiring Abroad*
© Michael Furnell 1986, 1988, 1989, 1990, 1991, 1992
Seventh edition published in 1994 entitled *Living Abroad*
Eighth edition 1995
Ninth edition 1996
Tenth edition 1997
Eleventh edition 1998
Twelfth edition 1999

Kogan Page Limited
120 Pentonville Road
London N1 9JN

The masculine pronoun has been used throughout this book. This stems from a desire to avoid ugly or cumbersome language, and no discrimination, prejudice or bias is intended.

British Library Cataloguing in Publication Data

A CIP record for this book is available from the British Library.

ISBN 0–7494–3095–8

Typeset by Saxon Graphics Ltd, Derby
Printed and bound in Great Britain by Bell & Bain Ltd, Glasgow

Contents

Contents _____

HOW TO ORGANISE YOUR INTERNATIONAL REMOVAL

The first steps you should take are to determine which of your household furniture and personal possessions you wish to take with you to your new home, and which you are going to leave behind, perhaps in storage until you return.

It is often useful to find out something about the kind of property available at your destination. Is it likely to have fitted wardrobes? Do UK electrical appliances work in the country you are moving to? If not can they be adapted and if so how much will this cost? The answers to these kind of questions can help you reach a decision. What is the value of items of furniture at your destination? If the item is expensive to buy new at your destination and the secondhand value in the UK is not good then it makes sense to take it with you. As a general rule furniture that has been purchased within the last five years, and all types of antique furniture are well worth taking with you as their value overseas is often greater than it is here.

When you have decided which items are going with you then it's time to phone your removal company and arrange for their representative to come to your home to survey your household effects. During the survey the representative will compile an inventory of the items that you wish to take with you, assess the packing requirement and estimate the weight and volume of your possessions. The weight and volume will be crucial to the overall price paid and is usually expressed in Cubic Feet/Lbs or Cubic Metres/Kilos.

Once the remover has completed the survey a cost estimate for the removal of your possessions can be prepared.

An international removal is comprised of three important steps. Firstly there is the packing of your possessions (the origin service) which involves carefully ensuring that all items are wrapped in protective materials and all small articles eg glassware, are boxed in sturdy export cartons and cases. For delicate items of furniture, eg a grandfather clock, a special custom built crate may also have to be made. Once the packing has been completed your possessions can then be loaded and for surface transportation this will be either into a removal van or a 20ft or 40ft steel container. For air transportation, and for some surface destinations the loading will be into a wooden case, often referred to as a lift van. A lift van gives additional protection to high value possessions and is constructed so that it can fit neatly inside either a removal van or a steel container.

The second step to be carried out is the transportation which will either be by road, sea or air. The remover will select the most appropriate vehicle, ship or aeroplane according to the route and your final destination.

Once the transportation has been completed and your possessions have arrived at their destination the third step (the destination service) can begin. The remover will, through his colleague at your destination, arrange customs clearance, delivery and unpacking of your effects into your new home.

In other words the reverse of the packing services at origin will take place during the destination service.

Many of the leading international removers are shareholders in OMNI, Overseas Moving Network Incorporated, which is a consortium of the leading removers of the World welded together into a tight knit organisation designed to give high quality service at many worldwide locations. If you choose to move with an OMNI remover then smoothness and quality should be the passowrds of your relocation. John Mason International, with offices in London, Liverpool and Manchester, are one of the leading OMNI members in the United Kingdom.

Introduction

In 1986, when I was invited by Kogan Page to write this book under the original title *Daily Telegraph Guide to Living & Retiring Abroad,* I hoped it might run to two or three editions, but I had no idea that 14 years later I would be revising the book for the 12th edition. It gives me much satisfaction to know that the information which I provide is still needed, and I try very hard to make each edition more useful and informative.

As we approach the 21st century I am very conscious that change is in the air, both in technology and in our way of living.

Already the Euro has been adopted as the currency for 11 of the 15 European Union member countries, although the actual Euro currency notes and coins will not be issued until the year 2002. Meanwhile the countries concerned will continue to use their own currencies for another two years. As the UK has not decided whether to adopt the new money, it seems sensible for this edition of the book not to make any attempt to convert the prices which I quote into the Euro currency. Thus I will still refer to pounds sterling, francs, marks, lire, etc throughout the relevant chapters.

When I first started work on this book, the property market in the UK and the major European countries in the 'sunshine belt' was enjoying a boom in demand for residential property. Then we went through a major depression between 1990 and 1996 when prices of residential property plummeted, both at home and overseas. Consequently many families with mortgages found themselves in a 'negative equity' position. Fortunately, during the past two years the property market has recovered most of its pre-1990 prosperity, and with falling interest rates is likely to enjoy a continuing brisk demand in the next 12 months or so.

As more and more families invest in computers and have the opportunity to surf the Internet, there are greater facilities to find information on a wide variety of subjects, including househunting. This source is being quite widely used when seeking homes for sale or to let in the UK, but not yet for overseas properties. This is probably due to the vast areas that have to be covered to provide a comprehensive selection of available foreign properties, but there is scope for this facility in the future.

Although the pound sterling has weakened a little against some currencies this year, it still maintains favourable exchange rates with many European countries and also with Australia and New Zealand, compared with five years ago. The message therefore is *buy your overseas home now* while current rates are available and before the new euro currency becomes fully operational.

If you are hunting for an overseas home one of the best sources of information is the glossy magazine *Homes Overseas*, which was founded in 1965. Every issue contains a wide variety of data about availability and buying procedures for villas and apartments in many European and other countries. Currently it is published six times a year (price £2.50), and can be obtained by ordering from newsagents, or by post from Blendon Communications, 46 Oxford Street, London W1N 9FJ.

Exhibitions devoted to overseas properties are another useful source of information and provide opportunities for personal discussions with agents and developers specialising in a variety of countries. *Homes Overseas* magazine organises a series of these shows in selected parts of the UK and Ireland including Birmingham, Harrogate, Brighton and Dublin. Several shows by other promoters are also held in the Greater London area. Watch the property columns in the national press for details.

ACKNOWLEDGEMENTS

My special thanks go to many long-standing friends who help to keep me up to date with the changing procedures and policies in the 20 countries that I cover in this book. Without their assistance it would have been nearly impossible to have produced the 12 editions that have appeared so far.

I am pleased to continue my co-operation with my co-author Philip Jones, who is very knowledgeable about France and the United States. For the fifth year running he has written the two chapters on these locations. My gratitude is also due to Blevins Franks International, Chartered Accountants, who have once again contributed the chapter on tax and financial planning.

Michael Furnell
March 1999

Part One:

Before You Go

1 Living Overseas

WORKING OVERSEAS

Many readers of this book may already have obtained a job in an overseas country and thus have a reliable source of information in their new employer, who can tell them about the rules and regulations, customs and facilities applicable in the country where they intend to work. Thus any problems they may experience can be quite speedily resolved.

If you are in the early stages of planning to live and work outside the UK then you probably have much research to undertake.

Perhaps you have an ambition to reside and work in a country with a pleasantly mild climate, but remember that it is possible that you may have to go to a location where it rains a lot or is perpetually cold, in order to get the most suitable job for your qualifications. Thus your profession or occupation may be an important influence on your final choice of destination.

A family man with a wife and young children will need to make decisions about the education of his children. Are the education facilities adequate in the country where you plan to live? (Chapter 6 on education overseas may be helpful) and will the youngsters and perhaps yourself and your wife have to learn a foreign language?

Alternatively, will you send the children to boarding schools (if they are old enough), and transport them to your new location for school holidays? This could involve much additional expense, and will the children be happy away from their mother and father for at least six months of the year? If the overseas job you plan to take is for a limited tour of duty, it may be preferable for your wife to stay at home and keep the children at their existing schools, thereby avoiding an interruption in their education.

Where the new job contract is for several years, you and your wife may prefer to retain your UK home and rent it (furnished or unfurnished) to a suitable tenant. In this case a reliable letting agent should be appointed (see Chapter 3, Letting and Insuring Your Home, page 43 for more details). You will then have a base to return to at the end of your overseas appointment.

Should you decide to sell your UK home before leaving the country, you will need to decide about the disposal of any furniture and personal effects that you do not take with you. Is it better to sell these before you depart, or store them in the UK, pending your return? The latter can be expensive.

Answers to many of your questions are given in the chapters that follow and also in the companion book to this *The Daily Telegraph Guide to Working Abroad,* by Godfrey Golzen, which includes advice on the job market etc in over 40 countries around the world.

RETIREMENT ABROAD

Those who are retired or approaching that enviable status may decide that they would benefit from living in a country with a warmer climate. To achieve this they are prepared to cut their ties with their homeland and start a new life overseas in one of the southern European countries or further afield.

How do they select the location for their new retirement home? Many of them will have enjoyed family holidays on the Continent, or further afield to the United States or Australasia over a period of years. Others will have travelled extensively to new countries on business. These experiences may influence their opinions about their most favoured locations for a life of leisure, without boredom.

The choice

Having given the matter much careful thought, the first essential is to narrow down the choice of location to one or two countries, where you think you will be happy to establish a new home and lifestyle. Depending on family commitments it may be essential to take into account accessibility to the UK if a crisis occurs back home, but as far as Europe is concerned the ease and speed of modern transport should not create any problem in this respect.

One important financial point not always realised by senior citizens going to live overseas is that pensioners living in some popular retirement destinations, including Australia, Canada, South Africa and New Zealand, do not receive annual index-linked pension increases from the UK Government for their State pension. As a result, it is estimated that nearly half a million pensioners in various parts of the world, who have been retired for many years, still only receive the same State pension as when they retired – and that can mean as little as £8 per week. Strenuous efforts have been made to lobby the Government on this injustice, but pleas have been ignored on the grounds of cost.

2 Tax and Financial Planning

Bill Blevins, David Franks and Khurshid Baqa
Investment and tax specialists of Blevins Franks, Chartered Accountants

This Chapter takes into account the Budget statement of 9 March 1999, which might be altered by the progress of the Finance Bill through Parliament.

UK RESIDENCE

The emigrant and expatriate are usually hoping to cease to be both 'resident' and 'ordinarily resident' in the UK, to avoid UK income tax and capital gains tax on their world-wide income and capital gains. To succeed, one has to understand the meaning of the terms 'resident' and 'ordinarily resident'. Ordinary residence is explained on page 15, and residence is explained below.

Resident in the UK has a very wide meaning. A tax year starts on 6 April and ends on the following 5 April. As a general rule, an individual will be resident in the UK in a particular tax year if:

1. he lives in the UK for more than 182 days in any one tax year; or
2. he lives in the UK for more than three months on average over four consecutive tax years; or
3. he normally lives in the UK and goes overseas for a period of less than one complete tax year.

In applying the three-month average test, the Revenue will ignore days spent in the UK for reason of 'exceptional circumstances beyond the individual's control', such as being taken ill shortly before returning abroad after a visit to the UK. This concession, which is wholly at the discretion of the Revenue, does not, however, apply to the 182-day test.

The above rules may be overridden by double taxation agreements where the individual is resident both in the UK and in another country. The third test is unlikely to apply unless the taxpayer is UK resident in both the preceding and succeeding years under one of the others.

If an individual who normally lives in the UK spends most of a tax year abroad, eg he goes on a working holiday travelling around the world for a year or two, the fact that he is present in the UK for less than 91 days in the tax year will not necessarily make him non-UK resident. If, however, he is working overseas full time for a complete tax year or longer in an office or employment or carrying on his own business he will, by concession, automatically be regarded as non-UK resident for income tax purposes for that year. It does not matter if an employment involves some UK duties provided that these are *merely incidental* to the overseas duties.

The Inland Revenue will take a harsh line on the definition of 'merely incidental' duties. The more senior the employee the harder it is likely to be to establish that UK duties are merely incidental. Visiting the UK to report to your boss is usually regarded as incidental. Attending a board meeting may well be such if you are a manager but will not be if you are a director as it is regarded as an integral part of your job.

The Revenue will look at the quality of duties undertaken in the UK rather than the time spent on them, to determine whether or not they are merely incidental.

A husband and wife are looked at separately. Thus it is possible for the husband to be non-resident while his wife is a UK resident. For example, if the husband is in genuine full-time employment overseas he will be regarded as non-resident even though he may visit the UK for short periods during the year. On the other hand, his wife, if she is not employed overseas, may remain a UK resident and therefore liable to tax on her income world-wide (even though she is living with him). This used to be a problem before 6 April 1993 but will rarely apply now if the couple are living together overseas, as the wife's normal place of residence will almost always have changed to her husband's new work location.

The diagram on page 14 will help you through the maze of rules on residence. However, it must be stressed that the residence rules are not defined precisely and your individual circumstances always need to be considered. In particular, if you plan your life so as to keep marginally within (1) and (2) above, or so as to remain outside the UK for a single tax year and a day or two on either side, there is a risk that the Revenue could successfully challenge your anticipated non-resident status.

It is important to keep a detailed record of all your time spent in each country, showing dates of arrival and departure and places stayed at. This could be important evidence in the event of a dispute – but also read 'How do they know where I am resident?', on page 15.

THE RESIDENCE MAZE

To help you to work out whether or not you are likely to be resident in the UK in a tax year, follow the maze on page 14.

For tax years ended before 6 April 1993 an individual was also regarded as UK resident if he had accommodation in the UK 'available' for his use and visited the UK during the tax year even, in theory at least, for just a few minutes. A person did not have to own residential accommodation or have a legal right of occupation for a property to be 'available' to him. Merely having a place set aside for his use (eg a bedroom in someone's home) could be sufficient.

THE DATE OF NON-RESIDENCE

Technically your UK residence extends for the entire tax year ending 5 April after you leave the UK. However, by concession, if you leave the UK to take up permanent residence abroad you are normally regarded as becoming non-resident the day after you leave the UK, even though this may be in the middle of a tax year. As explained earlier, a tax year starts on 6 April and ends on the following 5 April. This concession applies for income tax. If you leave to take up full-time work abroad for a period which will

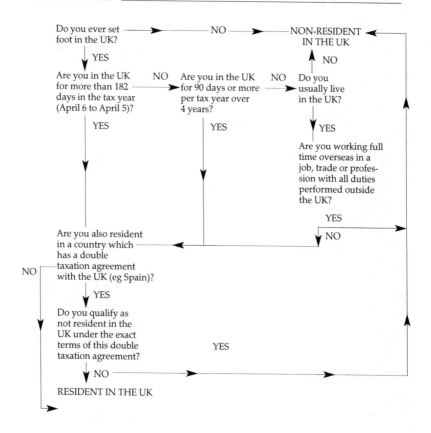

Do you ever set foot in the UK? — NO → NON-RESIDENT IN THE UK

YES

Are you in the UK for more than 182 days in the tax year (April 6 to April 5)?

NO → Are you in the UK for 90 days or more per tax year over 4 years?

NO → Do you usually live in the UK?

NO ↑

YES

YES

YES

Are you working full time overseas in a job, trade or profession with all duties performed outside the UK?

YES

NO

Are you also resident in a country which has a double taxation agreement with the UK (eg Spain)?

NO

YES

Do you qualify as not resident in the UK under the exact terms of this double taxation agreement?

YES

NO

RESIDENT IN THE UK

exceed a complete tax year you are regarded as leaving to take up permanent residence abroad for this purpose. By concession, so is your spouse if she goes with you and establishes that she is non-UK resident while she is living overseas.

For capital gains tax purposes, for those who leave the UK after 16 March 1998, gains realised during a 'temporary' period of residence overseas may be deemed to be taxable in the year of return to the UK. This only applies to assets that were owned by the individual whilst a UK resident and before leaving the UK, but which are sold whilst overseas. It is necessary to remain overseas for five complete tax years to ensure that the period of non-residence is not regarded as temporary. However, it may be possible to establish permanent residence in an overseas country within a period of less than five years, and to claim exemption from UK capital gains tax under the terms of a double taxation treaty between the UK and that overseas country.

ORDINARY RESIDENCE

Unlike most other countries, the UK recognises two forms of residence: residence and ordinary residence. *Ordinarily resident* is not defined by the Taxes Act, but is generally understood to denote the status of someone who is usually resident as opposed to extraordinarily or casually resident for one tax year only.

You will normally be ordinarily resident in the UK if you spend more than three months in the UK on average over four tax years. This concept is crucial for capital gains tax as you have to be *both* not resident and not ordinarily resident in the UK to be free from UK capital gains tax. You have only to be not resident to avoid UK income tax on income other than UK income.

Because other countries do not have a concept of ordinary residence, double tax agreements do not deem a person not to be ordinarily resident in the UK.

You are also likely to be ordinarily resident if you leave the UK for a year or two only and maintain your base in the UK while you are away. This particularly applies if you have accommodation available for your use and visit the UK for a short period each year. If you retain a house in the UK which is let out, it will not normally be available for your use during the period for which it is let. The Inland Revenue even consider that a person can be ordinarily resident in the UK for a tax year even though he does not set foot here during that year.

'HOW DO THEY KNOW WHERE I AM RESIDENT?'

In most countries it is your responsibility to make yourself known to the tax authorities if you are tax resident. If you are caught not declaring your tax residence you can be fined, or even gaoled. In

Spain, for example, the fine can be six times the tax, plus interest, plus a gaol sentence.

There is usually a huge amount of information which is automatically passed to your new country's tax authority. This may include yacht registration, becoming a company director, buying a property or receiving bank interest. Often you need a tax reference number just to open a bank account. Most double tax treaties enable information to be passed to the other country.

Many non-residents totally confuse tax residence with two other kinds of residence – immigration and exchange control. The definitions of tax residence, immigration residence and exchange control residence are normally completely different.

Being non-resident for exchange control or immigration purposes has nothing to do with your tax residence. Your tax residence is determined by completely different rules; therefore you must make no assumptions, but take good professional advice in order to understand your position.

It is no good saying to the tax man in country A that you are resident in country B unless it is true. He might well immediately ask for your tax identification number in country B, so that he can make contact to check out your story.

As you wonder how they can tell where you have been for the last 183 days (or whatever) as your passport is never stamped, think about the massive trail of paperwork which you leave behind you – telephone bills, electricity bills, bank statements, credit cards, parking fines, correspondence with professional advisers or files with doctors/dentists etc. All stand by to give evidence of your whereabouts on a daily basis. Airline manifests are not sacrosanct. In Spain a few years ago, American Express were forced to disclose to the tax authorities the names of all holders of their Gold Card. Most tax men have power to obtain this kind of information direct from third parties. Computers are phenomenal at storing and retrieving information easily.

Try firing your gardener, divorcing your wife, upsetting a neighbour or falling out with a business partner. These people are well known for shopping 'ghosts' (individuals who are tax resident in a country but never declare themselves). In many countries, such as Spain, there is a system of 'denunciation' where individuals may be rewarded for passing on information to the tax or rating authorities.

Most reasonably sophisticated tax authorities (although not the UK) have the right to interview you, and possibly your spouse. Quite often the onus of proof can be placed on the taxpayer rather than the tax inspector.

Moreover, if they have not asked the right questions during your lifetime, you may find that when your death certificate is filed an inspector of taxes becomes interested in how you managed to die in his country when you do not have a tax file number! You, of course, are not too interested at this point. But your wife may find that your estate disappears into paying large back-taxes, penalties and interest.

Finally, your assets can be frozen in your country if you are caught, making you bankrupt, and your debts may be chased into other countries.

Take good professional advice to avoid tax legally – there is no need to go the illegal route.

AVOIDING CAPITAL GAINS TAX – NON-RESIDENCE: THE GENERAL RULES

This section sets out the UK capital gains tax position for someone going to live *anywhere outside the UK.*

The definitions of 'resident' and 'ordinarily resident' are to be found on pages 10 and 15.

For UK domiciled	*Capital gains tax liability*
Resident	UK capital gains tax due on all assets throughout the world.
Not resident and not ordinarily resident and not a temporary non-resident	*Not liable* even if the assets are located in the UK (unless assets used for a trade in the UK; see pages 19–20).

By concession, an individual leaving the UK is treated as not resident the day after he has left. This concession can be refused if the Revenue think tax has been deliberately avoided. It is therefore safer to realise capital gains in the tax year *after* you have left (ie the year starting 6 April after you have left).

Note that the effective date a capital gain is realised is on the making of a contract, which in some cases can be even before a formal unconditional exchange of contracts, not on completion. A verbal agreement has been held to constitute an enforceable contract. Remember also that the Inland Revenue have the right to see all correspondence, file notes, memos etc, leading up to a contract, and often request such documents from you, your accountant, your solicitor, the purchaser and even from the purchaser's solicitor to check if a contract might have come into existence prior to the signing of the formal sale agreement.

If you realise a capital gain in the tax year during which you leave the UK and before the date you leave, the gain is obviously liable to UK capital gains tax, subject to the annual exemption and the other exemptions mentioned below.

To avoid UK capital gains tax, you have to be not resident and not ordinarily resident. For those who leave the UK after 16 March 1998, UK capital gains tax may remain on any UK assets that were owned before the date of departure and are sold whilst overseas. You should remain overseas for five complete UK tax years in order to avoid this change. Those who return earlier will be taxed in the year UK residence is resumed.

There was a possible exception for those who left the UK before 17 March 1998: if you work full-time overseas either under a contract of employment or in a trade, profession or vocation, and you are absent for a complete tax year, the Revenue's normal practice is to treat you as both not resident and not ordinarily resident in that year. However, you must genuinely work full-time overseas, and this is a concession which can be withdrawn by the Inland Revenue if they believe the employment or business has been created mainly to save tax. Furthermore, it was introduced for income tax purposes and you should be wary of relying on it if you intend to realise a large capital gain. The concession is not available for capital gains tax purposes for anyone leaving the UK after 16 March 1998.

Some people feel that it is not necessary to work full time during the year overseas provided that you live in one place throughout the year and do not set foot in the UK during that year. This is based on the decision in a court case, Reed *v* Clark, where the judge felt that a distinct break in the pattern of Dave Clark's life of just over a year was sufficient to say that he had not left the UK for the purpose only of occasional residence abroad. The judge also indicated that he thought that occasional residence is the converse of ordinary residence.

Accordingly, it can be inferred that an absence from the UK of just over a year spanning a complete tax year is sufficient for a taxpayer to be not ordinarily resident in the UK. However, as the case was concerned with a different aspect of the tax legislation it may be dangerous to rely on this. The Dave Clark case was decided many years ago and the Inland Revenue have not amended their standard test of ordinary residence in the light of it. Indeed, they specifically say in their booklet IR20 that a person who usually lives in the UK and, for example, goes abroad for a long holiday and does not set foot in the UK during a tax year may still be ordinarily resident in the UK for that year. This is, of course, merely an expression of their opinion, but expect a court appearance if you want to disagree with it.

ASSETS USED IN A TRADE: THE GENERAL RULE

If you own an asset used in a UK trade and the asset is situated in the UK, even if you become not resident and not ordinarily resident, you will remain liable for capital gains tax on it.

Example

Mr and Mrs Lowes owned a successful freehold nursing home which they operated as a partnership. They left the UK in February 1996, leaving a manager in charge of the home. In May 1996, the manager agreed to buy the nursing home, giving the Lowes a capital gain of £430,000. Unfortunately, Mr and Mrs Lowes remain liable for UK capital gains tax, even though they are both not resident and not ordinarily resident.

The reason why they are liable is that section 10 of the Taxation of Chargeable Gains Act 1992 continues to tax a gain made on assets situated in the UK where those assets are used in a trade – this includes business premises, work in progress, or goodwill. Thus a partner disposing of an interest in assets used in a UK partnership would remain liable to UK capital gains tax.

It is also worth pointing out that letting a UK property, held as an investment, is *not* a trade, and therefore not liable to be taxed by this trap. Even disposals of short-term holiday lettings, regarded as a trade for some sections of the Taxes Act, are not caught by section 10 of the Taxation of Chargeable Gains Act.

If you cannot avoid the tax based on any of the above points, there are some other tax planning hints set out below.

Tax planning

Mr and Mrs Lowes could have avoided UK capital gains tax by one of two methods:

(a) *Incorporation*. If the business had been incorporated, the property could have been transferred to the new company or left in their own names and let (at a market rent) to the company. In either case, the sale of the shares and/or the nursing home freehold would have been free of UK capital gains tax if sold in the tax year after leaving the UK, provided that the Lowes remained both not resident and not ordinarily resident (for five complete UK tax years, if leaving the UK after 16 March 1998). However, it is very important that the incorporation occurs *before* Mr and Mrs Lowes leave the UK, as section 25 of the Taxation of Chargeable Gains Act 1992 imposes a tax charge on a non-UK resident when he ceases to carry on a UK trade.

(b) *Renting the freehold*. An alternative way would have been for the Lowes to let the nursing home to the manager. He would sign a lease, paying a market rent. Later, having left the UK, established non-residence and non-ordinary residence, they could have sold the rental property to him free of UK capital gains tax if they remain overseas for five complete UK tax years. Because of section 25, the lease must be granted *before* leaving the UK.

There is one word of caution about such tax planning. There have been several tax cases (and one in particular called Furniss *v* Dawson) which enable the Revenue to ignore a series of transactions which have no real commercial purpose other than the avoidance of tax. They can impose tax as if the transactions have not occurred.

AVOIDING BOTH UK CAPITAL GAINS TAX AND THE OVERSEAS TAX

We have explained some methods of avoiding UK capital gains tax, but clever avoidance of UK tax could end up becoming a case of 'out of the frying pan and into the fire'. You also have to avoid paying tax on your gain in your new country.

There are several ways of achieving this: for example, by being a fiscal nomad for a few months. Alternatively, you can make your capital gains disposal during a period when you are living in the new country *but* neither resident there nor in the UK. Another plan makes use of the fact that some countries treat the individual as making notional disposal and reacquisition at market value of all assets at the time when he becomes, or ceases to be, resident there. Better still, some countries do not tax capital gains.

Professional advice should be sought to ensure that all taxes are properly avoided.

LETTING YOUR HOME – TAX-DEDUCTIBLE COSTS

If you decide to continue to own your UK house but to let it, you will continue to be liable to UK tax on the rental income even if you are not resident and not ordinarily resident in the UK. The UK includes England, Northern Ireland, Scotland and Wales.

A new system of tax on rental income came into operation on 6 April 1995. The income from letting of UK properties is calculated by the use of ordinary accounting principles and by applying the same computational provisions as apply to a trading activity. Adjustments may be necessary to both income and expenses to deal with prepayments and accruals.

In general, expenses incurred wholly and exclusively for the purpose of the letting are deductible and usually include the following:

☐ agent's fees;
☐ legal fees relating to the letting (including VAT);
☐ repairs and redecorations;

☐ postage and telephone costs directly relating to the letting;
☐ wear and tear;
☐ other services (electricity, gas, TV, paid by the landlord);
☐ insurance;
☐ inventory fees;
☐ ground rent;
☐ valuation fees for insurance purposes;
☐ gardening costs or window cleaner;
☐ accountancy fees;
☐ interest costs;
☐ VAT charged.

ACCOUNTS

The accounts need to be drawn up for the year to 5 April (although in practice, the Inland Revenue may accept 31 March).

Deducting interest on a UK property

Interest on a loan is deductible against the rental income if the loan was used only to purchase or improve the property, or to pay expenses of letting the property. There is *no limit* on the loan, unlike the £30,000 limit applied to your home mortgage when you live there. However, relief for the interest can be given only against UK rental income. It cannot be claimed against any other UK income. The Inland Revenue may ask for a Balance Sheet to evidence that loans have not been used to meet personal expenses of the landlord.

DEDUCTION OF TAX AT SOURCE

Where rent is paid to a non resident landlord, tax at 23 per cent is to be deducted by the agent for the property, or where there is no agent, the tenant. If this results in an overcharge on the landlord, he or she may claim a refund. However, the landlord may instead elect, with the agreement of the Inland Revenue, to file Tax Returns under a regime of Self-assessment and to pay the tax due by instalments on 31 January and 31 July. Such an election must be made *before* the start of the tax year when it will first apply, and will be accepted by the Inland Revenue if the taxpayers' affairs have been kept up to date and in order.

UK CAPITAL GAINS TAX – YOUR OWN HOME

If you sell the property in a tax year in which you are both not resident and not ordinarily resident, there is no UK capital gains tax due. If you are planning to return to the UK and have a potential UK capital gains tax liability on your house, you may be better off selling it in the tax year _before_ you return, when you are not resident and not ordinarily resident. That way, you will avoid UK capital gains tax. However, for those who left the UK after 16 March 1998, it is necessary to remain overseas for five complete UK tax years, in order for this to work.

Provided that a house has been your only or main residence at some time, the last three years of ownership are always exempt from capital gains tax.

There are many other rules about avoiding capital gains tax on a principal private residence (your own home) which are rather complex, but worth setting out in detail as this is often a key point for the working expatriate. Note that the rules for interest relief (MIRAS etc) and capital gains tax exemption are entirely separate.

More than one residence

It must be borne in mind that you can have two residences available to you without owning them both. A home which you rent counts as a residence. An overseas flat or house, whether owned or rented, is also a residence.

It is not wholly clear whether the house you live in overseas constitutes a second residence for the purpose of the exemption. As a person who is not resident and not ordinarily resident in the UK is outside the scope of capital gains tax it is arguable that a house owned while the person is living overseas is not one which is eligible for the private residence relief, and that therefore it can be ignored in applying the restriction on the relief. In practice the

Revenue seem to accept that the overseas house can be ignored, but if you want to be absolutely safe it would be wise to elect for the UK one to be treated as the principal residence.

If you own (or have available) more than one residence, you can elect which property should be regarded as the principal private residence for the capital gains tax exemption. Such an election, which must be in writing, must be made within two years of the acquisition of the second house. The election can be varied at any time by giving a fresh notice, but the variation cannot apply to any period over two years before the date of the new election. If no election is made, the Inspector of Taxes will choose, on the basis of what appears to him on his examination of the facts to be the main residence at the time. A second property which you let to bona fide tenants (or keep available for letting) is not treated as being your residence.

Time limit for election

It has been held by the High Court that the time limit for making the election is two years from the date the second residence first becomes available. Most people doubt this interpretation of the legislation but anyone who now wants to challenge it will have to go at least to the Court of Appeal. In the past elections were sometimes accepted outside this limit (but not to operate more than two years retrospectively). The Revenue have stated that where the taxpayer's interest in one of the properties has 'no more than a negligible capital value in the open market' and the taxpayer was unaware that an election could be made, they will extend the time limit to a reasonable time after the individual first becomes aware that he is entitled to make an election. They will then treat it as having effect from the date on which he acquired the second residence (Inland Revenue Extra-Statutory Concession D21). This concession is intended to cover the position where one of the properties is rented and the taxpayer did not realise that it constitutes a residence.

Husband and wife

A husband and wife can have only one main residence between them while they are living together. Where a private residence election affects both it must be given by both.

The capital gains computation

If you let your house (or leave it unoccupied) and sell it in a tax year when you are resident (or ordinarily resident) in the UK, you may have a capital gains tax liability for the period the property was let (or unoccupied). The amount of the gain which remains free of capital gains tax is:

$$\text{Total gain} \times \frac{\text{Number of weeks owned as principal private residence}}{\text{Number of weeks owned}}$$

Remember that:

☐ the number of weeks which count as your owning it as a principal private residence always includes the last 36 months, even if let;

☐ weeks prior to 1 April 1982 are ignored for both the numerator and the denominator of the above calculation.

Where part or all of your home has been let, up to £40,000 of the gain attributable to the let period is tax free. The amount of relief depends on various factors, including how long it has been let.

Periods of absence

In the above calculation, certain periods of absence can also count as being periods when the house is your principal private residence, even though factually it was not (eg it can even be let). These periods of absence are as follows:

1. Any period (or periods) not exceeding three years; *plus*
2. Any period where you worked overseas as an employee and all the duties were performed overseas. There is no time limit. Note that if the husband works but the wife does not, she would still be eligible for relief for her part ownership as long as she is living with the husband. Note that this exemption does not apply if you are self-employed, nor does it apply if any of the duties were performed in the UK, however incidental they might be; *plus*
3. Up to four years where your job in the UK requires you to live elsewhere (usually more than 100 miles away).

There are several major traps in obtaining any of the above three periods of relief. You must meet each of the following three conditions:

1. The house must be your main residence *before* the start of the period of absence; *and*
2. It must be your main residence at some time *subsequent* to the period of absence. This means that you must re-occupy the house before you sell it. There is no legal limit on the minimum time the house must be occupied, and some say that even one week is sufficient, so long as you have no other residence available. The Inland Revenue do not consider that such a short period of occupation is normally sufficient for the house to have become a 'residence', but their view has not been tested in the courts. There is one exception to having to re-occupy before you sell. The Inland Revenue have granted a concession where you are forced by your job to live elsewhere in the UK on your return; *and*
3. You must have no other residence eligible for relief during the periods of absence. Of course, while overseas you are bound to have your overseas house available for your use as a residence. In practice, the Inland Revenue tend to ignore this. You might consider submitting a written election to the Inland Revenue within two years of going overseas that your UK home is to be treated as your principal private residence. If you do not make the election, the Inland Revenue might claim that your overseas home is your main residence, and hence you will fail to meet this condition. In practice, an election is not needed.

Separation or divorce

Where a married couple separate or are divorced and one partner (usually the husband) moves out and subsequently, as part of a financial settlement, disposes of the home (or his interest in it) to the other, it can be regarded as continuing to be the husband's main residence during the period up to the date of the transfer, provided that it continues to be the wife's main residence throughout that period and the husband does not have another property which he is claiming as his main residence (Inland Revenue Extra-Statutory Concession D6). It should be noted particularly that this applies only where the house is ultimately transferred to the wife. If it is sold and all or part of the proceeds paid to her, the concession will not operate. In such a case it may be preferable to transfer the property to the wife and allow her to sell it.

Buying a UK home while overseas

An expatriate who buys a UK house while he is overseas would not have met the rule of using the house *before* and after a period of absence as his principal private residence. While there may be relief for interest purposes, there is no relief for capital gains tax purposes. Instead, the expatriate should consider selling the house in the tax year *before* he returns, while he is both not resident and not ordinarily resident, when he is exempt from all capital gains tax. By concession, if you work full time overseas, the Revenue will regard you as both not resident and not ordinarily resident until the day you return, in which case it appears unnecessary to sell the house in the tax year before you return; selling before you return, even in the same tax year, would be sufficient. However, if possible you should not rely on this concession as it can always be withdrawn.

Avoiding capital gains tax and keeping the house

As an alternative to selling to a third party in the tax year before return, you could transfer the property to a trust for yourself and your wife's benefit. The transfer into the trust will be tax free if the requirements of not resident and not ordinarily resident are met, and any subsequent disposal by the trust will also be tax free if the property is occupied by you under the terms of the trust.

WORKING ABROAD AND MIRAS

Keeping a house in the UK will not in itself affect your UK tax residence status. You may still even be able to continue with your MIRAS relief (Mortgage Interest Relief At Source) until April 2000, when the relief will be withdrawn entirely.

Since 6 April 1983 (or in some cases even earlier) mortgage interest on house loans may be paid after deduction of tax if the interest is 'relevant loan interest' paid by you as a 'qualifying borrower' to a 'qualifying lender':

1. 'Relevant loan interest' is interest paid and payable in the UK to a 'qualifying lender' and it is interest on loans for the purchase of a residence, including a residential caravan or houseboat in the UK, which when the interest is paid is used wholly, or to a substantial extent, as the only or main residence of the borrower. Before 5 April 1988 relief was also available for the purchase of a residence for a dependent relative or separated or former spouse and for home improvements. Interest relief will continue for such loans until they are repaid *or* replaced.

2. 'Qualifying borrower' is any individual who pays 'relevant loan interest'. There is an exception to this. If you or your husband or wife receive(s) earnings that are exempt from UK tax, eg certain Crown and Foreign Office appointments, neither of you can qualify for MIRAS. There are very few tax exempt occupations.

3. A 'qualifying lender' includes a building society, a local authority, the Bank of England, an insurance company authorised to carry on long-term business (eg life assurance) in the UK, a trustee savings bank, an existing lender under the mortgage option scheme, and any recognised bank or licensed deposit-taking institution authorised by the Treasury.

MIRAS enables you to reduce your mortgage interest payments by the tax relief due, which is at a reduced rate of 10 per cent. It is limited to interest on the first £30,000 of a loan to buy your principal private residence. Even though you, as an expatriate, are no longer living in the UK and may have no UK income, you can still obtain MIRAS relief because of an Inland Revenue concession.

Where you are required by reason of your employment to move from your home to another place either in the UK or abroad for a period not expected to exceed four years, any property being bought with the aid of a mortgage, which was being used as your only or main residence *before* you went away, will still be treated as such, provided that it can reasonably be expected to be so again on your return. It is *not* sufficient to claim the first four years of an expected five-year absence. The maximum period is four years, but if there is a further temporary absence after the property has been reoccupied for a minimum period of three months, the four-year test will apply to the year of absence without regard to the previous absence.

If you are already working abroad and buy a property in the UK in the course of a leave period and use that property as an only or main residence for a period of not less than three months *before* your return to the place of your overseas employment, you will be regarded as satisfying the condition that the property was used as your only or main residence before you went away.

If you let your property at a commercial rent while you are away, the benefit of the concession may be claimed where appropriate if this is more favourable than a claim for relief against letting income. You cannot, however, claim MIRAS relief and then claim further relief against letting income to bring the total relief back to 40 per cent. Since the relief was reduced to 10 per cent from 6 April 1998 it will rarely be beneficial to leave a let property within MIRAS. If you go abroad but leave your family in your UK house, MIRAS relief will not be subject to the above-mentioned four-year time limit.

COUNCIL TAX

Council tax is loosely based on property values by allocating properties to one of five tax rate bands. The tax is normally imposed on the occupier. In some cases, such as where the property is in multiple occupation or it has been unoccupied for more than six months, it is payable by the property owner.

UK RATES OF INCOME TAX

For 1999–2000, the rates are:

Income	Rate
First £1,500 of taxable income	10%
£1,501 to £28,000	23% (basic rate)
Over £28,000	40% (higher rate)

UK PERSONAL ALLOWANCES

The main allowances are:

	1998–99	1999–2000
Ordinary Personal allowance	£4,195	£4,335
Increased Personal allowance		
if age 65–74	£5,410	£5,720+
age 75 and over	£5,600	£5,980+
Married couple's allowance,		
additional personal allowance		
and widow's bereavement allowance		
Ordinary	£1,900	£1,970*+
age 65–74	£4,965	£5,125*+
age 75 and over	£5,025	£5,195*+

* Tax relief for these allowances is restricted to 10 per cent of the allowance.

+ Age related allowances are reduced by one-half of income over £16,800 for 1999–2000 (£16,200 for 1998–99) until the allowance is the same as the ordinary allowance.

Blind person's allowance	£1,330	£1,380

There is no restriction on an expatriate claiming personal allowances, and no need to declare your world-wide income to do so. However, claiming the allowance could prompt questions from the Revenue, so may not be wise if you will be abroad for a few years only. Both husband and wife are eligible for the allowance, and can each make a separate claim. With effect from 6 April 1996, citizens of all states within the European Economic Area are eligible to claim UK personal allowances which may result in a refund of UK tax deducted at source. Citizens of the Commonwealth and of the Irish Republic remain entitled to claim allowances as previously.

For a non-UK resident, there is no UK tax liability on income from UK State pensions, UK bank deposits, or dividends from UK share-holdings. However, such income is taken into account when personal allowances are claimed in the UK against UK income. It is advisable to keep deposit accounts outside the UK (eg in the Channel Islands) to avoid UK tax. Prior to 6 April 1996, income from UK State pensions and shareholdings was liable to tax, but the Inland Revenue did not collect tax on bank deposit interest by concession.

UK PENSIONS

UK pensions (other than a State pension) paid to a non-resident are liable to UK tax unless the pensioner is exempt by a double tax agreement or the pension is paid out under one of the following schemes:

1. India, Pakistan, Burma and colonial schemes;
2. pension funds for former public service employees of overseas territories;
3. the Central African Pension Fund;
4. the Overseas Service Pension Fund;
5. pension funds set up for overseas employees of UK employers.

Most double taxation agreements tax pensions only in the country in which the individual is resident, with the exception of pensions paid out of public funds in the UK, which remain taxable in the UK. Public funds include pensions paid to former servants of the Crown, and pensions paid for services rendered to a local authority in the UK. Such public fund pensions may be free of UK tax under the double taxation agreement if the pensioner is a national of the other country.

If your pension is going to be liable to UK income tax or foreign tax and you have the option to do so, it is normally better to elect to take a tax-free lump sum and to reduce the level of pension liable to UK tax.

If you are moving to an EU country, there are flexible agreements over pension and many other social security benefits. UK social security pensions are payable in your new EU country, including cost of living increases, though these will be related to the British cost of living index. There is a leaflet (SA29) produced by the DSS which discusses some of these points (for address, see page 379).

In addition, the UK has agreements with a number of non-EU countries, primarily covering retirement pensions.

UK DIVIDENDS

Dividends from UK companies constitute taxable income. However from 6 April 1996, a non-UK resident will have no additional tax to pay on dividends received. Until 5 April 1999, they carried with them a tax credit which covered the first 20 per cent of the shareholder's liability – and effectively, the whole of that liability where the shareholder is liable to basic rate tax. For example, a £100 dividend can be expressed as follows:

Dividend	*Tax Credit*
£100	£25

The £25 tax credit is 20 per cent of the aggregate sum. A basic rate taxpayer who receives the dividend has no further tax to pay. A UK resident higher rate taxpayer must pay a further £25 tax, to bring his total tax to £50 or 40 per cent of £125. A non-taxpayer may be entitled to reclaim the £25 tax credit. In general non-UK residents are not entitled to reclaim the tax credit. However, a British citizen and, since 6 April 1996, a European Economic Area citizen, who is entitled to claim personal allowances is also entitled to reclaim the tax credit against such allowances. In addition it is possible to reclaim part of the tax credit under many of the UK's double taxation agreements. The refund normally effectively leaves the UK taxing the non-resident at 15 per cent of the total of the dividend plus the tax credit. For example, on a dividend of £100 the UK can charge 15 per cent of £125 or £18.75. The balance of the tax credit, £6.25, will be reclaimable by the nonresident.

If an overseas company, but not normally an individual, controls 10 per cent or more of the company (whether directly or indirectly) the tax refund is generally higher. The agreement will normally only allow the UK to keep 5 per cent of the £125 aggregate figure, thus creating a refund of £18.75 of the tax credit on £100 of dividend.

After 5 April 1999, the UK system of ACT was abolished and dividends no longer carry a repayable tax credit. Individuals who are taxable at basic or lower rates only have no tax to pay on receipt of a UK dividend. Nor can any tax refund be claimed. UK resident higher rate taxpayers pay tax of 25 per cent of the dividend – ie £25 tax on a dividend of £100, as formerly. A non-resident can ignore UK dividends when calculating any liability to UK tax.

UK INTEREST (BANKS AND BUILDING SOCIETIES)

Normal 'onshore' building society and bank accounts are not advisable for UK expatriates. Many societies and banks advertise 'international accounts', suggesting that interest payments may be made gross without risk of UK income tax. At first sight these appear highly attractive when compared to the returns available on high interest money market bank accounts. From 6 April 1996, the UK tax liability of a non-resident has not been allowed to exceed the tax which would be payable if UK dividends, UK interest and UK state pensions were all disregarded. However, in effect, the UK personal allowances which can be deducted from other income are reduced by the amount of any UK interest and state pensions. The receipt of UK interest can therefore result in an increase of tax which is payable on other income from the UK, such as property income or occupational pensions, etc.

In addition, if the non-resident is not domiciled in the UK he would be putting his capital at risk unnecessarily to a charge to UK inheritance tax.

UK GILTS

Gilts are publicly quoted stocks backed fully by the British government. (The name 'gilt' comes from the original certificates which were issued with gilded edges.) At no time has a British government failed to meet any of its funded debt obligations whether in the nature of capital or income. But do not be fooled into thinking that gilts are always safe. If you have to sell before maturity, you can lose a lot of money. How much you lose or gain depends on what has happened to interest rates since you purchased your stock.

When you buy a gilt, you are lending the government money at a guaranteed interest rate (called the 'coupon'). Repayment is normally due at a specified date, so you can work out exactly how much you will receive and when, although the government has the right to repay some stocks at any time over a three- to five-year period. Rates of return are often higher than from a bank or building society, and the guarantee is stronger – the government is less likely to go bankrupt than Barclays Bank or the Halifax.

UK tax position

Interest on gilts is liable to UK income tax and the majority have tax deducted at source. However, there are a number of gilts on which there is no tax due either on income or capital gain if you are not resident in the UK, although it will be up to you to prove your non-resident status. It is not enough simply to provide a foreign address; you may have to give details of your tax reference number and district in the overseas country. In order to obtain approval, you should obtain Form A1 from the Financial Intermediaries and Claims Office, St John's House, Merton Road, Bootle, Merseyside L69 9BB. Unless you have already been cleared as not resident, expect some searching questions about your long-term plans, duration of visits, location of home and so on. The list of gilt stocks which are free of tax to residents abroad may be obtained from the Bank of England, Threadneedle Street, London EC2R 8AH.

SIXTEEN WAYS TO AVOID UK INHERITANCE TAX

UK inheritance tax is payable after death by:

(a) UK domiciled individuals on their world-wide assets, wherever they may be resident;
(b) non-UK domiciliaries on any assets situated in the UK.

It is very difficult to shed your UK domicile. Thus you may live outside the UK for many years, but *remain liable for UK inheritance tax on your death on your world-wide assets*. Here are some ways to avoid tax.

1. Giving it away tax free

If you give away no more than £231,000 (£223,000 before April 1999), there is no inheritance tax (IHT) to pay. After seven years, you can give a further £231,000 (and so on every seven years and one day). Both husband and wife each have their own £231,000 limit. In addition, each year you (and your wife) can give away £3,000. Thus over a period of seven years and one day you can give away:

	Husband	Wife	Total
2 × £231,000	£462,000	£462,000	£924,000
8 × £3,000	£24,000	£24,000	£48,000
	£486,000	£486,000	£972,000

2. Giving away 'in consideration of marriage'

Each parent can give away an additional £5,000 to a child or £2,500 to a grandchild and £1,000 to anyone else on the recipient's marriage. The rules are very strict and professional advice on how to do it should be taken, in advance of the marriage.

3. Normal income expenditure

Regular amounts can be gifted as 'normal expenditure out of income' representing perhaps as much as 10–50 per cent of annual income *free of IHT*. Careful use of this exemption can significantly reduce, or even eliminate, your IHT problem.

4. Unlimited lifetime transfers to an individual or trusts

You can give *unlimited* amounts to any other individual during your lifetime or to most trusts (but not discretionary trusts). The gift could be money, or shares in a company, or any other asset. If the gift is of unquoted shares or assets used in a business (or is of a controlling interest in a listed or AIM company) and the recipient is a UK resident, capital gains tax can be avoided by signing a holdover relief election, though there may be none to pay if the donor is both not UK resident and not ordinarily resident. In the event of the donor dying within seven years, there will be IHT to pay but at reduced rates. If he dies within three years of the gift, there is no tax reduction. Trusts can be very useful for giving wealth to grandchildren under the age of 25.

5. Avoid 'reservation'

Gifts 'with reservation' will not be exempt from tax under 4. above. The gift must be given absolutely. A gift where the donor enjoys any interest or rights is not acceptable. Thus the gift of a house, with rights for the donor to reside in it, is not an absolute gift, nor is the gift of shares with the right to an exceptional salary from the company. So avoid giving anything which has reservation of interest. This is a very technical area. It may be possible to carve out for oneself a right to reside in the house prior to making the gift. Professional advice should be sought before attempting such a gift.

6. Keep the back door open

You could give away any amounts into a discretionary trust, where you are *not* a beneficiary but other relatives, including your wife, are the named beneficiaries. You could remain as the controller of the assets in trust (called the trustee). A series of trusts is recommended for technical reasons. As long as your gifts are within the limits set out in 1. above, there will be no IHT due. Your wife can also establish a similar series of trusts.

7. Life insurance

Life insurance can be a surprisingly cheap way of covering any eventual IHT bill. For example, if your estate was worth £384,000, you and your wife were aged 50, and you left all your assets to her on your death, the IHT payable at the second death would be £61,200. For an annual outlay of about £900 per annum, a tax-free benefit under trust of over £90,000 can be obtained, and indeed is projected to be worth over £220,000 on the death at age 85 of the survivor.

Alternatively, at 65 you could invest £25,000 in a last survivor investment bond (under trust) with life cover of a sum assured at the second death of just under £100,000.

These costs can be reduced considerably by purchasing term life insurance which provides cover for a fixed number of years only. You choose how long. During the time you pay regular premiums, if you die, the policy pays out a fixed amount. If you survive to the end of the term, you receive nothing back and premiums cease.

8. Equalising estates

If the husband's estate is worth £600,000, the IHT payable is £147,600, leaving £452,400 as the net estate. If estates are equalised between husband and wife and each wills the estate to children/grandchildren/relatives, the IHT payable is reduced to approximately £55,200, saving £92,400. The estates do not actually need to be equal. The key thing is for each spouse to have at least £231,000 of the joint assets.

9. Residential property

If a donor gifts a property and continues to stay in it, or even visits it for other than short periods, the gift is treated under the 'reservation' rules, unless a commercial rent is paid.

Various solutions are possible. If a leasehold can be created on a freehold property, and gifted after seven years of its creation, the gift of freehold will be outside the donor's estate. Once the leasehold has expired, the donor would have to vacate the property or pay a commercial rent.

If a property can be sold and the proceeds gifted, the beneficiary could purchase a new property and allow the donor to live there rent free. Capital gains tax could be avoided subsequently if the beneficiary is not ordinarily resident.

10. Company shares, business assets and woodlands

Unquoted company shares are eligible for a special 100 per cent business relief, for IHT purposes. The effect is to take such assets out of the scope of inheritance tax completely. Before 6 April 1996 it was necessary to own 25 per cent or more of the company concerned.

A controlling interest in a quoted company attracts 50 per cent business relief. If you hold a little under 50 per cent of a quoted company, consideration ought to be given to increasing your holding to over 50 per cent to qualify for this exemption.

Another way to reduce the value is to form another company (owned by the ultimate beneficiaries) and build up this new company in preference to the existing one. Assets used in Lloyd's underwriting or in any other business you carry on are also eligible for 100 per cent reduction.

Certain other property used by a private company or a partnership is also eligible for business relief at the reduced rate of 50 per cent. Similar rules apply to agricultural property but the rate is increased to 100 per cent if there is vacant possession. Woodlands can also qualify for the 100 per cent relief.

11. Single premium bonds

An investment bond can be a useful way to reduce your estate yet retain an income. The beneficiary of the bond is a child or grandchild instead of the investor. Inheritance tax may be payable at the time of buying the bond, but is avoided on any growth in value of the bond.

Alternatively, a trust can be established and an interest-free loan made to the trustees, who then use the loan to purchase an investment bond. 'Income' can be taken in the form of loan repayments. No IHT is payable on the loan and, with the exception of any outstanding loan, the trust fund remains outside the settlor's estate.

12. Giving away shares of newly formed companies

Making gifts of assets likely to appreciate is an effective way of reducing your estate. The gift is normally valued at the date it is gifted, not the subsequent value.

13. Giving away when cheap

The best time to make gifts is when the value of an asset is depressed. Watch out for opportunities. For example, for about a year following the October 1987 crash, values of equities were low. In 1991 and 1992 property values were low.

14. Generation skipping

If your own children are already wealthy, pass your estate on to your grandchildren instead. This skips a generation and reduces the likely IHT on your children's death.

15. Writing in trust

Life insurances and death benefits from pension schemes may form part of your estate for IHT purposes. You can set up the policy to pay the benefits direct to your children, in which case they do not attract IHT. If you are concerned that your wife, should she survive you, should receive the benefit, it is advisable that you write the policy benefits in trust for your children, unless your wife survives you by 30 days, in which case she receives the benefit.

16. Interest free loans

An interest free loan is *not* a gift as long as:

☐ the loan is documented; and
☐ the loan is repayable on demand or at very short notice.

Such loans can be used to purchase assets from the donor. Professional advice should be sought before granting such loans.

WORKING ABROAD – UK TAX

If you work abroad and live abroad for a period of less than one year, you will normally remain liable in full to UK tax.

Until 17 March 1998, those who worked abroad for a period of at least 365 days were eligible for tax relief at 100 per cent of their foreign earnings. This relief is no longer available – it is generally necessary to be non-resident for at least one complete tax year in order to escape UK tax on foreign earnings.

There is a trap, however. To achieve your 365 days of continuous employment abroad, you cannot during that period:

☐ spend more than 62 days continuously in the UK for any reason;

☐ spend days in the UK which in aggregate exceed one-sixth of the length of the total period from the start of the 365 days up to each time you visit the UK.

Note in particular that just avoiding spending more than 62 days in the UK is not sufficient. You must also avoid breaching the 'one-sixth' rule each time you visit the UK.

A day will be considered to be a day of absence if you are outside the UK at midnight. If your flight leaves the UK at 11 pm in the evening, that is normally regarded as an entire day spent abroad, although there is no legislative basis for this and it is accordingly unwise to rely on it. If you return from abroad at 11 pm, even after a hard day's work, the legislation provides that this must nevertheless be taken as a day in the UK.

The legislation looks at days of absence from the UK, not days spent working overseas. It does not matter what the taxpayer is doing while he is overseas.

The one-sixth limit is applied very rigidly. An unplanned or unexpected visit to the UK can spell disaster in trying to establish the 365-day minimum period. Careful planning is required, as shown in the following example:

	Date	Days abroad	Days in UK	Total days
Leaves UK for Spain	12.08.94			
Returns to UK for Christmas	15.12.94	125		125
Leaves UK for Spain	20.01.95		36	161
Returns to UK for grandfather's funeral	07.02.95	18		179
Leaves UK for Spain	10.02.95		3	182
Returns to UK	09.12.95	304		485

The number of days spent in the UK between two periods of absence cannot exceed one-sixth of the total number of days in the period under consideration. In the above example, the individual spends 485 days from the time he leaves to work in Spain to the end of his assignment. On returning to the UK on 7 February 1995, there is a total period of 179 days. One-sixth of 179 is 30, but he has spent more than this in the UK as he was here for 36 days. Thus, the period from 12 August 1994 to 20 January 1995 is *not* a qualifying one. The calculation now starts again on 20 January 1995. He spends 18 days abroad, then three days in the UK, and finally 304 days abroad before returning permanently. Since this is a total of 325 days and is less than the required 365, no part of the 485-day period will count as exempt from UK tax. Instead, UK tax is payable in full, even though this taxpayer has been on an overseas assignment which lasted about 16 months. Thus, going abroad for a short period and then returning to the UK can be very dangerous.

The relief under the 365-day rule was given by a deduction of 100 per cent of the employment earnings. This is better than exempting the earnings from tax, as they remain relevant earnings for pension purposes. Thus, on your return to the UK you could use your earlier overseas earnings as a means of increasing your UK pension contributions in order to save even more tax. However, this relief does not apply if you are abroad for such a long period that you cease to be UK resident.

NATIONAL INSURANCE CONTRIBUTIONS

Social security and pension schemes

The system of UK social security, known as National Insurance, is administered by the Contributions Agency, an executive agency of the Department of Social Security (DSS) through a network of local offices around the country and specialist offices. Wherever you or your employer have any overseas involvement your National Insurance contribution position can become very complicated. All such matters are the responsibility of the DSS Overseas Branch, whose address is given on page 379.

TRAVELLING EXPENSES, AND BOARD AND LODGING

If you work in a job the duties of which are performed *wholly* outside the UK, the following expenses are not taxable:

(a) travel from any place to take up the employment;
(b) travel to any place in the UK at the end of the employment;
(c) board and lodging provided by or reimbursed by the employer.

If only *part* of the duties are performed outside the UK, the following expenses are not taxable:

(a) travel from any place in the UK to the place of performance of any of the duties outside the UK; or
(b) travel from the overseas place of performance of any of the duties to any place in the UK

provided that the duties concerned can only be performed outside the UK and the journey is made *wholly and exclusively* for the purpose of performing the duties or returning after performing the duties.

FAMILY TRAVEL

No tax is payable on travel costs provided or reimbursed by the employer for the taxpayer's spouse or children under 18 to visit overseas. To qualify for this relief, the taxpayer must be working overseas for a continuous period of 60 days or more.

'Continuous' means that even a single day back in the UK, for whatever reason, will debar the relief (or start a fresh 60-day period after the employee returns overseas).

This relief is only given for travel between a place in the UK and the place (or places) of performance of duties. It applies to not more than two outward and two return journeys by the same person in a UK tax year. A child must be under 18 at the beginning of the outward journey, and can include a stepchild and an illegitimate child.

3 Letting and Insuring Your Home*

Many home owners going to live abroad will be looking for a tenant to live in their house or flat while they are away.

The case for letting, as opposed to leaving your home empty or selling, hardly needs to be put today when vandalism and crime are constantly in the headlines. The Government, recognising the difficulties for owners leaving their homes and wishing to encourage the private landlord, introduced the Housing Act 1988 which came into force on 15 January 1989. This Act simplifies the many provisions of the various Rent and Housing Acts from 1965 to 1987. Landlords now have a choice between an assured tenancy and an assured shorthold tenancy. It is not possible here to define the various differences between these two forms of tenancy, but there are specific areas of which the owner-occupier needs to be aware. However, lettings to large companies where the occupier is a genuine employee being housed by the company temporarily are excluded from the Act. It should be noted that a letting to a member of the Diplomatic Corps who has immunity is inadvisable, as the individual would be outside the jurisdiction of British courts. It is essential, therefore, for the owner to obtain legal advice before deciding which form of tenancy to opt for.

---

*Adapted from *Working Abroad: The Daily Telegraph Guide to Working and Living Overseas*, 20th edition (Kogan Page).

ASSURED TENANCIES

1. An assured tenancy may be for a fixed term or periodic, ie month to month.
2. The tenant must be an individual, not a limited company.
3. The tenant must occupy the house or flat as his or her only or principal home.
4. There are various terms which should be provided in the agreement and in particular a provision for the rent to be increased by notice in writing.

The benefits of an assured tenancy are as follows: there is very little rent control; there is no restriction on the initial rent; premiums can be taken (although this is unlikely to be a marketable facility); rents can be increased during the tenancy, provided there is a term in the agreement; and even where not so provided the landlord may serve notice under the Act to increase the rent. In the latter instance, the tenant may go to the Rent Assessment Committee who must fix the rent at a 'market' figure, not at the previous imposition of what was perhaps unfortunately called a 'fair' rent.

Possession of the property can still be obtained by virtue of former owner-occupation and the service of the appropriate notice of the tenant before the commencement of the tenancy. Additional provisions for a mandatory possession order have been included in the new Act, such as three months' arrears of rent, and there are a number of discretionary grounds on which possession can be granted, even if the owner does not wish to return to the house. However, there is one specific disadvantage with the Act if the owner is unfortunate enough to have a tenant who refuses to leave when the owner wishes to reoccupy. This is the provision under the Act where the owner is obliged to serve two months' notice advising the tenant that the owner requires possession and on what ground(s) prior to any proceedings being commenced. This undoubtedly will extend the period needed before a possession order is granted by the Court and owners would be well advised to take out one of the various insurance policies now available to cover hotel costs, legal fees, etc and as a minimum to make sure that either alternative accommodation is temporarily available in the event of a return home earlier than expected or the tenancy is terminated well before the projected date of return.

ASSURED SHORTHOLD TENANCIES

1. These must be for a minimum term of six months without provision for a break clause, although after this period there can be two months' notice provided.
2. A notice must be served in the specified form at least four or five working days before the commencement of the agreement.
3. The tenant may apply to the Rent Assessment Committee during the period of the tenancy to fix the rental at a 'market' figure. However, on the expiry of the original term, the owner is entitled to require the tenant to pay a higher rental and the tenant is not entitled to go back to the Rent Assessment Committee. It is therefore preferable to have relatively short lease periods.
4. Two months' notice has to be served that the landlord requires possession before or on the day the fixed term comes to an end and, if the tenant refuses to leave, the Courts must grant possession, after the expiry of the notice.

As must now be obvious to the reader, the rules do nothing to encourage the owner to attempt to let the property or manage the home him or herself while away, and the need for an experienced property management firm becomes even more important than in the past. A solicitor might be an alternative but, although more versed in the legal technicalities than a managing agent, a solicitor will not be in a position to market the house to the best advantage (if at all) and solicitors' practices do not usually have staff experienced in property management, able to carry out inspections, deal with repairs, arrange inventories and to handle the many and various problems that often arise.

Having retained a solicitor to ensure that you have the correct form of tenancy, you now need to find an experienced and reliable estate agent (ideally, a member of the Royal Institution of Chartered Surveyors, the Incorporated Society of Valuers and

Auctioneers, the Association of Residential Letting Agencies or the National Association of Estate Agents) specialising in property management who will be well-versed in both the legal and financial aspects of the property market.

PROPERTY MANAGEMENT

Property management is a rather specialised branch of estate agency and you should check carefully that the agent you go to can give you the service you need, that he or she is not just an accommodation broker, and that the agent is equipped to handle the letting, collection of rental and management of your property, as well as the more common kinds of agency work. Your solicitor should be able to advise you here, but to some extent you will have to rely on your own judgement of how ready and satisfactory the agent's answers are to the sort of questions you are going to want to ask. There are several specialised firms well equipped to deal with your affairs. One such firm is Anderton & Son (5/7 Selsdon Road, South Croydon CR2 6PU and branches), which supplied much of the information upon which this chapter is based.

In the first place the agent you instruct should have a clear idea of the kind of tenant you can expect for your property, and preferably be able to show you that he or she does have people who are looking for rented accommodation of this kind. Obviously, the rental and the tenant you can expect will vary with what you have to offer. A normal family house in a good area should attract someone like the executive of a multinational company who is in a similar, but reverse; position to your own: that is, a person working here on a contract basis for a limited period who may well provide a stable tenancy for the whole or a substantial part of your absence. A smaller house or flat would be more likely to attract a younger person who only wants the property for a limited period or who, at any rate, might be reluctant to accept a long-term commitment because of the possibility of a change in professional circumstances or marital status.

For your part you should bear in mind that tenants, unlike house purchasers, are usually only interested in a property with almost immediate possession, but you should give the agent, wherever possible, at least two or three months' warning of your departure in order that interest may be built up by advertising, mailing out details, etc over a period of time.

Rent

How much rent you can expect will also vary with what you have to offer and where it is, but the point to bear in mind is that rents are not usually subject to bargaining like a house price. Bargaining, if there is to be any, is more likely to occur over the terms of the lease which are set out below. Do not, therefore, ask for an unrealistically high figure in the expectation that the tenant will regard this as a starting point for negotiation.

Your agent, if he or she knows the job, will be able to advise you on the rental you should ask, though if you have not had previous dealings with the agent it might be advisable to have your solicitor check out the figures or to ask the agent to give you some instances of rentals being charged for similar accommodation. On the other hand, an offer which is a bit less than you had hoped for, but from a good tenant, might be worth taking in preference to a better one from somebody who, for various reasons, looks more doubtful.

Terms of agreement

A property management agent should have, or be able to produce fairly quickly, a draft agreement to cover the specific situation of the overseas landlord. You should show this to your solicitor and how well it is drafted will again be a pointer to how effective the agent concerned is likely to be. The document should cover at least the following points:

1. The intervals of payment – monthly or quarterly – and the length of lease.
2. A prohibition from assigning the lease without your express permission; likewise from keeping animals on the premies or using them for other than residential purposes.
3. An undertaking by the tenant to make good any damage, other than fair wear and tear, to fixtures, fittings and furniture and to maintain the garden.

4. An undertaking by the tenant to pay for telephone and other services from the commencement of the lease.
5. An undertaking to allow the landlord, or agent, regular access to the property for inspection and repair; and two months before the expiry of the lease to allow the landlord to take other prospective tenants or purchasers round the property.
6. A clause stating that the lease is terminated if any of the other clauses are broken, although the wording has to be carefully drafted to avoid invalidating the agreement.
7. What you, as landlord, are responsible for in the way of repairs: usually the maintenance of the structure and furnishings of the property together with anything left in the property (eg the central heating boiler). You can exclude some items, such as the television, from your responsibility, but generally the tenant is only liable for specific damage to items left in the house and not for their general maintenance.
8. Any special restrictions you want to impose: if, for example, your house is full of valuable antiques you may wish to specify 'no small children'.
9. The conditions under which the tenancy can be terminated prior to its full period having run and without any breach having taken place.
10. Notice must be served under Schedule 2, Ground 1 of the Housing Act 1988 which notifies the tenant that you are an owner-occupier within the meaning of the Housing Act. This gives the landlord and those members of the landlord's family who occupied the house before it was let the right to reoccupy it when the lease expires or is terminated, and protects the mortgage.
11. Notice under Sections 47 and 48 of the Landlord and Tenant Act 1987. The former should be on all rent demands; the latter, notifying the tenant of an address in England and Wales at which notices can be served on the landlord, need only be served once on a tenant at the beginning of a tenancy.

Although the agreement is probably the central document in the transactions involved in letting your house, it does not bring to an end all the things you have to think about. For instance, there is the important matter of the contents insurance.

Letting your home to a third party is probably not covered in your policy and you will have to notify your insurers (and the people who hold your mortgage) that this is what you are doing. In many instances, insurance companies will not insure the contents if property is to be let, and you will need to check carefully that you have cover and can switch to another company if it becomes necessary. At the same time you would be wise to check that the contents insurance covers the full value of what you have left in the house. This check could be combined with making a proper inventory of the contents which is in any case essential before tenants move into a furnished property. Making an exact inventory is quite a time-consuming business and you should bear in mind that it will also have to be checked at the end of the lease, when you may not be there. There are several firms that provide a specialist inventory service at both ends of the lease, covering dilapidations as well as items actually missing, for quite a modest charge which, incidentally, is deductible from the tax due from the letting. Any good property management agent should be able to put you on to one of them.

Since 1 March 1993 it has been an offence to supply furniture which does not comply with fire resistance regulations. Upholstery and loose covers must pass a cigarette test, a match test and an ignitability test.

In addition to the Furniture (Fire) (Safety) Regulations, the Government has recently tightened up safety laws in respect of gas appliances. In November 1994 the Gas Safety (Installation & Use) Regulations 1994 were introduced forcing landlords to take greater responsibility for the safety of their tenants by regularly servicing and repairing any gas appliances through a British Gas or Corgi registered company. Once again, heavy penalties will be enforced for falling to comply.

Finding the tenant and getting the tenant's signature on the agreement marks the beginning rather than the end of the property management firm's responsibilities. Broadly, these fall under two headings: the collection of rental and the management of the property. The rent is collected from the tenant, usually on a standing order basis, under the terms – monthly or quarterly – as set out in the agreement; and, in the event of persistent non-payment, the agent will instruct solicitors on your behalf to issue a county court summons.

WHAT CAN YOU EXPECT FROM THE AGENT?

Management is a more complex subject but an experienced property management agent should be able to supply you with a list of the services that he or she can undertake. It is, therefore, also a checklist of the kind of eventualities that may crop up in your absence which, broadly speaking, relate to the collection of rent, the payment of charges such as service charges and insurance, arrangements for repairs to the fabric of the building and its contents, garden maintenance or when forwarding mail.

Thus, apart from the basic business of collecting the rent, the agent can also pay, on your behalf, any charges on the property (eg ground rent, water rates and insurance) that your contract with the tenant does not specify should be paid by the tenant. There may also be annual maintenance agreements to pay in respect of items like central heating plant and the washing machine.

Then there is the question of what to do about repairs. As we have indicated earlier, whatever you manage to get the tenant to agree to take care of under the terms of the lease, there are certain responsibilities for maintenance and repair that you have to accept by virtue of your status as a landlord. If repairs are necessary, you will simply have to trust the agent to obtain fair prices for you.

On the other hand, except in the case of essential repairs which affect the tenant's legal rights of enjoyment of the property, you can ask your agent to provide estimates for having the work carried out, so that your approval must be obtained before the job is put in hand. Bear in mind, though, that in certain parts of the world the postal system may not be all that reliable. You may, therefore, find it a good idea to put a clause in the management contract giving the agent freedom to proceed with the best estimate if the agent does not hear from you within a specified period. For the same reason it is also wise to ask the agent to send you a formal acknowledgement of receipt of any special or new instructions you have given the agent. An example of this might be an instruction to inspect the property at regular intervals.

Depending on how many concessions you have to make to the tenant to get him or her to sign the lease, there may be other articles for which repair and maintenance remain your responsibility. These may include washing machines, TV and the deep-freeze. Such responsibilities should be set out in the management contract and you should give the agent the details of any guarantees or maintenance contracts relating to them and photocopies of the actual documents for reference. If no such arrangements apply, you should list the manufacturers' names and the model number and age of each item so that the agent can get the manufacturer to send the repair people along equipped with the right spares.

It is very important that a third party, other than you and the tenant, should be in possession of all this information, particularly when there is likely to be more than one tenancy during your absence; and it is a competent management agent, rather than friends, relatives or even a solicitor, who will be best equipped in this case to find new tenants, to check their references, to draw up new agreements and supervise the hand-over of the tenancy.

COSTS AND TAX

The costs of all these services vary according to the nature of the package you need. The professional societies already mentioned recommend charges, which would be applicable in most circumstances. For example, letting and collection is usually 10 per cent of annual rental. In the case of management services, expect to find additional charges made (usually 5 to 7 per cent of the annual rent). These are reasonable fees for the quite considerable headaches involved. We have shown enough of them here to indicate that not only is it virtually impossible to administer a tenancy yourself from a distance, but also that these are not matters to be left to an amateur – friend or relative – however well intentioned. In real terms the agent's charges may be reduced because they are deductible against the tax levied in the UK against rental income.

Expatriates letting their houses also derive a further benefit in respect of capital gains tax. Generally, if you let your principal residence, when you come to sell it you can claim exemption from CGT only for those years in which you lived in it yourself. However, if you let it because you are absent abroad this does not apply, provided you come back to live in the house before you sell it (see pages 22–25).

Finally, in this context, it is worth pointing out that some building societies are now prepared to consider giving mortgages to expatriates for the purchase of a property in the UK *and* to allow them to lease that property for the period of their stay overseas. Up to 90 per cent of the purchase price is available at normal building society rates of interest.

This is an attractive proposition for expatriates, particularly for young executives and professional people who have not yet bought a home in the UK but are earning a substantial income in, say, the Middle East, and for older expatriates perhaps thinking of a retirement home in the UK.

Some agencies supply details of the building societies offering this facility, or you could approach a society directly and explain your position. Should you buy a house as an expatriate and then let it until you return, the earlier recommendation that you leave the management of the property to an experienced and competent agent still applies.

You should note that if a UK property is bought purely as an investment, you would have to time its sale carefully to avoid liability to CGT.

Taxation is a complex subject and varies considerably in its effects on the individual; such advice as can be offered is found on pages 10–42, and we stress the necessity of employing the services of an accountant in your absence. Changes in the Budget allow the use of personal allowances against property income, subject to some restriction, while the Revenue have tightened up the method and timing and collection of tax due in each year, with stiffer penalties for late payment, and refusal to accept postponements except on specific grounds. Should you have an agent collecting the rent, whether this is a professional firm or a friend, the agent will be liable to pay tax on your behalf and, without an indemnity from a UK-based employer or a chartered accountant, may be obliged to deduct tax from each monthly or quarterly rental payment, to enable payment of the amount requested by the Revenue on 1 January.

Similar liabilities now fall on an agent collecting the rental in respect of the Council Tax. The owner will be responsible jointly with the agent to meet the standard charge if the property is empty, or where the property is let for less than six months to an individual. In these cases expect the agent to retain sufficient money to meet this commitment on your behalf.

INSURANCE

One important point that is often overlooked by people who let their house or flat is the necessity of notifying the insurers that a change of occupancy has taken place. Insurance policies only cover occupancy by the insured, not the tenants, though it can be extended to do so on payment of what is usually only a small premium. As already mentioned, many insurance companies will not insure the contents of let property, so notifying the company becomes even more important.

What worries insurance companies much more is if the house is left unoccupied for any length of time. If you look at your policy you will see that it lapses if you leave your house empty for more than 30 days or so – a point that is sometimes forgotten by people who go away on extended holidays. If you are going abroad and leave the house empty – maybe because you have not yet succeeded in finding a tenant – the insurers will usually insist that you turn off the main services and that the premises are inspected regularly by a qualified person. That means someone like a letting agent, not a relative or friend who cannot be relied on 100 per cent. Even if you have let the house without an agent, it may still be advisable to get one to look after the place. A situation could easily occur where the tenant moves out, leaving the place empty and without satisfactory steps having been taken from an insurance point of view. Furthermore, if the worst happens and the house is broken into or damaged, it is imperative that the insurers are notified right away. The effects of damage can be made worse unless they are rapidly attended to, and insurers do not hold themselves responsible for anything that happens between the time the insured eventuality occurs and the time they are notified of it. For instance, if your house is broken into and, a few days later, vandals get in through a broken point of entry and cause further damage, you would not be covered for that second incident unless the insurers had been notified of the first break-in.

Valuable contents are best put into storage and insured there: Pickfords, for instance, charge a premium of 12½ per cent of the storage charge. For very high value items, safe deposit boxes are becoming popular, but from an everyday point of view, the important thing is to make sure you are insured for full values. If you insure contents for £15,000 and the insurer's assessors value them at £20,000 you will only get three-quarters of your claim. To keep insured values in line with rising costs, an index-linked policy would be the best buy for anyone contemplating a long stay abroad. A policy specially written for expatriates is available from the Goodhealth Worldwide Group: the Expatriate UK Home Owners' Insurance Contract. They also offer expatriate motor insurance on private cars being used overseas. All insurance premiums are now subject to insurance premium tax (IPT).

Insuring at full value, incidentally, is equally important when it comes to insuring contents and personal belongings in your residence abroad. Many items will cost much more locally if you have to replace them than they did at the time they were originally bought. It is possible to effect such insurance in the UK, but from the point of getting claims settled quickly it is better to insure in the country concerned, where possible.

Finally, but most important, you should insure against legal and hotel costs when letting your house. Although in principle the legal instruments for quick repossession exist, events have shown that a bloody-minded tenant with a committed lawyer can spin things out to his or her advantage for an almost indefinite period. Premiums, which can be offset against rental income, are in the region of £75 a year.

Rental protection policies are now available, some provide limited cover at relatively low premiums, others cover higher rental amounts, but are more expensive. However, many insurance companies insist on credit checks and the employment of managing agents, in addition to the usual references.

4 Learn a Language

Please learn the native language of the country where you intend to settle, even if you are of retirement age. Surely it is just good manners to speak even a few halting words of the language of your host country when you go to live there permanently or even just to spend long vacations?

You will enjoy the many benefits of closer contact with your neighbours, in business relations or with tradespeople. They will appreciate your efforts to communicate with them and will often go out of their way to help you, not only to learn the right words but also giving assistance in solving problems while shopping, visiting banks and post offices or dealing with officialdom.

There are many different methods of learning a language and if you persevere your efforts will be rewarded, although care should be taken to choose a method that will provide you with the up-to-date language you will require.

Before you go to live abroad, why not take a series of evening classes at a local college of further education or enrol for a 'crash course' at one of the many language colleges?

Other sources of spare-time language education include the Linguaphone system, which offers a wide variety of courses. It is one of the longest-established organisations specialising in teaching foreign languages, and is based at the Linguaphone Institute Ltd, 50 Poland Street, London W1V 4AX (tel: 0800 282 417). It has a range of more than 30 languages and also offers language training for businesses, with individual or group training.

Using audio cassettes or CDs supplemented by an excellent series of books and exercises, the courses are designed for students who want to learn in their own time and place. Some can speak quite fluently in just three months. An advisory service is available free of charge.

Hugo's Audio Language Courses take absolute beginners through to a good working knowledge of written and spoken language. Fairly proficient students also find the courses invaluable for revision and advancement. Each course includes four tapes and a copy of the appropriate 'Three Months' book.

There are 20 titles in the series, covering Arabic*, Catalan, Chinese*, Czech*, Danish, Dutch, French, German, Greek, Hebrew, Italian, Japanese*, Latin American Spanish*, Norwegian*, Portuguese, Russian*, Spanish, Swedish, Turkish* and Welsh. These books set out the rules of grammar which enable students to gain a practical knowledge of the language in a short time. Conversational sentences and selected idiomatic phrases are also included.

In addition to the book there are four tapes with about four hours of recorded time and an instruction leaflet.

Prices for the courses are £29.95, except for the less popular courses, which are marked on the list with an asterisk. These sell for £34.95.

Hugo's also publish phrase books covering 25 different languages (prices from £2.50) and travel packs, each of which contains a phrase book and a cassette of the phrases which are designed to help the traveller to understand and speak the language by familiarisation, without having to learn a lot of grammar. These are priced at £6.99 each. The books can be purchased from bookshops or directly.

Other audio courses with cassette and books are produced by the BBC in their 'Get By' series which comprises a book with key words and phrases, plus other useful information and two 90-minute cassettes. These are produced in the main European languages, as well as Arabic, Russian, Japanese, Chinese and Hindi/Urdu.

The popular 'Teach Yourself' series of books is available in various languages and there is a 'Beginners' series in French, German, Italian and Spanish. Prices are from £6.99.

The Berlitz organization specialises in language instruction and has been established for 120 years. They have 350 Berlitz centres in

50 countries and in the UK publish a wide range of aids to learning in a variety of languages. These include Pocket Guides to nearly 100 countries or cities, which include language and cultural tips; Business Phrase Books for French, Italian, Spanish and German with over 1,000 key business terms and phrases and a bilingual dictionary; Berlitz Phrase Books, with pronunciation guides for the average traveller are available in 33 languages and these are also available in packs with 90 minute audiocassettes. There is also a range of bilingual 'dictionaries'.

Berlitz Today is a new self-instructional course available in French, German, Italian and Spanish. These comprise four 60-minute audiocassettes, a full colour course book, learners guides to help students to maximise course components, a Verb Handbook and bilingual dictionary, plus a coupon for a free private lesson at any participating Berlitz Language centre to test students' progress. Each set costs £39.95.

The even more comprehensive Berlitz Think & Talk self-study language course offers six CDs and six audiocassettes, a 12-chapter course book, verb-finder diskette, handbooks plus dictionary. There is also a coupon for a free and reduced price lessons with a Berlitz instructor. These are available in several languages, including French, German and Spanish through Berlitz Language Centres. Intermediate and Basic Workbooks and special language books for children are also published by Berlitz.

The Champs-Elysées organization of FREEPOST LON295, Bristol BS1 6FA has a new service of language courses for advanced students of French, German, Italian and Spanish.

This comprises a series of audiomagazines consisting of hour–long programmes on audiocassettes, packed with news, features and interviews for each country. These give you the chance to hear your chosen language as it is actually spoken and helps to expand your vocabulary and improve your ability to understand the spoken language.

The audiomagazines are produced at monthly or bi-monthly intervals on a subscription basis and optional study supplements in printed form are also available. A 30-day money-back guarantee is offered to enable you to try out your first edition.

VIDEOS

Video encourages participation by students who can work at home and retain a stronger interest in the subject than by studying from books alone. The BBC market several video packs comprising book, cassettes, video and video handbook in French, German, Italian, Spanish and some other languages. The growing popularity of CDs and CD ROMs will ensure the marketing of a wide range of new language learning aids in the near future.

LANGUAGE SCHOOLS

There are many language schools offering full and part-time study via face-to-face instruction, in London and the provinces. Linguarama Ltd of 8 Queen Street, London EC4N 1SP (0171 236 1992) are among the well-known establishments. They organise training in over 30 foreign languages at all levels from their London headquarters.

Knowledge of a foreign language has other practical advantages, especially if you need to communicate with local authorities such as the police. If you are stopped by a traffic patrolman for an alleged infringement of the law, such as speeding in, say, southern Europe, it is very difficult to plead your innocence if the officer cannot speak your language and you are unable to understand his. In this sort of situation you may well decide to pay the fixed penalty rather than become more deeply involved; if you can speak the local language you may save yourself a fine.

If your home is burgled and you need to report the event to the upholders of law and order, you may find it necessary to pay for the cost of an interpreter to explain all the details to the police. A basic knowledge of the local language could avoid this problem.

5 Taking Your Pets With You

Many families are very fond of their pets, particularly cats and dogs, and are reluctant to leave them behind when they go to live abroad. Import regulations vary from one European country to another, so a summary of the rules for the more popular countries is given below.

If you are travelling by air to your new home, it is possible to have your cat or dog flown to the new destination too. Most major airlines provide these services for pets and their carriage is regulated by the International Air Transport Association and the regulations of government bodies.

It is advisable to employ an approved specialist animal travel agency, which can provide full facilities and care of pets being flown overseas. For example, Airpets Oceanic (tel: 01753 685571), who are based at Heathrow, provide a collection and delivery service for pets, including the provision of comfortable transit containers approved by animal welfare organisations. They will also deal with customs formalities and insurance cover. They supply clients with information regarding the veterinary requirements of the destination country, give guidance on the necessary paperwork, and arrange for consular visas where required.

BELGIUM, THE NETHERLANDS AND LUXEMBOURG

Cats and dogs exported to or in transit through the Benelux countries must be vaccinated against rabies at least 30 days before export and not more than 12 months in advance.

It is advisable to have a health certificate by a veterinary surgeon issued within seven days before export. This document should state that the cat or dog has been examined by the veterinary surgeon and found free of contagious and infectious diseases and is fit to travel.

CYPRUS

The authorities permit new residents to bring their cats or dogs into the island providing the animals have had all the necessary vaccinations and they are allowed to serve the mandatory quarantine period in their owner's new home instead of kennels.

FRANCE

No import permit is required, but dogs and cats not intended for sale in France have to be accompanied in transit, or met at the port of entry by the owner. You will be expected to verify that the animal is not for sale. A maximum of three animals, one of which may be a puppy, is permitted; all must be at least three months old.

An export health certificate should accompany all cats and dogs exported to France. To obtain this, form EXA1 (obtainable from the Ministry of Agriculture, Fisheries and Food, Hook Rise South, Surbiton, Surrey KT6 7NF) should be completed and sent to your local Animal Health Office, who will issue the certificate to the applicant's nominated Local Veterinary Inspector who will complete the certification. Rabies vaccination is only compulsory for animals entering the island of Corsica or being introduced to holiday parks, camping grounds or those participating in shows being held in areas affected by rabies.

It is recommended that dogs should be vaccinated against distemper, parvovirus and hepatitus, but this is not compulsory.

GERMANY

An import permit is not required to take dogs and cats into Germany, if not more than three animals, accompanied by the owner or the owner's representative, are imported for transit through the country or are imported because of a change of residence. Also, not more than three animals can be imported by air, accompanied or unaccompanied, because of a change of residence.

No import permit is required if the animals are over eight weeks old and have been vaccinated against rabies at least 30 days and not more than 12 months prior to their arrival.

GREECE

A permit is not required to import a cat or dog into Greece from Great Britain. Animals must however be accompanied by the following certificates:

1. A bilingual health certificate issued by a local veterinary inspector of the MAFF (Ministry of Agriculture, Fisheries and Food), confirming the breed and species of the animal, that the inspector has examined the animal and that it is in good health, free from symptoms and signs of contagious disease and it has been treated for echinococosis within 30 days of the proposed shipment date. The certificate will only be valid for 10 days from date of issue.
2. For dogs only, a certificate is required stating that the animal has been vaccinated against rabies not less than 15 days before or not more than 12 months before importation into Greece.

It is not necessary to have a dog under three months of age vaccinated against rabies before importation into Greece, provided it is vaccinated on reaching the appropriate age after entry.

ITALY

The Italian authorities do not require an import permit for cats or dogs, but the animals must be accompanied by an Export Health Certificate, signed by a nominated local animal health officer.

Animals accompanied by a traveller

Accompanied animals should be vaccinated against rabies not less than 20 days and not more than 11 months prior to export, but those under the age of three months are exempt from rabies vaccination.

Unaccompanied animals

Unaccompanied animals are exempt from the rabies vaccination, but must undergo an examination by an Italian veterinary officer on arrival at the Italian border and found to be disease free before being allowed to enter Italy.

NEW ZEALAND

An import health permit must be obtained prior to the importation of cats and dogs from a country (eg UK) approved for the export of these animals to New Zealand. Health requirements specify identification by microchip or tattoo prior to export and a period of 30 days post-arrival surveillance is required.

NORTHERN IRELAND, REPUBLIC OF IRELAND, ISLE OF MAN AND THE CHANNEL ISLANDS

Unrestricted movement of cats and dogs between Great Britain, Northern Ireland, the Republic of Ireland and the Channel Islands is permitted and no documents are required.

PORTUGAL, MADEIRA AND THE AZORES

An import permit is required for dogs and cats entering Portugal, together with appropriate certificates. The first is a health certificate issued by a local veterinary inspector of MAFF not more than 14 days prior to export, stating that the animals are free of signs of contagious or infectious diseases including distemper and rabies. Also required is the Ministry's export certificate issued not more than 14 days prior to export, declaring that rabies has not existed in any of the districts from which the animal originates and that it has remained in the area of origin since birth or for six months prior to the date of shipment.

A health certificate has to be sent to the Ministry at Surbiton for authentication.

On arrival in Portugal, dogs have to be kept in the home under the supervision of the Animal Health Services. The period of restriction may be specified on the import permit or by the Animal Health Services. All dogs in Portugal over four months of age must be vaccinated against rabies; this is undertaken during the period of home quarantine.

SOUTH AFRICA

Dogs and cats that have been kept in the UK for six months before departure, or are younger than six months and have been in the UK since birth, are not subject to quarantine, provided they are accompanied by a permit from the Director of Veterinary Services in Pretoria. Application for the permit must be made to Pretoria at least six weeks before importation and accompanied by a confirmation from a UK veterinary surgeon indicating that the animal is fit to travel.

Rabies injections are necessary where the animal is entering the province of Natal.

SPAIN, CANARY AND BALEARIC ISLANDS

An export health certificate should accompany all cats and dogs exported from Great Britain to Spain. This should be signed by a nominated local veterinary officer appointed by MAFF.

A maximum of two pet animals only may accompany travellers from the UK.

Rabies vaccination is not compulsory for accompanied pet animals entering Spain directly from Great Britain or for animals less than three months old.

Commercial exports

If rabies vaccination has not been carried out on cats and dogs for commercial export, they may be placed in quarantine for 14 days in Spain. Thereafter, if no symptoms of disease have been observed, they will be vaccinated and released. The cost of vaccination must be borne by the owner. Commercially exported animals may only be consigned to an approved zoological unit, sporting or commercial establishment.

SWITZERLAND

All cats and dogs aged five months or more, imported from Great Britain, are required to be vaccinated against rabies at least 30 days and not more than 12 months prior to export to Switzerland, and a valid certificate of vaccination must be produced on arrival.

Those aged less than five months may be imported without a rabies certificate but must have an Export Health Certificate from a qualified veterinary surgeon, issued not more than six days prior to export. This certificate must describe the animal and state that it is free from contagious and infectious diseases, and that it is fit to travel.

Cats and dogs passing through Switzerland to another country, by air or rail without stopping, only require an Export Health Certificate.

ARRANGING FOR RABIES VACCINATION

Although the use of rabies vaccination is not normally allowed in Great Britain, arrangements have been made for vaccine to be available for animals being exported. The owner or exporter may choose a veterinary surgeon to undertake the work and the surgeon should contact the Divisional Veterinary Officer well in advance of the export date, giving a description of the animal and its destination, and requesting that vaccine be released so that it can be administered. The owner must provide documentary evidence to the vet that the animal is being exported.

AN END TO QUARANTINE REGULATIONS?

The British government is still under pressure from Europe to abandon quarantine of animals entering the UK as a means of controlling rabies, a rule which currently applies only to Britain and Ireland.

The Royal Society for the Prevention of Cruelty to Animals and many other pet lovers are calling for an end to the six months' quarantine of cats and dogs who enter Britain from the EU and rabies-free countries.

Scientific evidence seems to favour identity and inoculation schemes. Animal tagging and blood tests are judged by many experts to be effective and they are less costly and distressing to pets and their owners. Another reform that may be considered is a reduction of the quarantine period to just one month, rather than abolish it altogether. It is claimed that many vets are in favour of scrapping the quarantine system entirely. The experts appear confident that quarantine will be abolished during the next year.

6 Education Overseas

Parents who go abroad for business reasons or retirement when their children are still of school age often arrange for their offspring to continue their education at a boarding school in the UK, so that they see them only during the holidays or at half-term.

This is a pity because it tends to break up the family and can be very expensive. What is more, it is not really necessary as there are excellent English-speaking establishments in most European countries where pupils learn not only the subjects normally studied in Britain, but also a wider curriculum which introduces them to the international scene.

Very young children who commence their education in a foreign country also have the opportunity of mixing naturally with local youngsters and soon become bilingual. (Some even become fluent in three languages if their parents are of different nationalities and the country where they reside speaks a third tongue.)

A long-established advisory service for UK education is offered by Gabbitas of 6–8 Sackville Street, Piccadilly, London W1X 2BR. This includes free impartial advice on the selection of independent schools throughout the UK. A careers counselling service is available on a fee-charging basis and a full guardianship service is offered in the UK for children whose parents live abroad.

The firm publishes annually through Kogan Page *The Gabbitas Guide to Independent Schools* listing schools in the UK. It costs £12.99 plus 10 per cent postage and packing and can be obtained from Kogan Page.

The Independent School Information Service, 56 Buckingham Gate, London SW1E 6AG, is another useful source of information. The International Schools Directory is a further useful source. It costs £35 and is available from The European Council of International Schools, 21 Lavant Street, Petersfield, Hampshire GU32 3EL (tel: 01730 268244).

A brief selection of overseas schools for English-speaking children is given below:

AUSTRALIA

New South Wales

Redlands Church of England School, 272 Military Road, Cremorne, Sydney, NSW 2090.
Co-educational, 5–18 years.
Queenwood School for Girls, 47 Mandolone Road, Mosman, Sydney.
Kindergarten (primary) to secondary, 5–18 years.
St Andrew's Cathedral School, 474 Kent Street, Sydney.
Boys, 3–12 years.
Sydney Grammar School, Sydney, NSW.
Cogee Boys Preparatory, Cogee, NSW.

CYPRUS

Nicosia

American Academy, 3A, M Parides Street, PO Box 1967, Nicosia.
Primary and secondary school for boys and girls; also a junior school.
English School, PO Box 3575, Nicosia.
Secondary day school for boys and girls.
Falcon School, PO Box 3640, Nicosia.
Reception, primary and secondary school for boys and girls.
GC School of Careers, PO Box 5276, Nicosia.
Secondary school for boys and girls.

Terra Santa College, PO Box 1546, Nicosia.
Secondary school for boys and girls.

Limassol

American Academy and Junior School, Limassol.
Boys and girls, 5–16 years.
Limassol Grammar School (Foley's), Homer Street, Ayios
Nicolaos, Limassol.
Junior and secondary school for boys and girls.
The Logos School of English Education, Nikocleous Street,
PO Box 1075, Limassol.
Secondary school for boys and girls.
Private Grammar School (Gregoriou), PO Box 1340, Limassol.
Secondary school for boys and girls.

Larnaca

American Academy, Afxentiou Avenue, PO Box 112, Larnaca.
Secondary school for boys and girls.
St Joseph, Mich. Parides Square, Larnaca.
Secondary school for girls.

Paphos

Anglo-American International School, 24–26 Hellas Avenue,
Paphos.
Primary and secondary school for boys and girls, 5–18 years.
International School of Paphos, PO Box 2018, Paphos.
Co-educational, day and boarding, kindergarten, junior and
secondary departments.

FRANCE

American School of Paris, 41 rue Pasteur, 92210 Saint Cloud,
Paris.
Boys and girls, 5–18 years.

British School of Paris, 38 Quai de l'Ecluse, 78290 Croissy-sur-
Seine, Paris.
Boys and girls, 4½–18 years.
International School of Paris, 6 rue Beethoven, 75016 Paris.
Boys and girls, 3–18 years.
Bordeaux International School, 53 rue de Laseppe, 33000
Bordeaux.
Boys and girls 4–18 years, including boarders.
Mougins School, Avenue Dr Maurice Donat 615, BP101, 06250
Mougins.

GERMANY

British Embassy Preparatory School, Tulpenbaumweg 42, D5300
Bonn.
Boys and girls, 4–13 years.
British High School Bonn, Friesdorferstrasse 57, D5300 Bonn.
European School Munich, Elise-Aulinger 21, D-81739,
München.
Berlin British School, Dickenswec 17–19, 14504 Berlin.
Bonn International School, Martin Luther King Strasse 14,
53175 Bonn.

GREECE

Athens College, PO Box 5, Psychio, Athens.
Boys and girls, grades 1–6; boys only, grades 7–13.
St Catherine's British Embassy School, c/o British Embassy,
Plutarchoul, 10675 Athens.

ITALY

Ambrit International School, Via Annia Regilla 60, 00187 Rome.
Boys and girls' kindergarten and primary school.
International School of Milan, 6 Via Bezzola, Milan.

International School of Naples, Mostra d'Oltremore, 80125 Naples.
Boys and girls, 4½–17 years.

St James Henderson British School of Milan, Via Pisani, 20134 Milan.
Boys and girls 3–18 years.

St George's English School, Via Cassia, Km16, 00123 Rome.
Boys and girls 3–18 years.

MALTA

A free state school education exists, with optional private education. Fees are less than in the UK for both day and boarding establishments. Lessons in private schools are in English and the curriculum is closely aligned to the British systems, with students sitting for GCSE and A level exams.

Chiswick House School, Sliema.
Junior school for boys and girls.

St Edward's College; De La Salle College; St Aloysius College.
Typical secondary schools with GCSE and A level courses for pupils up to 18 years old.

THE NETHERLANDS

British School in the Netherlands, Boerderji Rosenburgh, Rosenburgerlaan, 2, 2252 BA Voorschoten
Boys and girls, 3–18 years.

British School of Amsterdam, Jan Van Eijckstraat 21, 1077LG, Amsterdam.
Boys and girls, 3–12 years.

International School of Amsterdam, A J Ernststraat 875, Amsterdam 1081HL.
Boys and girls.

PORTUGAL

Barlavento English School, Espiche 8600, Lagos, Algarve.
  Boys and girls, kindergarten.
British School, Oporto (founded 1894).
  Prepares pupils for Cambridge and London Boards and
  Common Entrance.
Colegio International de Vilamoura, Apartado 856, 8125
  Vilamoura.
International Preparatory School, Rua do Boror 12, Carcavelos,
  2775 Parede.
  Pupils, 5–13 years.
International School of the Algarve, Porches, near Lagoa, Algarve.
  Boys and girls, 4–16 years. Centre in southern Portugal for
  Cambridge University GCSE examinations.
Prince Henry International School, Vale do Lobo, Almansil,
  Algarve.
  Boys and girls, 3–16 years.
St Anthony's International Primary School, Avenida de
  Portugal 11, 2765 Estoril.
  Boys and girls up to 12 years of age.
St George's School, Vila Conçalves, Quinta dos Loureiras,
  Estrada Nacional, 2750 Cascais.
  Boys and girls, 3–13 years.
St Julian's School, Quinta Nova, Carcavelos, 2777 Parede (about
  10 miles from Lisbon).
  Boys and girls, 3½–18 years.

SOUTH AFRICA

Cape Town

Diocesan College, Campground Road, Rondebosch.
  5–18 years.
St Cyprian's Girls School, Belmont Avenue, Oranjezicht.
  Girls, 6–18 years.

Durban

Durban Girls College, 586 Musgrave Road, Durban.
  6–18 years.
Durban Boys High School, St Thomas Road, Durban.
  11–17 years.

Johannesburg

Redhill School, 20 Summit Road, Morningside, Sandton.
  3–18 years.

Pretoria

Glen High School, Atterbury Road/Menlyn Drive, Pretoria.
  12–18 years.
Park Ridge Primary School, Bezuidenhout Street, Vanderbijl Park.
  6–12 years.

SPAIN

A large number of British schools have been established in Spain and many of these are members of the National Association of British Schools in Spain, Avenida Ciudad de Barcelona 110, Escalera 3–5° D, 28007, Madrid. A list of establishments in major resort areas is given below. Further information can be obtained from the schools direct.

Basque country

American School of Bilbao, Soparda Bidea 10, 48640 Berango (Vizcaya).
  American-style education for boys and girls, 3–16 years.

Costa del Sol

Aloha College, 'En Angel', Nueva Andalucia, 29660 Marbella.
  3–18 years co-educational.

Calpe College, Apartado 200 San Pedro de Alcantara, Marbella.
3–18 years, co-educational.

The English Centre, Apartado 85, 11500 El Puerto de Santa
Maria, Cadiz.
2–17 years, co-educational.

English International College, Urbanizacion Ricmar, CN 340,
Km 189, Marbella, 29600 Málaga.
3–18 years, co-educational.

International School, Apartado 15, Sotogrande, Cadiz.
Offers day/boarding facilities, 2–18 years, co-educational.

St Anthony's College, Apartado 119, Los Boliches, 29640
Fuengirola.
3–18 years, co-educational.

Sunny View School, Apartado 175, Cerro del Toril,
Torremolinos.
4–18 years, co-educational.

Swan's International Primary School, Urb. Capricho 1–2, 29600
Marbella.
3–12 years.

Costa Blanca

Caxton College, Carreterra de Barcelona, 46530 Puzol, Valencia.
3–14 years, co-educational.

Colegio Hispano–Norteamericano, Avda Sierra Calderona 29,
Los Monasterios, 46530 Pucol, Valencia.
Co-educational.

El Limonar International School. Calle General Sanjurjo 2,
30151 Santo Angel, Murcia.
2–10 years, co-educational.

Lady Elizabeth School, Apartado 298, Javea, Alicante.
3–18 years, co-educational.

Newton College, Camino Viejo Elche, Alicante Km. 3, Partido
de Maitano P1–82A, Elche, Alicante.
3–18 years, co-educational.

Sierra Bernia School, La Caneta San Rafael, Alfaz del Pi, Alicante.
3–18 years, co-educational.

Xadia International College, Apartado 311 03730 Javea.
3–18 years, co-educational.

Barcelona

Anglo-American School, Paseo de Garbi 152, Casteldelfels, Barcelona.
3–18 years, co-educational.
Benjamin Franklin International School, Martorelli Pena 9, 08017 Barcelona.
Co-educational for American and other students, 3–12 years.
English Academy Santa Claus, León XIII 12, Barcelona.
2–12 years, co-educational.
Kensington School, Carre del Cavallers 31–33 08034 Barcelona.
4–18 years, co-educational.
Oak House, San Pedro Claver 12, 08017 Barcelona.
3–18 years, co-educational.
St Paul's School, Avenida Pearson 39–45, 08034 Barcelona.
3–18 years, co-educational.
St Peter's School, Eduard Toldra 18, 08034 Barcelona.
2–18 years, co-educational.
John Talabot, Escuelas Dias, Barcelona 08017.
3–17 years, co-educational.

Madrid

British Council School, Urb. Prado de Somosaguas, 28223, Pozuelo de Alarcon, Madrid.
3–18 years.
English Montessori School, Avda La Salle, s/n Aravaca, 28023 Madrid.
3–17 years, co-educational.
Hastings School, Avenida Alfonso XIII, 117/9, 28016 Madrid.
Primary and secondary co-educational.
International College Spain, Vereda Norte 3, 28109 la Moraleja, Madrid.
3–18 years, co-educational.
King's College, Paseo de los Andes, Madrid 28760.
1½–18 years, co-educational.
Numont PNEU, Parma 16, 28043 Madrid.
2–11 years, co-educational.
Open University c/o Kings College, c/Serrano 44, 28001 Madrid.
150 courses in English.

Runnymede College, Camino Ancho 87, La Moraleja-
Alconbendas, 28109 Madrid.
2–18 years, co-educational.
St Charles College, Calle Guadalquivir 16 (E1 Viso), 28002 Madrid.
Business and secretarial college.

Valencia

English School Los Olivos, Avenida Pino Panera, 46110 Godella,
Valencia.
3–14 years.
Plantio International School of Valencia, Urbanizacion El
Plantiori Calle 233, s/n 46353, La Canada, Valencia.
3–11 years.

Canary Islands

American School of Las Palmas, Apartado 15, Tarifa Alta, Las
Palmas.
3–18 years, co-educational.
The International British Yeoward School, Parque Taoro, Puerto
de la Cruz, Tenerife.
3–18 years.
Canterbury School, Juan XXIII 44, Las Palmas.
3–18 years, co-educational.
Colegio Hispano-Britanico, Apartado 228, 35500 Arrecife de
Lanzarote.
3–18 years, co-educational.
British School of Gran Canary, Tafira, Las Palmas (tel: 928
351167).
3–18 years, co-educational.
El Tablero, South Gran Canary.
3–10 years, co-educational.
Kent College, Carretera del Centro 10, Veelta del Medico
Panuelo, Tafira Baja, Las Palmas.
3–11 years, co-educational.
Trinity School, Camino Montijo 16, La Carrera 38410,
Los Realejos, Tenerife.
2–11 years, co-educational.

Wingate School, Mirador de la Cumbrita 10, Cabo Blanco,
   Arona, Tenerife.
   4–17 years, co-educational.
Windale Nursery School, Finca el Lland, Sabinta Baja 38640
   Arona, Tenerife.
   2–4 years, co-educational.

Balearic Islands

Academy International College, Apartado 1300, Palma, Majorca.
   2–14 years, co-educational.
American International School, Oratorio 4, Portals Nous, 07015
   Majorca.
   3–18 years, co-educational.
Baleares International School, Calle Cabo Mateu Coch 17, San
   Agustin, 07015 Palma de Majorca.
   3½–18 years, co-educational day and boarding.
Bellver International College, José Costa Ferrer 5, Cala Mayor,
   07015 Palma, Majorca.
   3–18 years, co-educational.
Queen's College, Juan de Saridakis 64, Palma, Majorca.
   3–18 years.

SWITZERLAND

Aiglon College, 1885 Chesières Vilars.
   Boys and girls, 11–18 years.
College du Leman – International School,
   74 Route de Sauverny 1290 Versoux, Geneva,
   8–19 years, co-educational. Also a summer school.
International School of Berne, Mattenstrasse 3,
   3073 Gumlegen bei Berne.
   Boys and girls, 5–18 years.
St George's School, 1815 Clarens, Montreux.
   Girls, 11–19 years.

EUROPEAN SCHOOLS

Nine European schools were set up among EU states for multinational education of staff employed in EU communities. These day schools provide education for children aged 4–19 and can be found in Belgium, Germany, Holland, Italy, Luxembourg and the UK. Information from European School, Culham, Abingdon, Oxford OX14 3DZ.

7 Health Benefits and Insurance

Pensioners living in any of the EU countries are entitled to claim medical and health facilities that are available to nationals of the country concerned.

Benefits include free dental treatment, sickness benefit, free medicine and drugs. Widows' benefits are also payable on the death of a husband. Generally speaking, the benefits are available to pensioners who were, at some time during their working lives, employed in any of the EU countries, but there are exceptions. Details are given in the Department of Social Security leaflet SA29, *Your Social Security, Health Care and Pension Rights in the European Community*, available from your local Social Security Office or direct from the DSS Overseas Branch, Newcastle-upon-Tyne NE98 1YX.

Those drawing their pensions from the Department of Social Security should receive a copy of Form 121 whereon the Newcastle authorities certify the pensioners' entitlement and this is sent to the appropriate social security authority in the country of residence.

Adults and pensioners who stay temporarily in an EU member state and/or many other countries that have reciprocal arrangements with the UK, can obtain medical and hospital treatment free or at reduced cost if taken ill in one of these countries. But before they leave the UK they must take with them Form E111, issued by the Department of Social Security, and which has been stamped and signed by the applicant's local post office. The coverage offered in the different countries in the scheme is contained in an informative leaflet entitled *Health Advice for Travellers*, which can be obtained from the Department of Health, PO Box 410, Wetherby

LS23 7LN or by telephoning the Health Literature Line on Freephone 0800 555777. This is a most useful publication and should be in the possession of everyone from the UK travelling overseas.

Those planning to live and work in EU member states will find an information service entitled 'European Direct' most useful. This provides information on the general activities of the European Union, informs European citizens of their rights within the internal market and gives advice on selected problems encountered by citizens. A series of factsheets are published on jobs, taxation, education, social security, welfare benefits, seeking work, etc; also rights of residence, voting, driving licences and so on. The leaflets can be obtained from The Office for Official Publications of the European Communities, by telephoning 0800 581591. The service is also available on the Internet at http://citizens.eu.int.

Although free medical benefits are available, delays in obtaining treatment in hospitals and consulting doctors can be lengthy, as in the UK. Also, hospital wards often lack the desired privacy when a patient is seriously ill.

It is therefore highly recommended that those living permanently in an overseas country should subscribe to a private medical insurance scheme.

A private health insurance plan for expatriates is available from Exeter Friendly Society, Devon (see pages 81 and 82). This organisation, which has been writing insurance for 70 years, is a registered UK Friendly Society.

The Exeter scheme is particularly good value for retired persons because their premium rates do not automatically increase with advancing age. Members have the opportunity to renew cover every year for life irrespective of claims record.

There is a wide range of benefit options to choose from to match individual needs and budgets. The policy covers medical treatment received anywhere in the world (excluding North America).

Full details can be obtained from Exeter Friendly Society, Beech Hill House, Walnut Garden, Exeter EX4 4DG (tel: 01392 477200; fax: 01392 477235).

WPA Health International offer three full health schemes for expatriates with worldwide cover including USA/Canada and also

(*continued on page 84*)

A SURVEY OF CURRENT EXPATRIATE MEDICAL SCHEMES

Benefits	PPP healthcare International Health Plan (Comprehensive Option)	BUPA International Lifeline (Gold)
Overall maximum	£750,000	£500,000
Hospital accommodation	Full refund	Full refund
Home nursing	Full refund up to 14 days	£600
Surgeons' and anaesthetists' fees	Full refund	Full refund
Operating theatre fees	Full refund	Full refund
Hospital treatment (non-surgical)	Full refund (£3,000 limit on out-patient, with £20 excess per visit)	Full refund (outpatients £2000)
GP treatment	Full refund within £3,000 out-patient limit. £20 excess per visit	£600
Maternity care	Complications only	Complications only
Emergency dental care	Accidental damage within £3000 out-patient limit. £20 excess per visit	£400 per person per annum
Emergency evacuation/ repatriation Premiums	Full refund – included in all plans with no extra charge see over	Full refund
Other benefits	<ul><li>6 weeks' cover when 'out of area';</li><li>parent accommodation to 18 years;</li><li>£100 cash benefit per night if treatment is free;</li><li>£500 ambulance cover;</li><li>health information line</li></ul>	

Exeter Friendly Society *Interplan* (European level 3)	*Goodhealth* *Worldwide Ltd* *Foundation Module*
£100,000	US $1,700,000 per person, per annum
Up to £30,000 per condition per year	Full refund
Full refund up to 14 days per year	Full refund up to 30 days per condition
Full refund	Full refund
Full refund within benefit for hospital accomodation	As above
As above	As above
£100 per year	As above
Excluded	Optional extra
Excluded	Full refund (accidental damage)
Optional	Full refund

A SURVEY OF CURRENT EXPATRIATE MEDICAL SCHEMES (CONT)

Premium	*Goodhealth Worldwide Ltd International Healthcare Plan*			*BUPA International Lifeline (Gold)*	*Exeter Friendly Society Interplan (European level 3)*
	Age	Area 1 US $	Area 2 US $	Area 3 US $	Varies according to age.[2]	Age related on joining only.
	0–17	485	551	1,087	Lifeline Gold[1]	21–29: £288
	18–20	572	735	1,357	Under 21: £299	30–39: £371
	21–24	696	821	1,716	21–24: £437	40–49: £504
	25–29	747	893	1,872	25–29: £584	50–59: £733
	30–34	833	957	2,003	30–34: £634	60–69: £1098
	35–39	906	1,051	2,225	35–39: £685	70–79: £1756
	40–44	1,076	1,209	2,702	40–44: £782	
	45–49	1,284	1,359	3,052	45–49: £918	
	50–54	1,592	1,648	3,570	50–54: £1024	
	55–59	2,101	2,123	4,704	54–59: £1247	
	60–64	2,660	2,712	6,292	60–64: £1625	
	65–69	3,208	3,674	8,009	65–69: £2357	
	70–74	3,873	4,378	9,478	70–74: £2826	
	75–79	4,480	5,041	10,900	75–79: £3210	
	80+	5,289	5,697	12,361	80+: £3663	

Area 1 Europe and Middle East Excluding elective treatment in USA
Area 2 Worldwide
Area 3 Worldwide

Premium rates for optional modules are available on application.

1. Individual cover only.
2. Higher premiums apply for USA and Canada.

New members accepted up to 75 years of age.

	PPP healthcare International Health Plan (Comprehensive Option)	
Age range:	Comprehensive Area 2	Comprehensive Area 3
Child rate	328.30	262.20
Up to 24	657.80	527.80
25–29	710.20	570.00
30–34	761.50	615.60
35–39	823.10	668.00
40–44	880.10	715.90
45–49	928.00	804.80
50–54	975.80	850.40
55–59	1,152.50	1,016.90
60–64	1,418.20	1,317.80
65–69	2,103.30	2,030.30
70–74	2,471.50	2,318.80
75–79	2,775.90	2,606.00
80 plus	3,135.00	2,943.50

Area 2 = Worldwide excluding USA & Canada
Area 3 = Europe

excluding these two countries. In addition they have a cash plan which provides money benefit when in hospital, or towards dental, optical, consultation fees and maternity benefit.

The expatriate scheme includes hospitalisation, emergency medical evacuation and a no-claims bonus of one year free after five consecutive years without a claim.

PPP healthcare has provided expatriate health cover for over 20 years. The International Health Plan provides three options with varying levels of in-patient, daycare and out-patient cover. All options include emergency evacuation and repatriation cover, emergency out-of-area cover and a cash benefit of £100 per night if treatment is received free of charge.

The dedicated International Personal Advisory Team includes a number of multilingual staff who are available Monday to Saturday to help with membership queries and claims. They settle bills directly with over 300 hospitals outside the UK.

PPP healthcare's unique 24-hour Health Information Line has access to one of the largest electronic libraries in Europe, to give members the latest information on a variety of medical topics. It is staffed by health professionals such as nurses, midwives, health visitors and pharmacists, who can answer queries on medical issues, specialist organisations, health scares and much more. Health factsheets are also provided to explain various medical conditions, written in plain English.

These health factsheets can now be accessed for the first time via PPP healthcare's newly launched Web site: www.ppphealthcare.com. Members are provided with online access to the Directory of Hospitals, health plan details and topical health articles, and can even download claim forms from the Web site, to avoid postal delays.

Goodhealth Worldwide Ltd, Mill Bay Lane, Horsham, West Sussex, have introduced their new International Healthcare Plan, based on a comprehensive foundation module with the flexibility of option modules which enable clients to tailor-make cover to suit their requirements.

The standard benefits under the foundation module include full refund for in-patient and out-patient treatment; prescription and over the counter drugs and dressings; home nursing; reconstructive surgery; psychiatric illness; AIDS; accidental damage to teeth; complications of pregnancy; parent/newborn accommodation; hormone replacement therapy; and evacuation and transportation/additional travel/mortal remains.

Optional modules include chronic conditions; dental (routine and major restorative); normal pregnancy and childbirth; inpatient only; and USA elective treatment.

Premium rates vary according to age and requirements and are listed on pages 81 and 83.

International Health Insurance Danmark a/s offer worldwide coverage with their health and hospital plans. There are several choices of cover, ranging from hospitalisation only, top-up cover, dental treatment and spectacles, to a comprehensive plan (the top-up plan is designed to make up for any shortfall in benefits in an existing scheme). Medical evacuation can be included too. Complicated claim forms for reimbursement of medical expenses are not needed – the submission of original receipted invoices are all that are required. Cover is worldwide, including the country where you reside, and there is no limit on the time you spend abroad.

Children under 10 years of age are covered free of charge under the parents' policy (up to four children – two per paying insured) providing they are included on the application form.

The company has been established for more than a quarter of a century, has policyholders in 160 countries and is wholly owned by Sygeforsikringen Danmark, the largest medical insurance company in Scandinavia.

Full details of benefits and premiums can be obtained from the UK branch office, International Health Insurance, 64a Athol Street, Douglas, Isle of Man IM1 1JE.

Part Two:

Moving Out, Settling In, Coming Back

8 Moving Overseas

Moving house can be a traumatic experience at the best of times. At worst, with careless planning and trying to cut costs, it can be a disaster!

Before the actual move there are always weeks of preparation; bringing down old boxes from the loft and poring over their contents to see if they are worth keeping; clearing out the garage and throwing away the odd bits of wood and junk that you were keeping in case they proved useful. Ask any remover – we've all got much more in our homes than we think.

So imagine the additional problems facing a householder who is moving abroad. He (or usually she) has to go through the family's possessions and ruthlessly pare them down to manageable proportions for packing into a container for shipping or air freighting to perhaps the other side of the world.

Difficult decisions have to be made, such as whether to take the three-piece suite and dining room table/chairs or to buy new ones once you are settled in your new home. How do prices compare? Whom to ask?

Invaluable help can be provided by a reputable international remover who will be able to advise you as to what is best left behind and replaced at destination and what should be taken to save expense or because of supply difficulties and so on. It costs nothing to invite a remover to survey your household goods and personal effects and to provide an estimate of the removal costs; and it could also save you a lot of time and energy.

The first main danger which people can suffer is sending their possessions through a freight forwarding agent who delivers only as far as the port of entry of the destination country. This means that you will have to arrange Customs clearance and also find someone to transfer your belongings from the port to your new home or, if that is not ready, into store. Without knowledgeable help, finding proper local storage facilities is no easy task in a strange country.

Second, a surprising number of people rely on a remover with no financial or other backing who nevertheless quotes extremely attractive prices. Unfortunately, in the past this lack of financial base has often meant the remover going bankrupt and being unable to carry out the move for which the remover was contracted. In this case, the hapless customer, who will already have paid the first remover, will have to pay yet again for someone else to complete the move. Regrettably, the chance of redress is so limited as not to be worth considering.

Both these circumstances can be avoided if you choose a contractor from among the Overseas Group members of the British Association of Removers (BAR). All international member companies have links throughout the world with equally reputable removers, through their international trade association, the Federation of International Removers (FIDI).

Membership of FIDI means that a contractor can arrange a door-to-door international removal, working with a reliable and know-ledgeable firm in the destination country who will deal with the formalities relating to Customs clearance and (if pets are involved) quarantine regulations, store the consignment as long as necessary and finally deliver it to your new address.

While these relationships offer a comforting level of expertise, the BAR Overseas Group also provides tangible security, through its guarantee of the financial soundness of its members. Its BAR-IMMI advance payment scheme provides a written guarantee that, should a member company fail to fulfil its commitments to a customer, the removal will be completed at no extra cost or the money refunded.

So people moving overseas who use a BAR Overseas Group member need have no fear of settling in their new home with only the clothes they stand up in while the rest of their belongings are stranded in Britain – something which has happened to many people using non-BAR Overseas Group members which have gone out of business.

In addition, a qualified remover can also guide you through the minefield of documentation relating to import/export licences and Customs regulations.

Electrical appliances may not be compatible with voltages in your destination country and your TV and video will probably not be suitable. If you are moving to a warmer climate you will definitely need a larger fridge/freezer, so, unless you have recently bought a new one, the freezer, or fridge, is not worth taking. Many houses have built-in furniture, so you may not need your wardrobes either.

On the other hand, there are some items which cost less in Britain than elsewhere and it may be worth buying these before you go. Under the government's personal export scheme, people who are emigrating or who intend spending at least 12 months out of the country are allowed to buy certain goods free of VAT charges. Your remover will be able to give you details of this.

Take good carpets, high-quality furniture and fine china/glass if you wish, and remember to include some articles of winter clothing. Even in warmer climes the evenings can be chilly.

Take your tool kit too, as tools are costly to replace wherever you live. But think twice about taking cane furniture as this is viewed with grave suspicion in most countries. As a precaution the quarantine authorities may decide to have the furniture fumigated at your expense, and the cost is high.

English books are often expensive in foreign countries, so you may wish to take not only your present collection, but also some for future reading and reference.

Special provision usually has to be made for pets and cars. In some countries both may be banned; in others (such as the USA) the car will have to comply with exhaust emission legislation.

Finally, do not forget to make a complete inventory of everything to be moved and to give your remover a copy. Any discrepancy between the list and the contents of your consignment could result in Customs officials delaying clearance – and although there may be the temptation to slip a few 'extras' in, don't try it; Customs searches are rigorous and the penalties severe.

For more hints about moving abroad, a free leaflet is available by sending a stamped and self-addressed envelope (preferably 9 × 4 inches) to the British Association of Removers overseas, 3 Churchill Court, 58 Station Road, North Harrow HA2 7SA.

REMOVAL CHECKLIST

Don't forget to arrange a UK contact address and to tell the following that you are moving abroad:

Your bank.

Income Tax Office. Notify the Inland Revenue, giving the exact date of departure.

National Insurance/DSS. For benefits, allowances, pension. Send your full name, date of birth, full National Insurance number, details of country to which you are moving and duration of your stay to the DSS Overseas Branch, Newcastle upon Tyne NE98 IYX.

Vehicle licence. If you are taking your vehicle abroad for longer than a year this is regarded as a 'permanent export'. In this case you should return your existing (new style) registration document to the Vehicle Licensing Centre, Swansea SA99 1AB, filling in the 'permanent export' section. Alternatively, you can apply to your local Vehicle Registration Office for the necessary forms.

Driving licence. You should retain your British driving licence (European Communities Model). Many countries, in addition to those in the EC, recognise it as valid; a list of those which do not is available from the AA.

International driving licence. An international driving licence is obtainable from the AA or RAC (even if you are not a member) and is valid for one year. The licence is not valid in the country where it is issued so you must obtain it before leaving the UK. Most countries require residents to hold a local driving licence, so check whether this is the case on taking up your new residence.

Motor insurance. Notify your insurers of the date of your departure – your insurance should be cancelled from that date and you should obtain a refund for the rest of the insurance period. Ask your insurance company for a letter outlining your no-claim record to show to your new insurer.

Life and other insurances. Notify the companies concerned or your insurance broker if you use one. Remember to insure the contents of your new home immediately you move in.

Dentist. Let your dentist know you are moving, as a matter of courtesy; it will save him or her posting useless check-up reminders.

Optician. It may be useful to take a copy of your prescription with you.

Private health insurance. Notify subscriber records department.

Gas. If you use it, notify your local gas office, giving at least *48 hours'* notice. They will give you a standard form to fill in with details of the move and any current hire-purchase agreements. If appliances are to be removed the gas company requires as much notice as possible to arrange an appointment; there is a disconnection charge.

Electricity. Notify your local office or showroom at least *48 hours* before moving. Arrangements are much the same as for gas.

Water. The local water supply company should also be notified at least *48 hours* before the move. Drain tanks and pipes if the house is to remain empty in winter.

Telephone. Notify your local telephone sales office, as shown in the front of your directory, at least *seven days* before the move.

Local authority. Notify the town hall of your departure. You may be entitled to a partial refund of your council tax.

Libraries. Return books and give in tickets to be cancelled.

Professional advisers. Solicitors, accountants, stockbrokers, insurance brokers etc. Make sure they have a forwarding address.

Stocks and shares. Write to the company registrar at the address on the last annual report or share certificates.

Organisations and clubs. Any business, civic, social, cultural, sports or automobile club of which you are a member. For the AA write to Membership Subscription and Records, PO Box 50, Basingstoke, Hampshire; for the RAC write to RAC House, Lansdowne Road, East Croydon, Surrey.

Credit card companies. Advise them that you are leaving the country.

HP companies. Notify the office where repayments are made. You will need to settle your accounts.

Local business accounts. Department stores, newsagents, dairy, baker, chemist, dry cleaner, laundry, motor service station.

Publications. Cancel postal subscriptions to magazines, professional and trade journals, books and record clubs etc, and orders for news-papers.

National Health Service. Return your NHS card to the Family Practitioners' Committee for your area, giving your date of departure, or hand in the card to the immigration officer at your point of departure.

Pension schemes. If you have a 'frozen' or paid-up pension from a previous employer be sure to notify the pension trust of your new address.

TV and video. If you have rented equipment, make arrangements to return it.

Post Office. Notify day of departure and UK contact address, as letters can be forwarded for a fee.

Personal Giro. The Post Office have a special SAE for this.

Premium Bonds. Anything rather than join the sad list of unclaimed prizes! Contact Bonds and Stocks Office, Lytham St Anne's, Lancashire FY0 1YN to check the current position, because in a few countries Premium Bond holdings may contravene the lottery laws.

National Savings Certificates. It is important to notify any permanent change of address. Advise the National Savings Certificate Office, Durham DH99 1NS, quoting the registered number(s).

National Savings Bank. Notify at Glasgow G58 1SB.

Your landlord. If you are a tenant, give the appropriate notice to quit.

Your tenants. If you are a landlord, that UK address you've organised will be needed.

Your employer. Give new address details, or a contact address, in writing.

Schools. Try to give your children's schools a term's notice that they will be leaving. If you wish your children's education to be continued in Britain contact your local education authority or the Department for Education, Sanctuary Buildings, Great Smith Street, London SW1P 3BT, for advice.

Make sure your *removers* have any temporary contact address and phone numbers for you, both in the UK and abroad, so they can get in touch with you if the need arises. It is also useful to them if you can tell them when you expect to arrive in your new country.

Reproduced by courtesy of Allied Pickfords Ltd.

TAKING A CAR ABROAD

After a virtual lifetime of driving on the left, British people still tend to prefer right-hand drive and will therefore consider buying their car here and taking it with them. First check at the embassy of the country you propose to live in that private car imports are permitted.

Probably the best way to plan this is to make a list of what you will want your car to do. You may no longer be using it to commute, so there will be less stopping and starting; the road surfaces may be less good than those you are used to, so you may consider taking a good second-hand car rather than a brand-new one. You will not then be so worried about driving through very narrow streets. In some places drivers actually park by shunting the cars ahead and behind!

In the Channel Islands small old cars are fine if your budget is tight. The road network will limit the amount of driving you are likely to do and a good used car with a guarantee can be bought from a reputable dealer.

If you are used to driving a large, comfortable car in this country, when you go abroad you may feel happier with a new, luxurious, well-appointed small car rather than a very old model. If you buy a new car in the UK before going abroad, you can use it here for six months, run it in and have your first service before you take it overseas.

Check the servicing facilities in the area where you plan to live. It would be unwise to take a car abroad if the nearest dealer service is 70 miles away. This factor may well limit your choice.

A big car will be expensive on petrol consumption and difficult to park. If you will be living in an apartment and there is no garage, the car will usually be left in the street and possibly for long periods at that. Consider carefully the security of your car and what you may have in it. Choose a model with locking wheel nuts and high-quality locks so that it is hard to get into without smashing the windows. Radio thefts are prevalent in some countries; therefore you may wish to consider a demountable radio.

Should you decide to take a small car to a hot country, buy one with a sun roof because the smaller cars carry no air conditioning.

Lead-free petrol is now widely available and you should check whether your engine will take this quality. Some engines need minor adaptation.

If you plan to put small pieces of furniture in the car for your move abroad, a hatchback is easier. On the other hand, an economical way of organising a move to the Continent is to hire a transit van, load it up with your furniture and drive it there, returning with the empty van to pick up your own car and any remaining luggage, but make sure you have the correct documentation (see pages 92 and 97).

Personal export of new cars

Those who wish to buy a new car and use it in the UK before they go abroad to live can take advantage of a special scheme which allows the purchase without payment of VAT or car tax. Motor cycles and motor caravans can also be purchased under the scheme. UK citizens who use the scheme may have the use of the vehicle in this country for up to six months before it is exported.

Form VAT 410, obtainable from UK manufacturers and foreign manufacturers' sole selling agents approved by Customs and Excise to operate the scheme, must be completed and returned to the manufacturer or agent. Customs and Excise will need to approve the application, after which the vehicle can be delivered to you. It is wise to allow plenty of time for the procedure. Only the applicant may take delivery of the vehicle, and there are restrictions on who can drive it while it is still in the UK. It must not be disposed of in any way before it is exported.

The vehicle may be taken abroad temporarily before the export date shown on the documents, but must be declared to Customs on its return to the UK, and the documentation produced. If the car is not exported by the due date for any reason (even if it is stolen or damaged), then VAT and car tax will become payable on its value when new, so it is vital to insure it for its full value as soon as it is delivered to you.

It is worth making shipping arrangements well in advance of the due export date, to avoid last-minute problems which could involve you in payment of VAT and car tax. These payments will also be levied if the car is brought back into the UK within six months of the export date on the documents.

Details of the scheme are explained in Notice 705, available from your local Customs and Excise Office.

It is possible to take delivery of a new car outside the UK free of VAT and car tax if you do not want to use it before you go abroad to live; this is a direct export and the manufacturer or sole selling agent of a foreign manufacturer in the UK will be able to supply full information.

Taking your existing car abroad

If you take the car you own at present abroad for longer than 12 months, this is regarded as a permanent export and a certificate of export (V561) is issued by the Driver and Vehicle Licensing Agency to enable you to register your car abroad.

The following procedure applies to exports from England, Scotland, Wales and the Isles of Scilly only – not to Northern Ireland or the Isle of Man where cars are registered separately.

Complete section 2 on the back of the Vehicle Registration Document, entering the proposed date of export, and send the document to your local Vehicle Licensing Office or to the Driver and Licensing Agency, Swansea SA99 1BL. This should be done well in advance of your departure.

A different procedure applies in Northern Ireland as vehicles are registered locally; it is necessary to register and license a car taken *to* Northern Ireland permanently as soon as the current British tax disc expires, if not before. The Certificate of Export mentioned above will still be necessary.

9 Settling In

After the excitement of the move and the traumas of starting a new life in a foreign country, a period of calm ought to be enjoyed while settling down in your newly acquired villa or apartment.

Unless you are very experienced in uprooting your family and shifting them to an entirely new environment you are almost certain to have a few problems to solve before you are really accepted as a 'local' by your neighbours in your adopted country, so here are a few tips on the subject of settling in.

DOCUMENTATION

Most countries require the completion of some documentation by new residents from overseas. It may be as simple as having an up-to-date British passport, so make sure that yours has at least one year to run before it expires in order to give yourself a breathing space prior to having it renewed by the local British Consul or the passport office in Britain.

If you already hold a pink driving licence issued in the UK and endorsed 'European Communities model', you may use it to drive a car in any EU country.

The International Driving Licence issued by the AA or RAC contains translations in nine languages plus an identity photograph of the holder. This impresses officialdom in some countries, particularly if you are stopped by the police, but many nations now require new residents to apply for a local driving licence. This may involve the completion of a simple form and the payment of a fee, but in some instances it is necessary to pass a driving test and to repass that test on achieving the age of threescore years and ten or some other arbitrary figure.

Residence permits are required in many countries and before these are issued, certain qualifications need to be fulfilled. These may take the form of satisfactory certificates from the police or legal bodies in your homeland regarding social or crime-free behaviour. Bank certificates are also often necessary to prove that you have sufficient income and/or capital to sustain an appropriate standard of living, so that you will not become a burden to your host country.

Take care regarding technical terms used in some countries. For instance a _permanencia_ is not a permanent permit to reside in Spain but temporary permission to remain in Spain for a further 90 days after the first 90 days granted to tourists have expired. A _residencia_ is a permit to reside in Spain.

If you are hoping to take up some form of employment in your new home country, examine the laws regarding work permits. In areas of high unemployment these are often very hard to obtain and permission to work in your own business which you are planning to set up is sometimes required. Professional people such as doctors, lawyers and accountants may need to be accepted into membership of the local professional guild before being permitted to practise their particular skill and foreigners do not always find it easy to qualify, particularly if the profession is already over-staffed.

In EU countries mobility of labour should be unrestricted.

Remember, it is never worth while, in the long run, to flout regulations; if you are caught, a large fine can be imposed or you may be banned from living in the country of your choice.

The fees charged by local consultants such as the _gestor_ (an administrator who can deal with many financial and legal problems) or _abogado_ (lawyer) in Spain are generally money well spent when dealing with officialdom, for it is much better to solve any problem first time round.

The overseas placing unit of the Employment Service has a service to recruit British workers for vacancies throughout the European Economic Area. Details can be obtained from: Overseas Placing Unit, Employment Service, 123 West Street, Sheffield S1 4ER (tel: 0114 259 6052).

FINANCES

Few people have sufficient cash to purchase their overseas home outright, and a mortgage may be necessary. Conti Financial Services, 204 Church Road, Hove BN3 2DJ, have been established for 19 years and specialise in home finance using the overseas property as security, if it is located in the USA, the Caribbean and many European countries. In certain circumstances it is also possible to finance an overseas home by using a UK property as security.

Before departing for your new home make sure that you have settled your financial affairs and that your income will be sufficient for your requirements. The cost of living in countries with a temperate climate can be lower than in northern Europe as far less has to be spent on home heating and warm clothing. But food is more expensive if you insist on eating familiar brand names imported from the UK or USA.

In planning your finances do ensure that you have a reasonable reserve fund to cover unexpected or unplanned expenditure on setting up home, for it is impossible to anticipate each and every need for a new life-style.

KEEPING YOUR VOTE WHILE LIVING ABROAD

On moving abroad, you retain your right to vote in UK and European parliamentary elections; however, there are a number of conditions of which you should be aware. To be eligible you must be a British citizen and satisfy *either* of two sets of conditions:

Set 1

- you have previously been on the electoral register for an address in the UK;

- you were living there on the qualifying date;*
- there are no more than 20 years between the qualifying dates for that register and the one on which you now wish to appear.

Set 2

- you last lived in the UK less than 20 years before the qualifying date for the register on which you now wish to appear;
- you were too young to be on the electoral register which was based on the last qualifying date before you left;
- a parent or guardian was on the electoral register, for the address where you were living on that date;
- you are at least 18 years old, or will become 18 when the register comes into force.

You have to register every year on or before the qualifying date and you may continue to register while overseas for 20 years from the qualifying date for the last electoral register on which you appeared as a UK resident.

How to register

To register you must fill in an Overseas Elector's Declaration form, which you can get from the nearest British consular or diplomatic mission. The following information will be required: your full name and overseas address, the UK address where you were last registered and the date you left the UK. The first-time overseas elector will have to find someone to support the declaration who is aged 18 or over, has a British passport and is a British citizen, is not living in the UK, and who knows you but is not a close relative. First-time overseas electors who left the UK before they were old enough to register will also have to provide a copy of their full birth

---

*The qualifying date each year is 10 October in England, Scotland and Wales and 15 September in Northern Ireland. This is for the electoral register which comes into force on 16 February of the following year and remains in force for 12 months from that date.

certificate and information about the parent or guardian on whose registration they are relying.

How to vote and remain registered

You do not have a postal vote. Instead you must appoint a proxy who will vote on your behalf. He or she must be a citizen of Britain, the Commonwealth or the Republic of Ireland, a UK resident, and willing and legally able to vote on your behalf. The application form for appointing a proxy is attached to the Overseas Declaration form. Your declaration, proxy application and, if required, birth certificate should be returned to the electoral registration officer for the area where you were last registered. The electoral registration officer will write to tell you whether you will qualify as an overseas elector and be included on the register: if you do not qualify, the officer will explain why. You will be sent a reminder each year, enclosing another declaration form, which has to be submitted annually.

WHERE TO SHOP

Countries with an outdoor way of life mostly have regular weekly markets in the main square or some other convenient location in each town and many villages.

These are the places where you can learn to shop for fruit, vegetables and other products and get good value for money, but you do need some linguistic ability if you are going to have any meaningful conversation with the local traders.

Supermarkets abound in towns with a sizeable local or tourist population. These establishments may be a little more expensive than the markets, but they do stock prepacked products, all individually priced, which means that you can serve yourself to packs that suit your requirements and know immediately how much they cost.

Although you will miss familiar foods, local products are often just as satisfactory and fruit and vegetables are particularly good value. Fish caught fresh from the sea is much tastier than frozen slabs of produce whose origins are far distant from the area of consumption. Meat producers are also more skilled in marketing cuts of joints, chops and other meat products than in former years. Even British-type sausages can be found in some shops.

Specialised shops covering ironmongery, shoes, clothes, pharmaceutical products and many other household requirements demand a little more courage for shoppers unskilled in the local tongue, but practice makes perfect; if you do not make the effort to use these establishments you will never make progress in shopping, and some of the staff may be able to talk your language!

It is well worth while taking advice from local people when planning the purchase of luxury items such as leather goods and jewellery as they should know the shops which offer the best value.

LOCAL RELATIONSHIP

If you are ever to become accepted by your neighbours you must endeavour to mix and talk with them, irrespective of whether they are of the same nationality as yourself.

The apparent reticence of British people, particularly those from the large towns and cities, must be overcome when living abroad; otherwise new residents will find it almost impossible to establish the friendships which are so essential to a happy life in a new environment away from familiar places and people. Loneliness must be avoided if at all possible.

Much can be learned from those who have lived in a particular area for a number of years or a lifetime.

DOMESTICITY

Running a house in a strange country can produce problems for the housekeeper. Different types of food, new styles of catering, a much warmer climate, strange shops with unfamiliar product brands can all produce periods of uncertainty during the first months of residing in a different country. It is during this period that each partner should show a greater interest in the household routine by trying to assist with daily chores and shopping, to the detriment, if necessary, of work in the garden or even giving up a round of golf!

HOBBIES AND SPORTS

Most people should have interests that not only entertain them but also, if possible, produce some useful end results.

Woodwork, photography, painting, model making, needlework, floral decoration, sewing or music are just a few suggestions for acquiring or improving useful skills to occupy leisure hours, all year round.

In the summer everyone can enjoy walking, gardening, bird watching and nature studies in the open air. Those able to participate in sport will find opportunities for lawn bowls, swimming, archery, tennis and riding plus extensive opportunities for golf in an ideal climate.

Many of these activities have their own clubs which enable members to mix and meet.

VOLUNTARY WORK

In every country there are opportunities for voluntary welfare work among the young and the old, and also for looking after the welfare of animals. This can be a most rewarding full- or part-time occupation and the need is great, particularly with local underprivileged children and the elderly, who are often housebound and lonely. For them a regular weekly visit to do some shopping or just to have a chat is a kindness which is much appreciated. All able-bodied people should keep an eye on those who are physically handicapped or elderly, and frequent visits will help to allay their fears of being taken ill with nobody near to help them.

Organisations of expatriates often establish a service through their members to undertake this valuable welfare work and this should receive willing support from those who are capable of looking after others as well as themselves.

CLUBS AND SOCIAL ORGANISATIONS

In almost every location where there are a number of expatriates living in fairly close proximity, clubs covering a wide variety of activities become established.

These might include simple lunch clubs for males, females or both sexes, where a wide variety of topics can be discussed and differing opinions aired over a meal and a glass of wine or other refreshment. From this might emerge a debating club, or specialised clubs covering subjects such as gardening, music, chess, bridge, darts, amateur dramatics, film societies and table tennis to mention but a few.

Apartment blocks in Spain generally have a Community of Owners, so that individuals can have a say in the management of the communal facilities, public parts or gardens, and the expenditure on external maintenance, caretaking staff, refuse disposal and so on. These regular gatherings of owners provide an opportunity to meet other owners in the development, which might not occur in the normal way where there are a large number of units in the scheme.

EXPLORATION

Please do not settle too permanently in your new home, for there are almost certainly many sights to be seen and territory to be explored within easy reach of your base.

All who are active in mind and body should take the opportunity of visiting all the noteworthy historical monuments and modern 'wonders of the world' within, say, 30 miles of their home, so as to be aware of local attractions and knowledgeable about the history, flora and fauna of the territory where they live. This will make life much more interesting and it is to be hoped that the knowledge acquired can be passed on to newcomers who are ignorant of the local attractions.

Many of the foregoing remarks have been devoted to urging expatriates to get out and about, and to help not only themselves but others less fortunate. However, a word of warning – do not overdo these activities or undertake too many obligations which will make them all onerous. Just take life steadily so that you enjoy the daily round without getting too tired or exhausted. If you do this you will have greater enjoyment from all your activities.

APPOINTMENTS AND PUNCTUALITY

Do remember that you need a degree of patience when dealing with those who have a Latin or Mediterranean temperament. In business or even domestic life you may have considered punctuality to be vital, but those fortunate enough to live a more placid, easygoing life do not consider this trait to be of such great importance.

If you reside in, say, Portugal or Spain, you will soon discover that a meeting planned for 10 am may not take place until noon, or even the following day. No discourtesy is intended for 'there is always tomorrow for things not done today'. A charming philosophy if you can get away with it and one that gradually becomes acceptable when you get to know your contacts better.

NEWS FROM HOME

Migrants who like to keep in contact with happenings at home in the UK are now well served by no less than six British newspapers who publish weekly international editions of their papers which have a worldwide readership.

The well established *Weekly Telegraph* carries a wide variety of news and features which have been published in the *Daily Telegraph* and *Sunday Telegraph,* including reports on sport and all aspects of life in the UK.

Postal subscriptions to this publication can be ordered from: Subscription Services, PO Box 14, Romford, Essex RM3 8EQ.

The London based Express Group launched *International Express* in 1990. It features a weekly selection of the leading news items and features from the *Express* and *Express on Sunday* and claims a circulation of 300,000 readers worldwide. This 64-page tabloid is sold through newsstands, and in New Zealand, for instance, it is on sale every Tuesday, at NZ$3.20.

10 Coming Back to the UK

The biggest single event which causes emigrants to return to their native country is the death of one partner, when the survivor feels that he or she just cannot cope with life alone in another country.

Elderly people come to realise they are less able to care and cater for themselves with the passage of time and they feel that they would prefer to reside near the family and old friends in their declining years.

Another factor that makes people decide to give up the 'new life' and return to their former living conditions is the discovery that they are not really happy in a strange environment with all its contributory features such as different weather conditions, unfamiliar food, new traditions and ways of life, or perhaps just a deep dissatisfaction with the property purchased in the sun, or with one's neighbours.

There is no disgrace in admitting defeat and returning home, but there are certain factors which must be considered in advance of any plans to move. These include the following:

SALE OF THE OVERSEAS PROPERTY

For the best results, appoint a well-established, legally constituted estate agent to sell your home. He or she will value it for you and undertake the marketing. In some areas a speedy sale can be effected if the price is right, but remember agents' commissions are much higher on the Continent compared with the UK. Ascertain the agent's terms before giving instructions to sell and don't be surprised if you are quoted commission figures of between 5 and 10 per cent of the purchase price.

Once appointed, let the agent get on with the sales campaign, but make sure that you keep the house neat and tidy at all times so that it will look its best to any unexpected prospective buyers, no matter what time they call.

Grant a sole agency for a limited period whenever possible and leave the agent to appoint a sub-agency if this is thought desirable. In this case a commission-sharing arrangement will be worked out between the two firms.

Next, ascertain the current regulations regarding the repatriation of the sales proceeds and any capital gains. Make sure that permission will be granted to remit the money received from the sale back to the UK. Generally this is allowed but sometimes you have to produce evidence that foreign currency was imported to pay for the property in the first place.

An alternative is to sell the property to a non-resident of the country where it is located and have the proceeds remitted to your normal UK bank. This procedure works quite well and obviates the necessity for applications which need to be approved by officialdom. The change of ownership must, of course, be registered at the local Land Registry; also local legal fees and tax will have to be paid.

Check up on current procedures for pension and other receipts. Give the bank and other officials adequate time to make the appropriate arrangements.

TAXATION

On returning to the UK after a number of years abroad, your status for taxation purposes will probably change quite dramatically and it is essential to seek full advice from an accountant or tax expert.

_____

EXCHANGE CONTROL

Restrictions on the export of capital are imposed by a few countries. If you have substantial capital invested in shares or a local bank account, check the procedures and restrictions (if any) about the repatriation of your funds. A comprehensive review should be undertaken of all investments, with the aid of expert advice.

It is sensible to re-examine testamentary provisions on return to the UK, particularly if a will has been drawn up in a foreign country. Don't forget to advise relations, friends, business contacts and insurance companies of your new address on returning to the UK. Work through the removal checklist on pages 92–94 in case it applies to your move back.

11 The End

Death comes to us all eventually so it is wise to have made some plans in advance if you are living in a foreign country, and the following notes may be of some help to prepare for the ultimate eventuality.

A surprising number of people fail to make a will, or do not update one when it has become inappropriate because of the passing of the years and the arrival of new circumstances.

Everyone, no matter how large or small their estate, should make a will, properly drawn up by a lawyer; the fee expended on this advice is money well spent if it avoids any complications after death.

Both wife and husband should make wills and everyone moving abroad or retiring to a new country should take advice on the rules of what constitutes a valid will in the country in which they propose to reside in the future.

In some countries there are laws which protect the family of the deceased and, as a result, the estate has to be divided so as to ensure that the surviving spouse, and also any children, are adequately catered for; after this the testator can deal with the remaining estate in accordance with any particular wishes.

Every responsible person should compile a 'What I own and where it is kept' list giving details of investments, insurance policies and property etc. This will save next of kin and executors much work and worry, eventually.

As far as the actual arrangements for the burial are concerned, those who wish to be interred in the UK should realise that the cost of sending the body back to the homeland can be substantial, so adequate financial arrangements should be made in advance to cover this by setting up a separate fund, or taking out a special insurance policy.

If you are being buried in the place where you die, the arrangements regarding interment may vary from one country to another. Cremation is not always available in every country, so it may be necessary to purchase a plot in a cemetery.

SPAIN

On the death of a person in Spain, it is necessary to register the fact immediately at the local Civil Registry. This is generally undertaken by a friend or a relative who will need to have a doctor's certificate stating the cause of death. On receipt of a Spanish death certificate this should be taken to the nearest British Consul's office who will then register the death and issue a British death certificate.

A lawyer should be instructed immediately to deal with the payment of inheritance taxes, for the assets of anyone dying in Spain cannot be distributed until taxes have been paid.

Most cemeteries in Spain are Catholic, but people of any religion may be buried there. In fact, by tradition, bodies are often not buried, but placed in sealed niches above ground. There is a British cemetery at Malaga and an international cemetery at nearby Benalmadena. The latter has burial plots for those who prefer them. The law states that bodies must be interred within 72 hours of death, but not before 24 hours after the sad event. Those who prefer cremation will find that these facilities are scarce, but there are establishments at Madrid, Seville and Malaga. The ashes can be placed in an urn, which can easily be transported back to the UK.

It is advisable to have a Spanish will, but if this does not exist the estate can be distributed in such a way that it complies with the deceased's British will. Those who die intestate will have their estate distributed to the next of kin in accordance with Spanish law.

FRANCE

In France, a death has to be registered at the local *Mairie* within 24 hours and a doctor's certificate obtained from the doctor who attended the deceased person, or from a medical person who is retained by the local council.

It is not permitted to close a coffin within 24 hours of death; this act can only be undertaken with the authority of the official by whom the death is registered.

In France, cemeteries belong to the local authorities, who issue licences to undertakers to carry out the actual burial. Despite the fact that there are no separate Jewish or Protestant cemeteries, a tradition has grown up whereby parts of many cemeteries are used only by specified religious groups.

For religious reasons cremation has not been popular in France in the past, but it is now being used more frequently and there are a growing number of crematoria.

PORTUGAL

The tradition in Portugal is for burial to take place very quickly, generally within 24 hours of death. There are undertakers in many towns who have experience of arranging funerals for foreigners; deaths have to be registered at the local Civil Registry where a doctor's certificate showing the cause of death has to be produced.

It is recommended that the British Consulate be informed of the death, especially if a British death certificate is required.

In places where there is a substantial foreign population, cemeteries permit both Catholic and non-Catholic people to be buried.

Some Portuguese cemeteries permit graves to be occupied for only five years, so it is desirable to ascertain that the choice of final resting place is a permanent one. Cremation is permitted in the recently opened Lisbon crematorium.

ITALY

In Italy deaths should be registered within 24 hours at the local *municipo* in which the person died. The next of kin usually undertakes this duty, but anyone can do it. Two witnesses are required and a death certificate should be signed by two doctors. Coffins are closed within 24 hours of death and burials should take place within 48 hours.

Cremation is quite common, particularly in the north of the country, and special documents are required. Costs tend to be higher than for ordinary burial.

There are communal cemeteries in most *communes*, where residents have the right to a free plot when they die.

One final, essential point is the choice of a storage place for your will. Make sure that your next of kin know where this is located, and try at all times to arrange your affairs in a neat and tidy manner so as to make your executor's task as simple as possible.

Often the family solicitor keeps the will and it would be useful if information on bank accounts, insurance policies and so on is also deposited with your legal adviser.

GRAVE TENDING SERVICE

Unless they are regularly inspected and maintained, the church yard graves of close relatives or friends tend to be neglected and can become very untidy. A solution to this problem is often difficult to find for those who go to live overseas for any length of time.

However, there is now a grave tending service offered by Pilgrim Grave Tending Services of Alton Barnes, Marlborough, Wilts SN8 4JZ (tel: 01672 851851). The firm has a network of specialist gardeners who will maintain graves to a high standard throughout the UK, for a fixed annual charge. This covers general maintenance of a grave according to season, including monument cleaning, weeding, edge clipping and grass cutting. Arrangements can be made for flowers or wreaths to be placed on the grave on a selected date. Photographs of the grave are provided before and after each tending and a report is submitted if there are any structural problems to the grave.

Part Three:

A Home Overseas

12 Try Before You Buy

As already explained, nobody should consider the purchase of a permanent home abroad without carefully investigating the facilities, amenities and life-style of the chosen district in considerable detail before entering into any commitment to purchase a property.

Without doubt, the most satisfactory way to do this is to rent a property for a period of several months in the area where you think you would like to reside, if possible in the low season when most of the holiday-makers have gone home and the seasonal attractions are no longer available. This will enable you to experience life with local people and get to know some of the foreigners and your own compatriots who have already settled in the area.

From them it should be possible to obtain information and useful tips about the best places to shop, local medical facilities, clubs for the British or other nationalities, sporting amenities and a whole host of other useful data.

With the advantage of local knowledge and contacts, you will soon become experienced at living in a foreign country and have the opportunity of deciding whether you like the life-style or whether in fact you would do better to remain at home.

During the winter months there is generally a good selection of top-quality apartments and villas available for renting at very reasonable prices and information on these can be obtained from local estate agents or firms in the UK who specialise in self-catering villa and apartment holidays. First Choice Holidays & Flights Ltd Villas, whose Sovereign Villa Collection brochure is available from most travel agents, publish an excellent guide to villas and apartments to rent in Spain, Portugal, Cyprus, France, Malta, St Lucia, Barbados and Florida, USA, which are available through them for holidays between January and December. Prices quoted include return air flights, maid service and grocery pack.

Private Villas is a useful publication produced six times a year and available from newsagents, price £2.75, or from Private Villas, 6th Floor, Berwick House, 35 Livery Street, Birmingham B3 2PB. It lists private villas which are available for renting direct from the owners or their agents. Here again, an inclusive package can include flights from the UK.

For those interested in France, there is an annual, *Chez-nous*, which lists and illustrates hundreds of private houses and holiday homes to rent. Details are available from Chez-nous, Bridge Mills, Huddersfield Road, Holmfirth HD7 2TW, England.

Whichever method you adopt to rent a property, do make sure that you are aware in advance of the terms offered by the owner or the letting company. Points well worth checking are the following:

1. Does the quoted cost include maid service?
2. Do you need to take towels?
3. Are gas and electricity charges included in the rental, or do you have to pay the owner's agent for energy consumed during the time in residence?
4. Location of shops and amenities.
5. How far are the sea and airport from the selected property; are there satisfactory transport arrangements made on your behalf?
6. If your flight is delayed and you arrive later than expected, can you gain access to the property?
7. Does the owner or agent provide a starter pack of food for use on arrival at the property? (This is especially important if you travel at weekends.)
8. Brochures often describe a property as, say, 'sleeping six'. What extra charges will be levied if only three people travel and use the accommodation?

Some developers arrange to have a limited number of properties available on larger sites for renting to prospective purchasers; the use of this service is well worth while and is generally quite economical.

Having made the momentous decision to purchase a home abroad, do not charge into the transaction blindly, even though it is an exciting proposition which you feel you want to fulfil at the earliest possible moment.

Time will be well-spent reflecting on your immediate and future needs and may well ensure that you do not make any hasty decisions that could turn out to be disastrous later on.

Some people purchase an apartment in their favourite resort, and this may be an excellent choice for annual vacations. But will it be large enough for permanent living? And will you really enjoy residing during the summer months in a building where transient occupants provide a constantly changing scene, with no opportunity to make permanent friends and with the recurring problem of late-night parties? Arrivals and departures can disturb the early hours of the morning because of the whims of charter flights to the UK and other parts of Europe.

Security should be adequate in an apartment block with a resident concierge, but the winter life could be very lonely if there are only one or two year-round owners in residence.

If you buy an apartment, make sure that the block has one or more adequate lifts – as you get older, climbing several flights of stairs may become almost impossible and then you will be dependent on others to fetch your shopping and to undertake errands such as a visit to the bank or post office.

Villa ownership, especially if the property is detached, offers greater privacy, some protection from undue noise and a feeling of true ownership which never seems to come with an apartment.

Many overseas houses have patios or balconies and most have gardens, sometimes large and sometimes small. When you retire you will have more time to potter around your 'estate', but make sure it is planned and well laid out so that gardening tasks do not become a burden as you grow older.

The exterior maintenance of any home is an important point to consider in advance. Many units are finished in cement rendering which requires an application of white or coloured emulsion paint every year or two. This is easy to apply on a single-storey dwelling, but requires more effort for a two- or three-storey villa. You may need to employ some professional skill if you find the work too tiring, but the cost should not be too great and it will help to keep costs down if the job can be completed in a few hours.

Even a small villa can easily be made into a permanent home and the purchase price is often not a great deal higher than that of a flat. However, take particular care in your choice of location, for an isolated villa away from shops and facilities could prove particularly inconvenient and lonely, especially if you become less mobile with advancing years and do not possess a car.

HOW MUCH?

Undoubtedly your first consideration must be how much you can afford to spend on your new overseas home.

Property prices vary considerably in the sunniest countries of Europe and elsewhere, but you can get a good idea of costs by subscribing to the colourful magazine *Homes Overseas,* which was established in 1965. It is published six times a year and every issue contains many advertisements from developers and agents in the UK and overseas, offering a wide selection of villas and apartments for sale in the most popular European resorts and some of the less known, but attractive locations. In addition there are informative articles written by experts on the many aspects of property purchase overseas, features on selected areas, the legal aspects, and lifestyles in different countries. An annual postal subscription (six issues) costs only £15 and can be ordered from Subscription Department, *Homes Overseas,* Blendon Communications, 46 Oxford Street, London W1N 9FJ.

During the past decade, distinct changes have taken place in the attitudes of potential purchasers of overseas properties, who have become much more selective. Formerly they would have gone on an inspection flight to their chosen destination, inspected a few homes and made a decision to buy. Now they tend to compare propositions much more carefully and will take holidays in a number of countries to examine costs, accessibility and legal restrictions, and will make contact with local people and fellow expatriates who have already taken the plunge, before making the decision to buy a residence for holidays or retirement.

Having finally decided on the location of your new home you must re-examine your finances and decide on a sensible sum to spend, which will not dig too deeply into your capital, or cost you an excessive amount to maintain or to mortgage.

Abbey National has established Abbey National (Gibraltar) Ltd at 237 Main Street, Gibraltar to provide a UK-style mortgage service to clients purchasing a home on the Costa del Sol and Costa Blanca, Costa Brava, Almeria, Tenerife and Majorca, in Spain and Portugal's Algarve. Advice on insurance and other matters is also available.

Some overseas builders and developers are willing to offer short-term loans, generally for not more than 60 per cent of the purchase price and for periods not exceeding five years. Interest rates tend to be high.

Many older home-owners in the UK have considerable equity locked up in their main residences, with little or no mortgage outstanding. They are in the fortunate position of being able to re-mortgage their property and use the proceeds to buy a home abroad or use the house as security for a loan.

SHELTERED HOUSING

On the Continent, sheltered housing schemes for the elderly are becoming more numerous and several British based firms are involved. For example McCarthy & Stone, the UK's largest developer in this category, has completed and sold three schemes in France, one each in Ireland and Jersey where resales become available locally from time to time.

Near Faro on Portugal's Algarve, Monte Da Palgagueira is a village for the retired with 30 traditionally built one- or two-bedrooms houses with full back-up service, large swimming pool, sun terrace and fine views. An adjoining nursing home has 22 rooms with en suite bathrooms, air conditioning, television and telephone. Staff are on duty 24 hours a day and facilities include lounge/dining room, physiotherapy, hairdressing salon and shop. Telephone 01980 622957 for more information.

Sheltered housing schemes in Spain include Interpares which was established 23 years ago, near Malaga on the Costa del Sol. This self-governing community, a non-profit organisation, comprises 72 spacious one-, two- and three-bedroom apartments, mostly individually owned and each having central heating and air conditioning. Services include restaurant and meal delivery, house-keeping and laundry, alarm bell and intercom, handyman and medical assistance. There are extensive gardens and a swimming pool. A nursing service for up to six weeks per illness per year is included in the monthly charges which are based on the size of the apartment. Apartments are for sale from time to time or may be leased for life-time occupation.

Santa Barbara is a complex for senior citizens situated in 20 hectares of land at Alhaurin de la Torre, away from the tourist areas, yet convenient for the beach, a golf course and the facilities of Malaga and its international airport. The first phase comprises service flats, spacious terrace apartments, terraced bungalows, and a service centre and some sports facilities. Medical attention is available if needed. Further details are available from Residencia Santa Barbara SA, Apartado de Correos 57, 29620, Torremolinos, Malaga.

On the Maltese island of Gozo Sunblessed Horizons Promotions Ltd have launched their Leisure Lifestyle Plan, which offers single people or couples lifetime use of a luxury apartment providing they are 50 years-old or over. Membership is purchased at prices that are based on the ages of the applicants when they join the scheme. The older they are, the lower the price charged. An annual management fee is payable to ensure the upkeep of the building – this is agreed with members in advance and based on the annual rate of inflation in Malta. On death of both members, or where they wish to give up membership, between 70 and 100 per cent of the membership fee is refunded (based on the length of occupancy), providing the managers are able to reassign the membership to a third party.

The two developments currently being offered are at the picturesque fishing village of Xlendi Bay, close to the sea, and at Marsalforn Bay, both on the island of Gozo. Further details and prices can be obtained from Cassar & Cooper (Real Estate) Ltd, PO Box 36, Sliema, Malta.

13 Property Organisations

When purchasing an overseas property there are inevitably greater risks than when buying a home in the UK.

Different laws, contracts in foreign languages, varied financial arrangements, local building methods and firms whose authenticity is difficult to check, all add difficulties and hazards to property transactions.

How can members of the public, who are sometimes very gullible and quite ignorant of procedures in the country they have chosen as a place for their home, be protected?

The Federation of Overseas Property Developers, Agents and Consultants (FOPDAC) is a UK trade association of agents and developers who specialise in marketing overseas property.

FOPDAC requires its members to comply with a code of conduct and to fulfil certain entry qualifications. It investigates complaints by the public against members and takes disciplinary action against member firms who are proved to be treating clients in an unsatisfactory manner.

Many problems arise because members of the public fail to take adequate legal and financial advice before committing themselves to a purchase. The very thought of owning a home in a chosen resort or country area seems to cause normally sensible business or professional people to throw caution to the wind. As a result, legal documents in a foreign language are often signed without recourse to proper expert advice and substantial sums of money are paid over to relative strangers, either individuals or firms, before any check has been made about their bona fides.

To minimise the risk of an unsatisfactory transaction, careful preliminary planning and caution throughout the acquisition period should be adopted by all buyers.

FEDERATION OF OVERSEAS PROPERTY DEVELOPERS, AGENTS AND CONSULTANTS (FOPDAC)

FOPDAC was formed in 1973 with the aim of establishing a code of conduct for its members in their dealings with the public and to try to educate prospective purchasers of overseas residential property on the dos and don'ts of buying villas and apartments outside their native land.

Chartered surveyors, architects, planners and developers, as well as tour operators, travel experts, finance and currency exchange companies, lawyers and, of course, selling agents and builders, are now included in the membership. Areas covered by the membership include mainland Spain, the Balearic Islands and the Canaries, Cyprus, France, Italy, Greece, Malta, Portugal, Switzerland, Czech Republic and Thailand.

To join FOPDAC, firms or individuals must have well-established businesses and have an integrity that is beyond reasonable question. Principals of companies are required to have sufficient professional expertise and experience to meet the strict requirements of the Federation's code of ethics, a summary of which is given below:

> Members shall make honesty and integrity the standard in all their dealings with their clients and customers. They shall avoid misleading property descriptions, concealment of pertinent information, and exaggerations in advertising. They shall not market property for specific purposes if that property is not accessible and usable for such purposes. Members shall comply with all financial and legal obligations relating to their transactions in overseas property and their clients or customers.
>
> Members shall use their best endeavours to enlist all the professional talents available to them in the fields of ecology, engineering

and architecture for the design of a development that strives for the best employment of the land and protection of the environment. They shall use their best endeavours to encourage developments with due consideration for open space and proper environmental controls. Members shall report in writing any violation of the by-laws, whether their own or those of others, whether members or not, to the Committee.

All member agents must recommend to a prospective purchaser that they seek independent legal advice in order to effect their purchase. Such recommendation will be given before any legal binding contract is entered into. If the prospective purchaser asks the agent for the name of a person to provide independent legal advice, the agent should provide a choice of names.

Where Federation members accept clients' money for payment, whether partial or full, for land or property, they must maintain a legally separate client's account which must be properly conducted and disclosure must be given, to the Secretary of the Federation, of the name and address of the bank at which the account is maintained.

Should any member of the general public conducting business through a member of the Federation complain that the member has not acted in accordance with the code of ethics, then the committee will investigate the complaint and arbitrate where necessary. If the committee should decide that a member is in default and the member subsequently fails to rectify the matter, then the member would be liable to immediate expulsion from the Federation.

The Federation symbol should be displayed on all advertisements and literature distributed by members.

The Federation publishes an informative brochure and list of members. These can be obtained (price £2) from the Secretary, FOPDAC, 3rd Floor, 95 Aldwych, London WC2B 4JF (tel: 0181 941 5588).

Before inspecting any overseas property the Federation suggests that each prospective buyer obtains answers to the following questions:

1. (a) Is the property being offered by its owner, its developer or an agent acting on their behalf?
   (b) Does the British agent have an association with an agent or agents in the chosen locality who is legally licensed in

that country? Does the British agent represent the vendor or the purchaser?

(c) What are the risks in dealing with an unlicensed local agent?

2. Is the property being offered with clear title? Is it 'free and unencumbered'?

3. (a) Are the costs of connecting water, electricity and drainage included in the selling price of a new home? If not, what are these costs likely to be?

(b) What are the acquisition and conveyancing costs usually incurred by the purchaser under the traditions and regulations of the locality?

4. (a) What are the formal stages of property purchase in the country in which the property is situated?

(b) Is the purchase contract binding? Is it in a foreign language?

(c) What essential points should be covered by the purchase contract to ensure that both parties are adequately protected?

5. (a) Should legal advice be sought on the purchase of an overseas property?

(b) Must a solicitor draw up the conveyance of an overseas property?

(c) Can the overseas property be sold freely and the proceeds transferred abroad without difficulty?

6. (a) What are the annual costs likely to be incurred by the owner of the property in the country or area chosen?

(b) If the property is in a development complex are there any charges for communal facilities?

(c) Is there a Community of Owners? Is membership obligatory? What are the benefits? What are the costs? Are the statutes in a foreign language?

7. Can a bank account be opened locally? What are the advantages of having a local bank account?

8. Can the property and its contents be insured? What are the rates of premiums to be expected?

9. Can the property be let to friends? Can a formal rental agreement be made with a rental agency? What return can be expected? Will this restrict the owner's use of the property unduly? Is tax payable on rental income?

10. Could the view from the property or its amenities be affected by unsightly future development? Is there a zoning plan for the surrounding area?
11. Are there any local regulations which affect the purchase of property by foreign nationals? If so, what are the formalities?
12. (a) If a plot of land is bought on which to build in future, are there any conditions of building permission? Are there time limits for such building? Are there height or size limitations?
    (b) Must a local architect be used? Must an architect be used who is nominated by the vendor? Must a nominated building contractor be used?
    (c) Are there any other formalities which should be observed when building a home on a plot purchased?
13. (a) Is furniture included in the price of the property, or does the owner arrange to furnish it? What is the approximate cost of furnishings to a basic or a high standard?
    (b) If the property has a garden, is the cost of planting included in the sale price? If not, what is the cost likely to be? Who maintains the garden in the owner's absence? Could a garden be planned and planted which requires little or no maintenance?
    (c) How much external maintenance is the property likely to need? Who is responsible for this maintenance? How much is it likely to cost?
    (d) Can a company be appointed locally who will manage the property during the owner's absence and supervise cleaning etc for the owner and guests when they visit?
14. What is the most economical and reliable means of travel to the property? Are there privileges to be obtained for owners and their guests?

FOPDAC has appointed European representatives in some countries where members transact business, including Switzerland, Ireland and the United States.

Other organisations of interest to overseas property owners include:

THE ROYAL INSTITUTION OF CHARTERED SURVEYORS

Some UK estate agents who operate overseas property departments are members of the Royal Institution of Chartered Surveyors. They are subject to a strict code of conduct and are bonded, so far as their operations in the UK are concerned, but this protection does not cover transactions or work undertaken abroad.

However, a degree of security for buyers does exist, as the majority of individuals who are members also have well-established practices in England, Wales, Scotland or Ireland and are unlikely to jeopardise their reputation and professional qualifications by involving themselves in unwise foreign deals.

THE NATIONAL ASSOCIATION OF ESTATE AGENTS

The National Association of Estate Agents has been established for 36 years and its membership comprises mainly estate agents and individuals who specialise in the sale and renting of residential property. New members have to pass examinations in general estate agency practice and are required to have a minimum of three years' experience in estate agency.

The Association is a founder member of CEI (Confederation Europeenne L'imobilier) an elected member of FIABCT, the international real estate organization and has links with the profession in a number of other European countries. An overseas grade has been introduced for agents who live and work overseas. Further details about NAEA can be obtained by telephoning 01926 496800.

THOMAS COOK RESORT PROPERTIES

In 1998, Thomas Cook travel agents launched a new service, Thomas Cook Resort Properties, to act as agents for the purchase of freehold overseas homes for their clients. They claim to have properties for sale all over the world, but are specialising in offering homes from developers in Cyprus, France, Portugal, Spain and Florida, United States. A wide choice of villas and apartments are offered at prices from about £20,000, with a range of ownership options from outright purchase to a quarter share.

They invite prospective clients to telephone 08702 425525 in the first instance, when they can talk to specialist staff about their requirements. When they need more detail they can meet a fully trained consultant in their own home or at one of Thomas Cook's World Travel Lounges, which are situated in 100 of their branches in many parts of the UK. Brochures and videos will be available for consideration from many developers, all of whom have been carefully vetted by Thomas Cook, who can guarantee the quality of their buildings.

Having decided on the location where they wish to purchase a home, clients can arrange inspection flights through the dedicated travel service, which offers discounted fares and car hire.

The office address of Thomas Cook Resort Properties is PO Box 36, Thorpe Wood, Peterborough, Cambridgeshire PE3 6SB.

THE INSTITUTE OF FOREIGN PROPERTY OWNERS

Norwegian-born Per Svensson founded the Institute of Foreign Property Owners in 1983, and for nearly two decades this organisation has been an invaluable aid to foreigners purchasing property in Spain and elsewhere. Membership costs about £40 a year, and includes advice on a wide variety of subjects plus a regular newsletter containing vital information for owners of property in Spain. Changes in the law and local authority regulations are explained in detail, and much other valuable data is circulated.

An associate company, InfoService, is able to act as a fiscal representative for any members needing this facility.

Details of the Institute can be obtained from the Institute of Foreign Property Owners, Avenida de L'Ait Rei en Jaume I, 15 20–29, Altea 03590, Alicante, Spain (tel: 00 34 65 842312; fax 00 34 65 841589).

14 Timesharing

Timesharing is a useful method of acquiring experience in living abroad for short periods without the expenditure of large sums of money.

This method of property ownership has been in existence for over 30 years. The first scheme was offered in a French Alpine ski resort in 1967. In the following year timesharing was offered by a co-ownership scheme in Spain promoted by two British businessmen who had built and sold two blocks of apartments in the main street of Javea, on the Costa Blanca, and then decided to construct a third block whereby clients could purchase part-ownership of a freehold, two-bedroom flat with names registered on the deeds. The cost of the use in perpetuity of a two-bedroom unit for a fortnight in June was £250, or £500 would purchase the use for all the winter months from November to March. This scheme is still operating successfully. Resales now fetch about £3,000 for a week in the summer.

In the UK, a pioneer scheme was started 20 years ago in the Highlands of Scotland, at Loch Rannoch. This operates very successfully, with nearly 100 units ranging from luxury three-bedroom lodges with huge living areas on the first floor enjoying the fine views across the Loch, down to small apartments. Features on the site include a dry ski slope, hotel and club, boating and fishing opportunities, swimming facilities and various other sports and pastimes.

It is estimated that nearly half a million families now own timeshare weeks in about 100 resorts spread throughout the UK from the north of Scotland to Wales, the Midlands, the South Coast, the West Country and in many overseas countries.

The term 'timesharing' originated in America and has also been called 'interval ownership', 'vacation ownership' and 'co-ownership'. There can be up to 50 owners of a single unit of accommodation, each having purchased seven days or more at the time of year when they wish to use their accommodation.

Having paid the purchase price, which can sometimes be spread over two or three years, no further capital payment is required but there are annual charges which range from about £100 to £500 per annum and these cover maintenance and management expenses.

In the UK and some other countries it is not possible to transfer legal title to the freehold ownership of a property to more than four people. To overcome this problem many timeshare developers adopt the club trustee system, whereby an independent trustee is appointed to hold the land and buildings on trust for the timeshare owners. Should the promoter get into financial difficulties, timeshare owners' rights are not affected and title cannot be taken away by creditors of the bankrupt company.

An alternative method is to grant a 'right to use' licence. Here the developer who holds the legal title provides the timesharer with a licence which permits use of the accommodation for the period purchased, over an agreed number of years or in perpetuity, the maximum in England and Wales being 80 years.

Normally at least two weeks in the year are not sold by the developers in order to provide a suitable period to cover maintenance and redecoration of properties. The average period of time purchased is between two and three weeks.

To ensure proper management of the scheme, and to spread general outgoings over sufficient owners, a minimum of 16 units is considered to be necessary and, if this is achieved, maintenance fees can be kept to a reasonable level.

Variations to the standard scheme include 'floating weeks' whereby there is no entitlement to a selected week each year and it is necessary to book your period in advance. Those wishing to take a holiday in the peak season may find availability a problem.

Two-owner, four-owner and six-owner schemes provide occupation of the selected villa or apartment for six, three or two months each year respectively. The time segment is usually divided into several periods, so that each owner can enjoy peak weeks, mid-season and low-season periods each year. The periods allocated generally rotate so that each participant has the opportunity to enjoy holidays at differing times each year over, say, a four-year time span.

McCarthy & Stone, the well-known UK developers of retirement homes, have introduced a 'Holiday Partnership' method of owning a holiday home for two months a year at their seaside development with swimming pool on the Balearic island of Majorca, Spain. Here, one- and two-bedroom luxury fully furnished apartments are priced from £8,950. Further details can be obtained by telephoning 01425 461985.

An objection that some people raise about the purchase of holiday accommodation is that they may tire of going to the same place year after year. This is not a problem experienced with timesharing, for most developments are in membership with one of the two major exchange organisations whereby owners can exchange their accommodation for similar size and quality apartments or villas in upwards of 1,000 timeshare developments in most parts of the world.

The best-known organisations are Interval International and Resort Condominiums International. They both have offices in the UK, as well as in the USA where they were founded. They carry out quality checks on all the schemes which apply for membership and have been known to reject a number of sites which do not come up to their strict standards of quality.

Established 25 years ago, Resort Condominiums International has about 3,000 resorts worldwide, and many of these are in Europe. The RCI Directory is published in many languages.

RCI's European Headquarters are at Kettering Parkway, Kettering, Northamptonshire NN15 6EY.

To ensure that a development will be a success and will sell readily throughout most of the year, a wide variety of facilities, including sporting activities, shops, restaurants, health clubs and live entertainment, is essential.

Every bit as important as the amenities is the standard of furnishing and the design of the properties themselves. All furniture should be very hardwearing, and attractive in appearance; kitchens should be furnished and equipped to luxury standards; bathrooms should be designed and equipped to first-class specification.

During the boom years between 1984 and 1989 some of the time-share marketing firms adopted hard-sell tactics to persuade reluctant members of the public to commit themselves to the purchase of time segments which they often could not afford or did not, on reflection, really want. Methods adopted included inducing holiday-makers to visit sales centres and show properties with promises of valuable free gifts, which were not always honoured, or complimentary meals and drinks for attending sales presentations which often lasted up to three hours. Participants were then expected to sign contracts and pay deposits without any opportunity for reflection or consultation with professional advisers.

There are many bona fide timeshare developments in the UK and overseas where prospective and actual clients are treated fairly, but a decade ago the black sheep brought the whole industry into disrepute.

In 1993 The Timeshare Act was passed by Parliament to ensure that buyers of timeshares who sign contracts in Britain, are given a 14-day 'cooling-off period' during which they can have their money refunded should they decide not to proceed with the purchase. Under an EU directive made in April 1997, Timeshare purchases in Europe are subject to a 10-day cooling-off period.

In recent years, a number of well known builders have either purchased existing or developed new timesharing schemes. For example, Barratt International Resorts have three extensive schemes on Spain's Costa del Sol. Hotel and tourist groups are also now promoting timeshare developments. These include the Hilton, Disney and Hyatt groups in North America; plus Marriot Vacation Club International, who are active in Spain and the USA; tour operator Airtours plan to be a major influence in the timeshare industry and currently offer developments in Florida and Grand Canary; the Ilkeston Co-Op Travel, a well known travel agent, has timeshare schemes in Tenerife. The involvement of all these renowned firms is helping to rebuild the public's confidence in timesharing.

Properly organised, developed and managed timesharing schemes will undoubtedly prosper in the future, for they do give families and individuals a safeguard against the escalating cost of vacations. It should be borne in mind that timesharing is not an investment in money terms, simply in future holidays.

Although capital profits have been achieved by some owners who invested at the early stages of the most successful schemes, no capital appreciation should be expected while the developers are still selling the units, or in the immediate future.

Other specific points to bear in mind, before signing any documents which commit you to purchase, are as follows:

1. Adequate management and maintenance of the development are of vital importance to the future. Ascertain who is going to undertake this work and the proposed charges, including any increase in costs in future years. Will they be based on the cost of living index, or will the figure be fixed annually at the whim of the management organisation?
2. Get details in writing of the facilities that will be offered on the site and, if possible, ensure that these will be available as soon as occupation is offered on timeshare units.
3. Details of the furnishings, fixtures and fitments to be included in each unit should be presented to each buyer in inventory form. Check the maximum number of people permitted to use each timeshare unit.
4. If you are paying cash, you may be entitled to a discount if settlement is made by a specified date. If you are financing the purchase on credit, check up on the interest rates to be charged for the period over which repayments are permitted.
5. Investigations into the track record of the project developers are a wise precaution; with already completed developments, endeavour to speak to one of the existing owners and get his or her opinion about how well the scheme is organised.
6. Check the terms on which the scheme is being offered, ie either freehold or club trusteeship, and whether segments are sold by the week or multiple weeks, whether they are for a fixed period every year or for a floating period whereby the weeks vary or rotate each year.

SELLING YOUR TIMESHARE OR BUYING A RESALE

Having owned a timeshare segment for several years, it is likely that some owners will decide they would like to dispose of their existing entitlement and purchase in another location, while others may want to recoup some of the money they have spent, due to changed circumstances.

When marketing of new timeshare schemes was at its height during the 1980s, it was not always easy to find a buyer for a 'secondhand' period, but now there are a number of firms who specialise in handling resales. Generally, they operate like estate agents and compile details of timeshare units which owners wish to sell and advertise these in the press and elsewhere to find purchasers.

As with all real estate transactions it is advisable to ascertain the *bona fides* of any organisation through whom you propose to try and sell your property. Some agents have been known to charge a substantial, money-back guarantee fee for achieving a sale within a stated period, then make no attempt to find a buyer and suddenly disappear at the end of the period, with all the fees.

The UK's oldest and most successful resale company is PrimeShare International Ltd of Broomvale Business Centre, Little Blakenham, Ipswich, Suffolk IP8 4JU, which celebrated its tenth anniversary in 1997. It operates internationally and handles over £10 million worth of sales a year. On top of extensive advertising, the company is the subject of regular articles in the national press. It also sells via the Internet (www.primeshare.com).

Their charges are reasonable and they arrange the transfer of titles to the new buyer on behalf of the vendor.

From the purchaser's point of view a resale is almost always cheaper than buying new from a developer because the latter is heavily involved in marketing and promotion costs which can amount to around 40 to 50 per cent of the original purchase price. The individual owner, on resale after say five years, is not involved in such heavy expenditure and can therefore accept a figure well below the current 'new' price, thus offering an attractive proposition.

PrimeShare offer a 14-day cooling-off period for purchasers, like other members of Timeshare Council, and hold their clients' money in an independently-contained client account. The vendor is paid out once a new title is issued. Purchasers currently receive two years free exchange company membership (RCI/Interval).

ORGANISATION FOR TIMESHARE IN EUROPE (OTE)

OTE was established in June 1998 to unite the interests of all the existing national timeshare associations in Europe, who will continue as 'Chapters' of OTE and which will include Timeshare Council (see below). OTE has been created to represent all the interests of those involved in the industry Europe-wide and to uphold common professional standards in all countries. As a pan-European trade association it is committed to representing the best of timeshare and developing the highest standards throughout the industry to meet the needs of consumers. The European Timeshare Directive granting, *inter alia*, a minimum 10-day cooling-off period is now in force in the majority of EU states, including Spain. In the UK, national legislation provides for a 14-day cooling-off period and there is a ban on deposit-taking within those 14 days. OTE has offices in Brussels, Madrid and London, sharing the latter with Timeshare Council.

OTE now has a 28-page Web site located at http://www.ote-info.com, which gives information on OTE, plus statistics on the timeshare industry and guidelines for those thinking about buying a timeshare week.

TIMESHARE COUNCIL (TC)

The Timeshare Council was established in April 1990 to protect the interests of both the consumer and all those with legitimate interests in the industry. It is re-establishing the credibility of the industry, after an initial period of bad press and unsatisfactory marketing experiences.

The UK Timeshare Act of October 1992 with its mandatory 14-day cooling off period, together with worldwide recession, hastened the departure of the less reputable operators. The Council has found it necessary to expel and reject some members for failing to comply with its standards of good industry practice.

TC membership includes timeshare developers, marketers, exchange organisations, management firms, finance providers, solicitors, consultants, and also leisure and hotel operators with timeshare interests.

The Council is the industry voice in dealing with the UK government, the EU and other government bodies, as well as the media, the public and other trade associations.

Useful information and advice leaflets together with a list of highly respectable resale category members are obtainable from TC by sending a stamped self-addressed envelope to: Timeshare Council, 23 Buckingham Gate, London SW1E 6LB.

HOLIDAY PROPERTY BOND

An excellent method of investing capital to provide first class self-catering holiday accommodation in the UK and abroad is offered by the Holiday Property Bond which is marketed in the UK by HPB Management Ltd of HPB House, Newmarket, Suffolk (tel: 01638 660066).

The scheme comprises a life assurance bond which invests in holiday properties and in securities producing income towards management charges. The Bond is underwritten by the Isle of Man Assurance Ltd and Midland Bank Trust Corporation (Isle of Man) Ltd holds all the assets of the Bond on behalf of investors.

Money is not borrowed by the Bond to finance the purchase of properties, and expansion of activities is funded from new premium income.

Established in 1983, HPB now claims to be one of the fastest growing property co-ownerships in Europe. It now has over 24,000 bondholder families who have collectively invested in excess of £170 million and have a financial interest in more than 700 luxury holiday properties at 25 locations in 13 countries, including

England, Scotland, Wales, Austria, Cyprus, France, Italy, Portugal, Spain and USA. Expansion plans for 1999/2000 include a 24 per cent increase in the number of fully owned bond properties.

The units include delightful cottages in the English Lake District, an 18th-century _manoir_ in France, a hilltop hamlet in the Dordogne and another near Siena in Italy, holiday homes in the Canary Islands, chalets near ski facilities in Austria, villas in Florida, a converted castle in Wales and a restored former hotel in the Highlands of Scotland. Many of these developments have exceptional holiday facilities, including swimming pools, and every unit is equipped to luxury standards. There are also six narrow boats for hire and fishing rights on a river in Perthshire.

The Tenancy Programme was introduced five years ago to widen the scope of holiday destinations, particularly in locations which only enjoy fairly short seasons. Every effort is made to ensure that chosen units provide a higher standard of accommodation than is normally found in rented apartments and villas. The programme for 1999 offers over 200 villas and apartments in destinations such as Venice, Gozo (Malta), Turkey, Greece, France, Portugal, Ireland, Spain, Florida and South Africa.

The minimum investment is £2,000 and a points system (one point per £1 invested) is operated. The points required to obtain occupation of each holiday home varies according to location, accommodation and the time of year chosen. There is no fixed annual fee, just a no-profit 'user charge' when a property is occupied, to help cover cleaning, fuel, taxes, insurance and administration charges.

Unlike timesharing, 'hard-sells' tactics have never been employed and there is a 28-day cooling-off period to enable investors to change their mind if they so wish. The Holiday Property Bondholders Committee, which includes a number of elected owners, provides the management with information on the possible selection of new sites and keeps in touch with Bondholders to help solve any possible administrative problems.

15 Title Insurance and Trustees

TITLE INSURANCE

For many years title insurance in the United States has been an important aspect of house purchase procedure and there are many companies which offer this facility. This precaution has not received the same attention in the UK, although a number of American-backed companies have endeavoured to market schemes in Britain, but to date they have not met with conspicuous success. Two well-known UK insurance companies, The Royal and Sun Alliance, do offer this facility to a limited extent and a new entrant, London & European Title Insurance Services, which is underwritten at Lloyd's of London, will provide cover to mortgage applicants of a few building societies.

Title insurance is, in effect, an insured statement of the condition of a title to a property which is being transferred to a new owner. It has two advantages, namely that the company issuing the insurance pays for any losses incurred should the title subsequently be found defective, and also that it will provide an additional cover for the cost of any litigation in defending claims. Purchasers do not have to prove negligence.

TIMESHARE TRUSTEES

One of the largest timeshare companies operating in the timeshare field is FNTC (First National Trustee Co Ltd) part of IGF Group plc (a quoted company of the Dublin Stock Exchange). FNTC is incorporated in the Isle of Man and provides services to developers and, where appropriate, to committees of timeshare clubs in the UK, Europe and India. One of the duties of this organization is to ensure that taxes are paid and buildings insured for all properties held in trust. Computerised records are maintained in respect of ownership of weeks and payments for time purchased. The Group also has two subsidiaries which are authorised under the UK Public Trustee rules. The main purpose as trustee is to ensure that timeshare purchasers obtain and always have a good legal title to occupation of a completed timeshare property and furthermore to maintain the good legal title throughout the period of trust.

Developers are requested to transfer clear legal titles to fully completed properties to the trustee, who holds them on behalf of timeshare owners. Before transfer of the title, all money actually paid by the purchasers to the trustees is held in a blocked account and not released to the developer until the title is transferred or, alternatively, until satisfactory completion guarantees have been given.

FNTC also helps management companies to collect maintenance charges from owners and ensures that annual accounts of property-owning companies are prepared satisfactorily. It will also organise general meetings of the clubs on behalf of the owners committee, and because of its position in the industry is able to offer consultancy and advice to people with timeshare interests. Although FNTC does provide important services to timeshare resort operators, it is also responsible to owners and cannot be replaced except by a vote of the owners themselves at a general meeting of the club.

Further information regarding First National Trustee can be obtained from the Legal Director FNTC, International House, Victoria Road, Douglas, Isle of Man IM2 4RB (tel: 01624 630630; fax: 01624 676266).

16 Flights and Sea Travel for Owners

To get maximum benefit from their overseas homes, many owners are keen to obtain the most reasonably-priced flights to their chosen destination, not only for themselves but also for their tenants, when they rent out their property in the summer. There are a number of clubs which provide members with low-cost travel by air and other benefits.

Flight Club has a sophisticated database which holds many thousands of discounted fares from local airports to a variety of popular European destinations. Quotations can be obtained by telephoning 01903 231857 and bookings can be accepted over the telephone, with payments made by credit card, with no additional charges, or by cheque if the date of departure is at least three weeks in advance. Flightclub is a bonded ABTA member.

For those who prefer to cross the Channel or Bay of Biscay with their car to reach their second home in France, Spain or Portugal, the Property Owners Travel Club may be of interest. This is operated by Brittany Ferries who have a fleet of six passenger ships operating out of Portsmouth or Plymouth to St Malo, Caen and Roscoff, and from Poole to Cherbourg, France. They also have a service to Santander in northern Spain which departs from Plymouth in the summer months and Portsmouth or Poole during the winter.

Their largest vessel, the *Val de Loire* (32,000 tons), can carry 2,100 passengers and 600 cars, with onboard accommodation for 1,700 passengers. It serves the Plymouth-Roscoff and Plymouth/Portsmouth-Santander routes.

Club members receive discounts of up to 33 per cent on the normal fares, plus reductions on on-board meals and bonus travel discounts for friends. For membership application forms and timetables, telephone Brittany Ferries, 0990 143555. There is a once-only joining fee and an annual subscription.

Those who own one or more rentable properties abroad may be interested in the services offered by Villa Owner Service (a subsidiary of 'Flight Club') whose offices are at Guildbourne Centre, Chapel Road, Worthing, West Sussex BN11 1LZ (tel: 01903 215123).

This organisation is a fully bonded ABTA member which specialises in booking flight seats worldwide for villa and apartment owners and their tenants. Owners, who can book a minimum of 20 seats per year, receive a commission of four per cent on all seats booked. The Club's computerised technology enables them to obtain almost instant flight availability worldwide at competitive rates.

The Villa Owner Service can also offer reliable worldwide flights from all UK airports for individuals on charter and scheduled services, plus related travel services such as car hire, travel insurance (including annual multi-trip polices) and airport car parking.

The alternative to club membership is to use one of the cut-price flight specialists, many of whom publicise their offers in the national press. However, it is advisable to ascertain if the flight you select is operated under an ATOL number (Air Transport Operators' Licence) and whether the agent making the offer is a member of the Association of British Travel Agents (ABTA). The reputation of certain uncontrolled 'bucket shops' (as they are known in the trade) has been poor, because of irresponsible behaviour over cancelled flights, late surcharges, unreliable aircraft, and even bankruptcies which have left holiday-makers stranded abroad.

The Air Travel Advisory Bureau, with offices in London, offers a data system which discloses details of the operators offering the best-value seats, at the time of application, to numerous destinations. Information can be obtained by telephoning 0171 636 5000.

Tour operators also dispose of surplus seats from time to time to selected destinations in southern Europe. Many airlines operating scheduled services are prepared to quote reduced fares to stand-by passengers, but the snag here is that you can rarely be certain that you will depart on the flight of your choice until the last minute and you may have to wait patiently for several days at the airport.

'NO FRILLS' AIRLINES

The low-cost flight services now offered from England to a number of the more popular holiday destinations in southern Europe are ideal for property inspection trips and for property owners who want to visit their overseas homes fairly frequently. Aptly described as 'no frills' flights,[1] these are currently offered by Debonair, Easyjet, GO (British Airways), Virgin and Ryanair, from Gatwick, Heathrow, Luton and Stansted. They serve airports in France, Spain, Portugal, Germany, Denmark and Italy as follows:

Debonair – Barcelona, Lisbon, Madrid, Nice and Rome;
EasyJet – Geneva and Zurich;
GO – Bilbao, Bologna, Copenhagen, Faro, Lisbon, Madrid, Malaga, Milan, Munich, Rome and Venice;
Ryanair – Carcassonne (southern France), Pisa, Rimini and Venice;
Virgin Express – Barcelona, Madrid, Milan and Rome.

Fares are well below those charged for scheduled services, but it should be remembered that to achieve this these operators often add extra seats to their aircraft, so that leg-room tends to be somewhat limited. However, the flights are all short haul, with journey times of around two hours or a little more, so any discomfort should be tolerable.

Remember too that the number of cut-price seats on each flight is limited and they tend to get booked well in advance, so it is not always possible to enjoy these concessions on the days when you want to fly. Early booking is advisable, although seats do some-times become available at short notice if an airline finds it is likely to have empty seats. Departures on Tuesday mornings are often the most fruitful as this day of the week is least in demand, whereas

---

[1]'No frills' concessions generally mean no in-flight meals or entertainment, and probably no free in-flight drinks. Baggage allowances range between 20 and 25 kilos per passenger.

Friday evenings are generally in the greatest demand for outward journeys and Sunday evenings for return trips.

There are no refunds if you have to cancel a flight, and you cannot alter the day and time of your departures.

FLYING TIMES FROM LONDON

The average flying times to European destinations from one of London's airports are as listed below:

Amsterdam	1 hour	Athens	3 hours 40 mins
Barcelona	1 hour 55 mins	Berlin	1 hour 40 mins
Brussels	55 mins	Dublin	1 hour 15 mins
Faro (Portugal)	2 hours 30 mins	Geneva	1 hour 25 mins
Gibraltar	2 hours 50 mins	Istanbul	3 hours 20 mins
Lisbon	2 hours 30 mins	Madrid	2 hours
Malta	3 hours 10 mins	Milan	1 hour 45 mins
Nice	1 hour 45 mins	Oslo	1 hour 55 mins
Paris	55 mins	Rome	2 hours 15 mins
Stockholm	2 hours 20 mins	Vienna	2 hours 10 mins
Zurich	1 hour 30 mins		

17 Security and Safety

Unfortunately vandalism, violence and burglary are on the increase in most countries, so it is wise to take appropriate counter-measures if you own a property abroad or intend to live overseas.

As far as property is concerned, the precautions you take with an overseas home are much the same as in the British Isles. If you live in a block of apartments with a full-time caretaker your problems are substantially solved, provided that the person in charge is reliable and conscientious. Of course, it is wise to have good strong locks on all external doors, plus a spy hole for use when you are in occupation and an unexpected visitor arrives at the front door. Then you can see who is calling, and if you have a chain you can open the door a little without allowing direct access.

The concierge or a close friend should have door keys when you are away, so that the property can be aired regularly and checks made to ensure that there is no problem with water, either from a leak in the pipes or a flood from a neighbouring property.

Villas, particularly if they are in a somewhat isolated position, require more detailed planning. In addition to a high standard of door locks, every window that is accessible from the ground should be fitted with security locking devices. In Spain and some other countries metal window grilles are installed as decoration; these also become effective deterrents to housebreakers and burglars.

Anyone living alone should have a telephone to call emergency assistance, plus an alarm system with panic button. A loud whistle could also be useful, plus a well-trained house dog. A mobile phone is another worthwhile purchase for use at home and abroad.

One of the first tasks on settling into a new home is to ascertain the best methods of alerting the security authorities. Discover the telephone number of the local police station and find out if it is manned 24 hours a day. Place this information in a prominent position in the dwelling so that it can always be found, and add to it instructions for contacting the fire and ambulance services. List the nearest doctor and hospital in case of sudden illness.

On some modern estates where there are perhaps more than 50 dwellings, a private security service may be provided permanently and paid for by the owners as part of their community charges.

18 Household Insurance

Prudent owners of overseas property make sure that they have adequate insurance cover not only for the building but also for the contents.

When considering insurance for overseas holiday homes, it is perhaps natural for the average Briton to feel happier with a policy underwritten in the United Kingdom and prepared in the English language. In the event of either a major or minor disaster to the property, the policy conditions can be fully understood and perhaps, more important still, communication with those whose job it is to resolve the problems is streamlined.

However, the single market of the European Union has now imposed regulations which decree that property in an EU country, owned by a UK resident, must be covered by an insurance company that is licensed to underwrite in the country where the property is situated. Furthermore, the taxes and charges that are applicable to that country must be paid.

The style of policy that is available within the UK market, which meets all the criteria, is similar to the familiar UK home policy and can be obtained from a specialist company – Holiday Homes Insurance, Scottish Mutual House, 27–29 North Street, Hornchurch, Essex RM11 1RS. This firm has provided cover for holiday homes for the past two decades.

A contract to meet all the requirements of the EU has been made available, with the policy document being issued in English, premiums and claims paid in sterling, but with full translation into the language of the country where the property is situated. The contract is arranged with a major UK insurance company in conjunction with their European partners.

A specimen quotation to cover a building in France for a sum insured of £50,000 for the building, with public liability indemnity of £1 million and £1,000 emergency travel expenses, would amount to about £196. The French national premium tax and common fund for victims of terrorism is included in the annual premium.

To cover an apartment in Spain for £50,000, plus contents of £8,000, indemnity liability of £1 million requires an annual premium of about £196, included in which are Spanish fire brigade charges and taxes.

In both quotations there is a policy excess of £25 on each claim, but this is not applicable to fire, cash in meters or emergency travel claims.

Another firm with a personal insurance scheme tailor-made for the expatriate is John Wason (Insurance Brokers) Ltd, 72 South Street, Reading RG1 4RA. Their 'Overseas Personal Insurance' is a UK policy which has been designed to insure the contents of and personal property contained in homes overseas, as well as the buildings themselves. It provides a wide range of covers and permits you to choose those which best reflect individual needs. There are sections offering cover for contents, personal belongings, personal money and personal liability. Optional medical and personal accident sickness insurance cover is also available to provide a complete solution to working expatriates. Cover is available worldwide except to those living in North America. The policy is written in English and insured through Lloyd's of London. Premiums and claims (the majority dealt with inhouse) are paid in sterling and there is a £50 excess applied to each claim.

You can, of course, place your insurance with an insurance company overseas, but you might have difficulties in understanding the proposal form and the policy in a foreign language (although some companies now provide English translations of their documents). Another point to remember is that policy wording may not always be as comprehensive as that obtainable in the UK. However, well-known insurance companies such as CGU and Sun Life are represented in most European countries.

The Spanish group OCASO Insurance Services Ltd claims to be the only Spanish insurance firm with a UK branch. Ocaso S.A. was established in 1920 and is the only Spanish insurance company with a UK branch which has the approval of the British Department of Trade and Industry to carry out building and contents insurance. All administration is transacted in London and they will handle telephone calls to Spain if necessary. Should an insured property need repairs they can make the necessary arrangements without the client having to travel to Spain. Policies are index-linked to the cost of living in Spain.

The address of OCASO in London is 110 Middlesex Street, E1 7HY (tel: 0171 377 6465).

19 Letting Your Overseas Property

Many families purchase an overseas home with the intention of using it for perhaps only four to six weeks a year for annual holidays and, perhaps at a later stage, when retirement is in prospect, plan greater use by the parents as they have more leisure time. Grown-up children can possibly have the advantage of using a family-owned property overseas at certain times of the year.

The property will not improve if it is closed up for long periods and not inspected and aired at regular intervals. Damage may occur as a result of freak weather, so some owners decide it is worth going to the trouble of letting their property on a commercial basis.

It should be realised that, generally speaking, this can involve quite a lot of work and the annual return will perhaps not be more than 5 or 6 per cent after all expenses have been paid. To achieve satisfactory results, it is essential to have a good local agent on the spot to see that the property is in a satisfactory condition and ready for occupation as tenants arrive and that it is tidied up after they depart, ready for the next tenant.

Cleaning and maintenance are of great importance, and having a local person available at all times to deal with any emergencies such as electricity breakdown or a malfunction of domestic appliances is highly desirable.

Some new developments have their own management service which they offer to purchasers for a competitive fee, and in the main resort areas there are firms willing to undertake management on behalf of individual owners as a specialist service.

It is unlikely that a property, even in a popular resort, will be let for more than about half of the year. Villas in country or remote locations will probably be occupied even less frequently.

The reputation of the management organisation is of paramount importance as it is not unknown for dishonest or careless operators to find a tenant for a week or more and not report the letting to the owner; thus the opportunity is there for them to pocket the rent themselves.

Before deciding finally on letting your property for the weeks or months that you don't require it for yourself, draw up a list of conditions for tenants and have these incorporated in any publicity material that you prepare to assist you in letting the property.

Decide on the maximum number of people you want to occupy the property. Do you expect tenants to pay an additional charge for gas and electricity consumed, or do you include this in the rent? Decide on arrival and departure times for tenants and ensure that there is adequate time between the two to allow for the property to be prepared satisfactorily for the arrival of the new occupants.

If you arrange lettings through a major tour operator there will probably be quite a wide assortment of people using your home and possibly a fairly quick turnover. However, these companies wish to protect their reputation and will ensure a high standard of maintenance and cleanliness. In any case, can you really expect higher standards from people recommended to you than from strangers? Even friends in whom you have complete faith sometimes have lapses and leave places in a horrible mess.

An alternative, although not always a satisfactory one, is to ask a neighbour to manage the property for you in your absence. This means relying on that person's goodwill to undertake the job properly. Don't forget that the neighbour may want a holiday away from home, just at the peak period when you have several tenants arriving within a short period. Will the job be done to your satisfaction if your 'volunteer' suffers a period of illness, and how much should you pay as recompense for his or her trouble? In the long run, professional management is probably more satisfactory.

In some countries, such as Malta, Cyprus and Florida there are government restrictions on letting holiday property, so check the facts in advance. Also, do not forget that the tax collector will demand a share of your 'profits'.

20 Look Before You Leap

As a final reminder, the following checklist should be studied by everyone before buying a property in a foreign country:

1. Visit the property you plan to buy wherever it is situated. If it is not already completed, ask to see a similar design that is furnished and ready for occupation. Check on the materials and finishes being used and get assurance that any proposed amenities such as swimming pools or tennis courts will be available for use immediately the building programme is completed.

2. Before signing any documents or paying over substantial sums of money, seek advice on the contract, the specification and the terms of business from qualified legal experts and an accountant. Ask the developer or agent for English translations of all documents which commit you to purchase.

3. Don't be in too much of a hurry to buy a property. The vendor will obviously encourage you to make a quick decision and sign up during your first visit, but it is better to lose the opportunity of purchasing a property which seems to attract you immediately than to make a hasty decision which you may regret later.

4. When purchasing an apartment, obtain written confirmation of maintenance charges and management arrangements.

5. Where estate facilities such as swimming pools, clubs and tennis courts are promised in brochures and publicity, but have not been provided at the time you purchase your property, get confirmation that these will be available within, say, 12

months. In some countries, developers are required to provide the bulk of the amenities and access roads before they launch the sales programme.

6. Ensure that you obtain a proper title to the property you are buying and, where a Land Registry exists, that there are no encumbrances, such as a mortgage, registered. Where a legal expert is employed, these checks will be part of his or her routine work.

7. A completion date in the sales contract is very desirable, but not always easy to obtain.

8. At an early date, compile a list of costs and taxes you will be expected to pay when you purchase the property – then you should not suffer any shocks.

9. When buying a new property still under construction or not yet started, obtain information about stage payments as the work proceeds and check if you are permitted a 5 per cent retention for six months to cover any building faults and if any guarantees are offered for, say, two years to compensate for bad building.

10. Make sure you comply with the fiscal rules of the country of your choice so that you can repatriate your capital on the sale of the property. Also examine the regulations regarding taxation of foreign residents, payment of pensions, medical facilities and so on.

Part Four:

Country Surveys

Tourist rates of exchange quoted are those applying
on
5 June 1999

Readers are advised to check information about the
country they are particularly interested in, as
changes occur daily.

21 The Islands Around Britain

The Isle of Man and the Channel Islands are offshore islands around the coast of Britain that offer interesting financial benefits but, sadly, lack a climate which is significantly better than on the mainland.

However, they do attract considerable numbers of tourists and some new residents each year. The very strong protective legislation imposed in Jersey means that this island is virtually closed to most new residents.

ISLE OF MAN

The Isle of Man is situated in the Irish Sea midway between the Republic of Ireland and Cumbria. It has an area of 572 sq km (221 sq miles) and measures 52 km from north to south by 22 km east to west. The coastline extends to about 160 km and has many long, sandy beaches in the north, which contrast well with the rocky cliffs and sheltered bays elsewhere. A range of hills stretches across the island, the highest of which is Snaefell (621 m) and between these there are well-defined valleys which provide a variety of scenery.

The population totals about 70,000 people, of whom 22,200 live in the capital, Douglas. Other major towns include Onchan, Ramsey, Peel, Castletown, Port Erin and Port St Mary. With a population density of just 122 people per sq km there is space for everyone.

The Isle of Man is not and never has been part of the United Kingdom, but an internally self-governing dependent territory with its own two-tier parliament, the Tynwald, founded by the Vikings, a thousand years ago. It makes its own laws and oversees all internal administration and social and fiscal policies. External matters including foreign representation and defence are administered by the UK government on the island's behalf, for which the island makes an annual contribution.

The legislature comprises:

1. The House of Keys, with 24 members who are elected annually, the majority of whom are independents. As a result there is a virtual absence of party politics.
2. The Legislative Council of 11 members, includes as *ex officio* members, the President of the Tynwald, HM Attorney General and the Lord Bishop. The Council generally acts as a chamber which revises Bills initiated in the Keys. Royal Assent to Tynwald Bills is given by the Queen, but now more often by the Lieutenant Governor, who is the Queen's personal representative on the Island.

A special relationship exists with the EU which allows the free movement of goods between the island and the Union, but the Isle of Man neither gives to nor receives anything from EU funds.

Economy

A well-balanced economy combining traditional industries such as farming, fishing and tourism with new areas of growth including financial services and manufacturing, has enabled the Manx Government to maximise the local standard of living and at the same time safeguard its environment and quality of life, the aim being to create a prosperous, law-abiding and caring, free society.

The government's initiative to stimulate population growth and economic activity by increasing awareness of the island's advantages has produced a significant influx of new residents and businesses, to the advantage of all the residential facilities available on the island. A rapidly rising national income, low levels of unemployment, and excellent education, social and health amenities, provide residents with a unique quality of life that is appreciated by everyone. All this is enhanced by favourable taxation, a low crime rate and a relaxed way of life.

The fact that everyone speaks English and uses a similar currency to the UK are further advantages.

For those seeking jobs there is a varied choice. Banking, insurance, asset management, trusts and stockbroking are now major employers of local staff. Traditional mass tourism has declined and, following the upgrading of many hotels, the accent is now on quality tourism and conferences. Shipping registration and management is expanding, and new industries are being encouraged by capital allowances on new buildings, plant etc. A film industry is being developed and there is a freeport adjacent to the main airport.

Taxation

The standard rate of income tax is 15 per cent on the first £8,750 of taxable income for a single person or the first £17,500 for a married person, after the following allowances to resident individuals have been granted:

Single person £6,600; married couple £13,200 and life assurance allowance 50 per cent of premiums paid. A higher rate of 20 per cent is charged on incomes exceeding the standard rate thresholds.

VAT is charged at 17.5 per cent on all goods and services except those which are zero rated.

Death or estate duties, capital transfer or gift taxes, capital gains tax and wealth tax are not charged in the Isle of Man.

Currency and cost of living

The island issues its own £1 notes and pence coins, which are on a par with £1 sterling.

The cost of living and inflation are about the same as in the UK.

Legal system

English law does not extend to the Isle of Man, but the Manx legal system is based on the principles of English Common Law.

Education

There are excellent facilities for primary and secondary education throughout the island, maintained by the Isle of Man Department of Education.

For those requiring independent education the merged King William's College and Buchan School provides continuous education for boys and girls, day pupils and borders from the ages 4 to 18.

Further education is available at The Isle of Man College which caters for over 6,000 full- and part-time students.

Work permits

Any person who is not classified as an Isle of Man worker must obtain a work permit, before taking up employment.

Health and postal services

The Manx National Health Service is under the control of the island's Department of Health and Social Security. A range of services from hospitals and medical specialists to district nursing are provided, for health takes a high priority in government expenditure plans. Newcomers to the island are entitled to the full range of health services as soon as they take up residence.

The island's post office authority became independent of the British Post Office in 1973 and issues its own stamps. A comprehensive and efficient range of services is provided.

Recreation

Apart from 95 miles of coastline offering a variety of beaches and rocky headlands, the Isle of Man has many other attractions for outdoor recreation. It is a golfer's paradise with no less than eight golf courses, all within 45 minutes drive of each other. There are good facilities for fishing, sailing, and other watersports, and opportunities for long-distance walks. Birdwatching and other wildlife viewing can also be enjoyed. The annual TT motorcycle races are known worldwide.

There are five separate Victorian Railway and Tramway systems with locomotives dating back over a century and these provide access to some of the islands special beauty spots.

Indoor facilities include a new multi-million heritage centre, the restored late Victorian Theatre at Douglas, plus arts and crafts centres.

Communications

Manx Airlines have been providing air services to and from the island for over 50 years. The current programme provides flights from 12 airports (London Heathrow and Luton, Southampton, Birmingham, Cardiff, Liverpool, Manchester, Leeds/Bradford, Newcastle, Glasgow, Jersey and Dublin).

By sea, the Isle of Man Packet Co provide a daily SeaCat service from Liverpool (journey time: 2.5 hours) and a conventional ferry from Heysham during the summer, plus a SeaCat service from Belfast and Dublin.

In winter there are conventional ferries from Heysham on Monday to Thursday and from Liverpool on Friday, Saturday and Sunday.

Property purchase

There are no restrictions on the purchase of residential property by non-islanders. A wide range of homes is available at prices comparable with many areas of England and Wales, but certainly much cheaper than in the Home Counties and south east of England. Frequently offered are bungalows, apartments, terraced and semi-detached houses and some country cottages. Prices range from about £15,000 for a one-bedroom converted flat; around £60,000 for a two-bedroom detached bungalow and from £75,000 for a four-bedroom semi-detached house.

All title deeds, including mortgages and other charges, are recorded and held in the Isle of Man Deeds Registry. A charge is made for registration but there is no stamp duty on conveyancing. Legal fees are controlled by a scale of charges imposed by the Tynwald.

The island introduced legislation in 1996 to control timeshare sales companies' activities, whereby purchasers' deposits are protected and they have the right of cancellation, which they can exercise within 10 days in Spain and the Isle of Man and within 14 days in England and Wales.

Climate

The island's climate is temperate and lacking in extremes, due to the influence of the surrounding Irish Sea. In winter snow and frosts are infrequent. The coldest month is generally February, when the average daily temperature is almost 5°C, but it is often relatively dry. July and August are the warmest months, with an average temperature of 14.5°C.

GUERNSEY

Guernsey (population 59,500) is the second largest Channel Island. It does not attract as many holiday-makers as its neighbour Jersey, but is a very pleasant place in which to live. Excellent shopping facilities are available in St Peter Port and there are plenty of recreational facilities.

Economy

The financial sector has expanded, and Guernsey is an offshore tax haven. A large banking sector with over 70 institutions is licensed to undertake deposit business. Many well-known financial institutions have local offices.

Tourism is the second largest industry, together with a very active conference business. Light industry has developed into an important employer and exporter. Fishing and 'high-tech' industries are also of importance.

Taxation

Income tax – 20p in the pound – has not changed for more than 30 years; there is no VAT, corporation tax, capital gains tax or inheritance tax. There is a double taxation agreement with the UK as well as Jersey. A special relationship with the European Union exempts Guernsey from most EU law, and there is no need to harmonise taxation and other internal policies with those of the EU.

Medical

Everyone in the island now pays a percentage of their income to cover all specialist care given by locally based specialists in Guernsey hospital. For the majority of people the contribution totals 1 per cent of their income up to a maximum income of about £22,000 per annum. Hospital services remain free. Most local residents have private insurance to cover the cost of treatment and consultation with general practitioners.

Education

Administered by the States Education Council and broadly similar to England. There is an excellent grammar school for boys and girls. Well-known private schools include Elizabeth College for boys and Ladies College for girls. There are also some small fee-paying schools and a college of further education.

Housing

New residents may occupy 'open market' properties only. These are inscribed on the Housing Control Register and amount to about 10 per cent of total housing stock (19,000). The aim is to protect bona fide locals from speculative purchasers of lower-priced properties. A wide variety of properties is available, ranging from larger town houses to country residences. Little scope exists for new building owing to land shortage.

Period or Victorian-style homes or estate houses cost approximately £180,000 to £250,000, while good-quality, detached houses in pleasing locations usually range between £400,000 and £600,000. There is also a limited number of superior properties costing up to around £4 million.

Conveyance charges amount to approximately 4.25 per cent of purchase price. Rates are very low and in three categories: occupiers' rates levied by the parish, tax on rateable value payable annually to the States, and quarterly water rate. Open market houses with a market value of £250,000 pay combined rates, including water, of about £200 per annum.

The Bristol & West Building Society has an office in Guernsey. The laws of inheritance differ from those of the UK and it is advisable to make a new will on taking up residence. Advice should be obtained from a local advocate.

Purchasing procedures

Verbal contracts are no longer legally binding in Guernsey. The purchaser is represented by an advocate who undertakes the title search and drafts the conveyance. Completion normally takes about six weeks and is effected by appearance before the Royal Court. A *congé* of 2 per cent of the consideration is payable on conveyance plus document duty and an advocate's fee of about 2.25 per cent.

JERSEY

This is the largest of the Channel Islands and the most southerly of this group of islands.

It is a very popular resort for holiday-makers from the mainland and attractive as a low tax area for wealthy individuals and international businesses. The island has also become a major international banking community with a wide selection of banks, mainly in St Helier.

Property purchase and residency

In order to protect local people and to maintain a balance between economic development and the preservation of the environment, it has been necessary to impose severe restrictions on the movement of people into the island.

This is achieved by local licensing laws which prevent individuals who do not have birth or marriage qualifications from buying or leasing freehold or leasehold residential accommodation unless approved by the Jersey Housing Committee.

One way of obtaining this approval is to be essentially employed in one of what are considered to be the most important professions, such as medicine, accountancy and banking.

Having obtained the Committee's permission, the employing company can then purchase or rent a property for the employee to live in. The individual cannot buy a property in his or her own name unless resident in the island for 20 years or more.

The only other way of obtaining a residence permit is as a wealthy immigrant. Each application is considered on its merit and requirements do vary. As a general guide, an annual tax liability of £100,000 is required and total wealth in the region of £10 million. Very few people of this status are accepted each year, and they must spend a minimum of £750,000 on a property.

Under Jersey law the legal title to property does not depend on deeds. Title passes only when the Royal Court of Jersey decrees. The Court will do this only when the parties have indicated their mutual agreement to the terms and have also previously satisfied the Housing Committee that the proposed new occupant has the necessary residential qualifications. Thus the housing purchase regulations are enforced without undue difficulties.

ALDERNEY

Alderney is the most northerly of the Channel Islands and lies only eight miles off the French Normandy coast. It has a population of about 2,147 and is the third largest in the group (measuring 3½ by 1½ miles). Many of the inhabitants are of French descent and some of the street names are in French, but English is the common tongue. This is a location where peace and serenity can be enjoyed in abundance, amid some delightful scenery. There is much natural beauty with fine sandy beaches, attractive bays, cliff walks and country lanes.

St Anne, 'the town', is little more than a sleepy village with cobblestone streets, colour-washed cottages and a surprising variety of small shops. It is inland, yet within easy walking distance of the harbour at Braye.

There are a number of sports clubs and a nine-hole golf course.

Administration

Alderney is a self-governing territory and one of the constitutive islands of the Bailiwick of Guernsey. The legislature, known as the States, comprises a President and 10 elected members. Each person who has lived on the island for at least one year is entitled to vote and is qualified to stand for the States after three years in residence. The Court of Alderney, which is administered by six Jurats and a Chairman, deals with all civil, criminal and company law matters. More serious crimes are referred to the Royal Court in Guernsey.

Economy

Tourism is important during the summer, yet the island is never overcrowded and visitors are made very welcome. Local crafts include pottery, spinning, weaving and knitwear, and also fishing.

Like its larger sister islands, Alderney is now an offshore financial centre and has the same modern banking, insurance and investment laws as Guernsey. The island has its own company law with about 500 firms currently registered. Costs of forming and operating a company compare favourably with the other Channel Islands. There are three branches of UK clearing banks.

The Guernsey Post Office has provided special stamps for Alderney since 1983.

Cost of living

The cost of living is probably about 15 per cent higher than in the UK, due to freight charges and the fact that there are no subsidies. But duty on cigarettes, liquor and luxury articles is much lower.

Taxation

There are no death duties or capital gains taxes for residents. VAT is not charged and local rates average about £200 per annum. Income tax is 20 per cent, with allowances similar to those in the UK. Other revenue comes from modest import duties on alcohol, tobacco, petrol and the sale of the island's own postage stamps.

Medical

The Social Insurance Scheme is administered by the States of Guernsey Insurance Authority, PO Box 39, Guernsey, and there are reciprocal agreements with Jersey and the UK. Patients are required to pay for treatment by doctors and dentists. The small local hospital has fully qualified nursing staff and modern equipment and the compulsory health insurance scheme covers all costs at this hospital. Routine surgical and more serious cases are referred to the Princess Elizabeth Hospital in Guernsey, and accident and emergency cases are generally flown by charter aircraft to Guernsey or Southampton.

Education

Children between the ages of 5 and 16 can attend the modern local school where nationally recognised examinations can be taken. Further education can be taken in Guernsey where there are excellent schools for girls and boys. Alderney also has nursery schools and playgroups for under-fives, and a fully independent preparatory school.

Work permits

For non-islanders wishing to settle and work in the island an employment permit system operates, but certain categories of occupation are exempt. Further information can be obtained from the States Office, Queen Elizabeth II Street, Guernsey.

Importations

Domestic pets from other Channel Islands, the Isle of Man and the UK mainland can be imported without a permit. All other animals require a permit and must be quarantined. Caravans cannot be imported.

Housing

There are no restrictions on the purchase of homes in Alderney by UK or EC passport holders. There are about 1,000 residential properties on the island and prices are generally more expensive than in Southern England. Local estate agent Mitchell & Partners Ltd, PO Box 46, Ollivier Court, Alderney report that small houses start at about £85,000, town houses and bungalows range from about £125,000 while family homes with four bedrooms may sell for in excess of £200,000.

To protect the environment and in view of the scarcity of sites, the law requires anyone applying to build a new residential property to have been resident in Alderney for more than 10 years. New residents are, however, encouraged to rebuild or convert buildings registered as dwellings.

Purchasing procedures

Verbal contracts are legally binding having signed the conditions of sale. No advocate is required but a title search should be undertaken. Completion generally averages four to six weeks and is effected by appearance before the Alderney Land Registrar.

Expenses comprise *congé* (the local property purchase tax) – 4 per cent of the purchase price – and a stamp duty of 1.5 per cent.

Communications

There are scheduled air services throughout the year from Southampton, Jersey, Guernsey, Caen and Dinard. There is a weekly freight service to Guernsey and fortnightly services direct to Weymouth. More comprehensive passenger sea links to France and

England are being negotiated for 1999. Details can be obtained from the tourist office (tel: 01481 823737; Web site: www.alderney.gov.gg).

SARK

Sark is the smallest of the four major Channel Islands. It lies 7½ miles east of Guernsey and 22 miles west of the Normandy coast of France. It measures just 3 miles in length and 1½ miles at its widest point. Sark enjoys outstanding natural beauty, with a variety of rural scenery and many rocky bays with sandy beaches.

The population totals about 580 and there are six hotels, a number of guest-houses, some self-catering premises and two campsites.

There are no metalled roads and cars are not permitted, so internal transport is on bicycles or horse-drawn carriages. There are a limited number of tractors used for farm work and the conveyance of visitors' and residents' luggage from the harbour to the 350-foot-high plateau where the majority of accommodation, the shops and the pub are situated.

There is no airport and aircraft are not allowed to fly over the island below 2,000 feet. The only access is by sea from Guernsey, Jersey or France. As a result living on Sark is more peaceful than in many other places.

Administration

The island's constitution dates back to 1565. Queen Elizabeth II is Sovereign and her government is responsible for law and order and defence, but Sark is not part of the British Isles or the United Kingdom, nor a Sovereign State.

The island is governed and administered by 'Chief Pleas', which consist of the island's 40 landowners and 12 elected Deputies of the People. Chief Pleas meet three times a year and are presided over by the Seigneur, who holds the island from the Crown in perpetuity.

The 40 sections of land into which the island is split are called tenements and each tenant (tenement owner) is expected to attend

Chief Pleas on a regular basis. The tenants must be British subjects and be resident on the island for a major part of each year. There are a few 'freeholds' on Sark which do not have a seat on Chief Pleas, but which are subject to the same restrictions as tenements. If a tenement or freehold is sold, the purchaser must have the approval of the Seigneur.

Only the eldest son of a family is entitled to inherit land or property, but if there is no son a daughter may inherit, but from then on if there is no heir apparent for 7 degrees of affinity, the land reverts to the Seigneur. This ensures that the tenements are never divided or split.

There is a ground rent on each leased house which is payable annually to the landowner. Leases can be purchased by people of any nationality.

Except where existing foundations are being used, permission to build a new house is only given to people who have resided on the island for at least 15 years. Planning control committees have to approve the style and site of new houses.

Economy

Tourism is an important source of income and employment, with many visitors enjoying long or short vacations in the summer and also day trippers visiting from the other Channel Islands and France. Agriculture is another source of employment.

Both Midland and National Westminster banks have branches in the main street and there is a post office. The official currency is the Guernsey pound, but Jersey and British currency is accepted, as well as major credit cards. There are no automatic cash machines in Sark.

Cost of living

This is about the same as in the other Channel Islands.

Medical

There is a doctor in the local medical centre and Sark has reciprocal arrangements with the British National Health Service, but residents should have private health insurance. There is no local dentist.

Education

Education is compulsory between the ages of 5 and 15. The Sark schools currently have three teachers and about 36 children. Youngsters over the age of 11 years are encouraged to attend boarding schools in Guernsey or elsewhere for a wider education.

Local restrictions

Transistor radios may not be played in any public place. Pubs do not open on Sundays and tractors or horse-drawn carriages are not allowed on roads (tracks) on Sundays without special permission. Electric Invalid Carriages are permitted subject to a doctor's certificate. Only the Seigneur is permitted to keep a bitch that has not been spayed, so dog breeding is not permissible.

Housing

A small number of attractive houses and sometimes a bungalow are normally on the market. At the time of going to press, Sark Estate Agents, of L'Atelier, Sark (tel: 01481 832360) were able to offer, with unrestricted occupancy, a leasehold self-contained 3-bedroom chalet with swimming pool and gardens of 1.75 acres, on the north-east coast, for offers in the region of £230,000 (lease 66 years). On the east coast of the island a long lease of 95 years was offered for £395,000 on a four-bedroom house and a detached two-bedroom bungalow with letting potential. Occupancy was unrestricted.

A few rental properties are also generally available.

Taxation

Sark is virtually a tax-free island, for residents. There is no inheritance or capital gains tax. The property tax and visible wealth tax are very modest.

Communications

There is a daily boat service to Guernsey almost throughout the year and a catamaran service to and from Jersey in the peak season.

Telecommunication services are adequate.

22 Europe and the Mediterranean

ANDORRA

General information

Status

Co-principality

Capital

Andorra la Vella

Area

468 sq km (180 sq miles)

Population

65,000

Location

Latitude 43°N; longitude 0°E. Landlocked territory in the eastern Pyrénées, surrounded by France and Spain, roughly the same size as the Isle of Wight and having very mountainous terrain.

Political stability

Andorra has a unique record of peace and diplomatic non-intervention in European affairs which stretches back for 700 years. As a co-principality it has been run on largely feudal lines, with the President of France and the Bishop of Seu d'Urgell (a nearby Spanish town) as joint sovereigns. Early in 1993 Andorrans voted at a referendum for a more democratic constitution. This maintained the co-princes as heads of state, but limited their powers. It is now a sovereign state with its own constitution, thus able to make its own foreign policy and join international organisations. Membership of the United Nations was obtained in July 1993 and the Council of Europe in November 1994.

Economy

Currency

The French franc and the Spanish peseta comprise the official currency as Andorra does not have its own monetary unit, and the euro will be adopted in 2002. Coins and bank notes of these two countries circulate freely and travellers' cheques in various currencies can be cashed at local banks. Access, Amex and Visa credit cards are accepted by many traders. Credit Andorra, a local bank has 10 branches with English-speaking staff and there are six other independent Andorran banks, which all operate with complete confidentiality. Foreign banks are not permitted to operate locally.

There are no exchange control restrictions.

Cost of living

This compares favourably with many other European countries. Food and other living expenses are roughly on a par with Spain, while fuel costs are very competitive as electricity is generated by hydro-electric power. Telephone charges and property insurance are not high, while luxuries such as alcohol, jewellery and electrical goods are quite cheap due to low import duties.

Taxation

There are no income, inheritance, profits, capital gains or value added taxes. The normal rate of duty on goods imported into the country is 7 per cent and this provides the bulk of the government revenue. Telephone calls and electricity bills attract a duty of 10 per cent.

Exchange rate

As for Spanish pesetas and French francs (see pages 194 and 277).

Exchange control

None.

Language

Catalan, Spanish and French are the main spoken languages, but English is spoken and understood in some areas, especially tourist parts.

Expatriate community

Only about 17,500 of the population are true Andorrans, the rest being 28,500 Spanish residents, 6,600 Portuguese, 4,400 from France and the rest a mixture of other nationalities, including about 1,000 Britons.

Security

Andorrans are generally law-abiding citizens, with a few 'black sheep' who are mostly visitors and foreign workers. The crime rate is very low and the country itself has no army.

Residence permits

In December 1996 the government finally passed the long awaited amendment to the act covering *Residents Passius* or foreign residents. New resident applications, and renewals of existing permits will require a deposit of 4,000,000 pesetas per head of family, plus 1,000,000 pesetas for the spouse and each dependent, to be made with the government finance agency INAF. This deposit will not attract interest but will be returnable on relinquishing the permit, which will be valid for an initial period of one year with a 'rubber stamp' renewal for a further three years thereafter. A person who spends 183 days or more each calendar year will be considered a resident.

Work permits

People wishing to seek employment face great problems in gaining a work permit, unless the applicant is setting up in business with an Andorran or is engaged in tourism.

Personal effects

No duties are payable provided that there is no intention to resell.

Housing

Only about 8 per cent of the country's total area is available and suitable for residential development, so there are restrictions on how much property a foreigner may own. Currently this comprises one unit, ie one apartment or villa or one plot of land not exceeding an area of 1,000 square metres. Husband and wife count as one entity in this respect, but children over the age of 18 may register a property in their own name.

Many ski apartments and some excellent villas have been built for foreign owners over the past three decades, so there is a good selection of resales on the market, also some newly built homes. Prices range from about £27,500 for a one-bedroom ski apartment, with chalets and town houses costing upwards of £120,000.

Buying property

A property can be reserved verbally, but once a 10 per cent deposit has been placed with the vendor's agent, the purchaser is committed and will lose the deposit if the deal is not completed by the buyer. A receipt for the deposit is issued and, about six weeks later, after the necessary enquiries have been made and government approval has been obtained, both parties appear before a local notary to sign the purchase contract. At this time the balance of the purchase price is paid over and the title deeds are then issued.

Fees charged by the notary amount to about 1 per cent of the purchase price.

Local councils collect annual rates to cover services such as street lighting, snow clearance and refuse collection from each household. The annual average bill is likely to be about £110 for an apartment and £200 for a four-bedroom chalet.

Mortgages of up to 80 per cent of the purchase price are normally available. Fixed interest rates are 5.5 per cent at present.

Where to live

The best residential districts include Ordino, Erts, La Massana, Sispony and Sant Julia. Avoid areas near the highway which traverses the main valley through the country as this is used by heavy goods traffic and is consequently noisy.

Inspection flights

Not available, but independent travel facilities are adequate (see below).

Communications

Air

Daily air services from Heathrow and Gatwick to Barcelona (flight time about two hours), which is about 130 miles south of Andorra. Then a road journey by an excellent public shared taxi or minibus at a reasonable fare. Alternatively, it is possible to fly to Toulouse in France and continue the journey by train or hire car.

Rail

By train, the journey from London via Paris and Toulouse to Hospitalet, close to the Andorran border, takes about 24 hours, or even quicker if you travel via the Channel Tunnel.

Road

The journey by car is via the trans-Pyrénéean highway which links Toulouse with Barcelona and passes within 40 km of Andorra la Vella, the capital. From the Channel ports the distance is about 600 miles, and with a morning crossing it is possible to cover about two-thirds of the journey on the day of departure, spend a night in a hotel en route and arrive in Andorra about the middle of the next day.

Recreation and residential amenities

Andorra is a mountainous country with more than 60 peaks over 7,500 feet high. Even the 'lowlands' are about 4,000 feet above sea level, so there are plenty of opportunities for winter sports. From December to April there are excellent facilities for skiing with a number of good ski stations and over 130 pistes suitable for all levels of the sport. Enthusiasts can undertake snow-biking, surf-skiing, heli-skiing and mono-skiing. After an outdoor session it is possible to enjoy swimming in Olympic-size pools, visit an ice rink, play squash and tennis, athletics and football.

Walking, hiking, biking, fishing, canoeing and horse riding can be enjoyed in summer through beautiful scenery and along the banks of numerous rivers.

The most spectacular facility is the recently opened Caldea aquatic thermal centre at Escaldes. Claimed to be the largest in Europe, the building covers 25,000 square metres on three levels, dedicated to water, fun and body care. Under an immense glass dome there are heated swimming pools, geysers, fountains, waterfalls, power showers and steam baths, as well as a Turkish bath, saunas and jacuzzis. The Caldea Club on the second level provides members with a more personal atmosphere and facilities for relaxation treatment, a repose area, beauty salon, gym and restaurant.

The exterior of the building is dominated by an 80 metre high tower.

The main shopping centre is at Andorra La Vella. Here there is an excellent range of retail establishments including some large department stores.

BBC World Service Radio enables residents to keep in touch with happenings in other countries. TV addicts can watch BBC and BSkyB programmes and ASTRA with satellite dishes. Local French and Spanish TV programmes can also be received.

Health services

In the centre of Andorra La Vella, the capital, a new, well-equipped hospital has been opened recently. In addition there are three clinics and some of the doctors speak English. Specialists from Barcelona visit Andorra regularly and there are opportunities for major treatment in a hospital at Toulouse. A private room in any of the hospitals may cost only £125 per day and most new residents subscribe to a British or other private medical scheme.

The healthy mountain climate with very low levels of humidity is particularly beneficial to sufferers from chest complaints and rheumatic problems.

Climate

Spring (April–May)

Maximum temperature 22°C, minimum 4°C. Generally warm but with variable rain or snow showers.

Summer (June–September)

Maximum temperature 26°C, minimum 10°C. Mostly dry hot days, with cooler nights. No humidity.

Autumn (October–November)

Maximum temperature 18°C, minimum 2°C. Clear skies, fresh mornings and evenings. No fog.

Winter (December–March)

Maximum temperature 15°C, minimum 7°C. Snow on most higher altitudes, mostly sunny days and not damp.

AUSTRIA

General information

Status

Republic

Capital

Vienna

Area

83,855 sq km (32,367 sq miles)

Population

7,555,338

Location

Latitude 48°N; longitude 10°E to 16°E. Austria is situated in southern central Europe, covering part of the eastern Alps and the Danube region. Though landlocked, the country has a wide variety of landscape, vegetation and climate, ranging from Alpine highlands, through the foothills, to lowland plains.

Political stability

Despite a history of political and territorial instability, post-war Austria has gained a reputation for comparative continuity and stability, although party politics have created some problems. It is a federal republic which gives considerable autonomy to the regions.

Austria's neutrality does help to enhance a policy of cordial relations with other nations. In economic matters, Austria is a member of the EU.

Economy

Cost of living

The Austrian economy is undoubtedly very stable. Prudent policies and efficient industry have combined to protect employment. Generally, a high standard of living is enjoyed by most of the inhabitants.

Taxation

Income tax rates are progressive from 10 per cent to 50 per cent, with a pay-as-you-earn system. A double taxation agreement exists between Britain and Austria. VAT varies from 10 per cent on food etc, to 34 per cent on some cars. The annual local tax is 0.8 per cent, based on the value of land. The social security system is comprehensive and contributions are approximately 17 per cent of salary.

Exchange rate

Austrian schillings 20.77 = £1.

Exchange control

There are no limits to the amount of foreign currency which can be imported or exported.

Language

The language of 98 per cent of the population is German, so a knowledge of the tongue would be useful. However, knowledge of English is fairly widespread in Austria, especially among the well educated.

Expatriate community

There are few expatriate Britons in Austria.

Security

Austria is a secure nation and faces no specific problems.

Residence permits

There are no restrictions on entering Austria for citizens of the EU countries, but they need a valid passport and must apply for a residence permit on arrival.

Work permits

EU citizens do not require a work permit to take up employment in Austria.

Personal effects

Household goods may be imported duty free, so long as they are accompanied by a household goods inventory (see Chapter 8).

Housing

In order to protect local inhabitants from growing shortages and escalating prices of residential property, all nine Austrian provinces have regulations which require the acquisition of real estate by foreigners to be subject to the approval of the Land Transfer Authorities. The restrictions imposed vary from one province to another. Property prices appear to be expensive but Austrian homes are normally built to a high specification. The owner occupation figure is about 50 per cent, but there is a shortage of homes to buy.

Currently, it is virtually impossible to purchase property in some regions of the country if you are not Austrian. In other communities the restrictions are not severe.

Buying property

The property agreement is written in German, with an English translation, and this can be signed in either Austria or the UK. A copy is given to the purchaser. The lawyer acts for both parties and can have power of attorney to act on behalf of the purchaser. He or she can also prepare a mortgage agreement if a loan is required.

Deposits are not normally necessary. The documents are signed before an official of the Austrian Embassy and then returned to the lawyer with a draft or cheque for the purchase price. Meanwhile the new title to the property is registered at the land registry and this may take four months or more. When registration is complete the taxes and fees are paid and the purchase price released to the vendor.

Expenses total about 8–8.5 per cent of the purchase price and comprise land tax at 3.5 per cent plus a separate fee for the Land Registry Court, depending on the price of the property, but it will be around £175–£270; title registration 1 per cent; stamp duty 0.5 per cent; notary fees 3.5 per cent.

Where to live

See 'Housing' above.

Communications

Austria has excellent communications both internally and externally, including six commercial airports, well over 1,000 km of motorways and 5,800 km of railways, plus large stretches of navigable waterways as well as thousands of cable-based mountain lifts. There are frequent flights to Vienna from Gatwick and Heathrow. Public transport in Austria is well developed.

Austria has a dense network of postal communications and news media, including fully automatic telephone, telegraph and telex as well as radio and television.

Recreation

Leisure facilities in Austria are good. The environment is one of stunning beauty, which encourages outdoor pursuits such as walking, camping and climbing, not to mention the ideal Alpine skiing conditions which make skiing Austria's national sport. Other popular physical pursuits include football, swimming, judo and motor racing. There is also a very strong tradition of horse riding. In general, sports facilities are excellent.

Culture and the arts also provide a rich source of interest for residents. Literature, opera, choirs and festivals combine with the fine architecture to promote Austria's cultural image. The main cities such as Vienna and Salzburg are especially fascinating.

Education

Education is compulsory for children aged 6–15 but there are very few independent schools.

Driving

Driving in Austria is on the right and passing on the left. Tolls are charged on some mountain roads.

Social security

A compulsory social security system for all employees covers health, accident, pension and unemployment insurance. Cover is granted not only to the employee, but also to dependents.

The Austrian health service is well equipped. Each province has its own health administration and health office. In principle, everyone is entitled to make use of the health service facilities as the costs are borne by the social insurance and social welfare scheme, but private health insurance is recommended for foreigners.

Climate

Austria belongs to the central European climatic zone, with the influence of the Atlantic felt in the west and the continental influence more strongly in the east. In general, the climatic seasonal changes are far less pronounced in the west than in the east. For the purposes of describing climate, Austria can be divided into three areas:

East-continental Pannonian climate: mean temperature for July above 19°C; annual rainfall less than 800 mm.

Central Alpine region: high precipitation with long winters and short summers.

European climatic zone: wet and temperate, July temperature 14–19°C, annual precipitation 700–2,000 mm.

CYPRUS

General information

Status

Independent Republic

Capital

Nicosia

Area

9251 sq km (3570 sq miles)

Population

approximately 700,000

Location

Latitude 30°N; longitude 32°E. The island of Cyprus, at the eastern end of the Mediterranean, is a land of contrast. In the south, where the majority of Greek Cypriots live, there is considerable prosperity; and vast sums have been invested in the construction of new roads, hotels and residential accommodation. The second airport, at Paphos has been modernised and the facilities at

Larnaca have been extended to include new arrival and departure areas.

The main business centre is Nicosia, the capital, which is approximately in the centre of the island. Unfortunately, it is still split into two sectors, the northern half being the Turkish section and the remainder the Greek area.

The Turkish Cypriots administer the northern part of the island, including the once popular resorts of Kyrenia and Famagusta and are supported by a contingent of the Turkish army. As a result tourism is at a low ebb in this area, compared with the rest of the island.

The southern coastal towns of Limassol, Larnaca, Ayia Napa and Paphos are all controlled by Greek Cypriots. They have a multitude of sandy beaches and many residential and touristic facilities, and so enjoy considerable business activity.

In the centre of the island is the Troodos mountain range, where in about three winter months it is possible to enjoy skiing in the morning and then descend to sea level and have a swim in the Mediterranean during the afternoon.

Political stability

Although the island has been partitioned for nearly 30 years, with Turkish soldiers in the northern sector, there are still hopes that the problems will eventually be resolved.

A contingent of United Nations peace-keeping troops are based locally and the British Army and the RAF have bases on the island.

Cyprus is an independent sovereign country with a democratic-presidential system of government. The island is a member of the Commonwealth, the Council of Europe, the United Nations and an associate member of the European Union (full membership is anticipated in the future).

Economy

Cost of living

Prices may seem somewhat lower than in England, but remember that the exchange rate is slightly in favour of Cyprus, with Cyprus £1 being equal to about £1.20 sterling. Inflation has been kept low, thanks to thriving manufacturing and agricultural industries, and also offshore business, such as banking, insurance and marine. These, together with tourism, are the main foreign currency earners. Local produce such as fruit and vegetables is reasonably priced, but some imported items are more expensive than in the UK, due to transport costs. Heavy winter clothing is not required, due to the year-round agreeable climate.

Taxation

Income tax commences at 20 per cent on chargeable income in excess of C£2,000, but for expatriates special rules apply. Expatriates' income of up to C£2,000 from pensions for services rendered abroad and also from investments acquired when the owner was outside the island is tax exempt, and thereafter the tax rate is only 5 per cent.

Cyprus has a double taxation agreement with the UK, many other European countries, the USA and Kuwait.

On the sale of a property the owner is liable to capital gains tax on the difference between the price achieved and the original price paid. This works out at 20 per cent of the profit, but the first £50,000 is exempt for non-Cypriots. The exemption figure is raised to £67,000 if the owner has resided in the property for five years or more. Should the owner be non-resident in Cyprus for tax purposes and foreign money was used originally to buy the property, exemption from capital gains tax is granted.

VAT is charged at 8 per cent on many items, but food, children's clothing, certain other essential items and real estate are exempt.

The Off-Shore Business Centre is successful, with some thousands of off-shore companies operating from Cyprus, enjoying low taxation and other benefits.

Exchange rate

Cyprus pound (C£) 0.87 = £1.

Language

English is spoken by practically everybody. About 70 per cent of local TV programmes are in English and there are two English language papers. In addition, the local British Forces radio broadcasts round the clock every day.

Expatriate community

Links between the UK and Cyprus have always been strong and are illustrated in many ways, such as the similarity of property registration procedure, driving laws and the existence of a substantial Cypriot community in Britain. It is estimated that over 3,000 Britons are resident in Cyprus and many more own holiday property there.

Security

The Cypriots themselves are generally open and honest and so personal property is not especially at risk. According to Interpol statistics, Cyprus has an incidence of crime that is only one sixth of the average for European countries.

Residence permits

Foreigners owning real estate in Cyprus do not need a resident's permit, but it is more convenient to obtain one as it avoids having to renew a visitor's permit every three months and ensures that they receive the tax concessions mentioned above. Permanent residents' permits can be obtained by applicants of independent means by completing a form from the Immigration Office and providing certificates from an overseas bank showing a minimum qualifying income of £10,000 (UK) per annum for a married couple.

Work permits

Aliens wishing to work in Cyprus require a permit from the government under the Aliens Immigration Law.

Personal effects

Personal baggage, household goods and furniture can be imported free of duty. A duty free car can also be imported for both husband and wife if desired.

Housing

A large number of new villas and apartments have been built in southern Cyprus over the last two decades, particularly in the vicinity of Limassol and Paphos. Leptos Estates, one of the leading property developers on the island, builds in the Paphos area. Their current projects include Poseidon Beach Village, a seafront scheme with communal pool where special villas cost approximately £120,000. Other sites in this part of the island include apartments of varying sizes priced from about £20,000. Leptos have a London office at Leptos (UK) Ltd, 555 Green Lanes, London N8 0RL. Another well-established developer is Cybarco Ltd of Nicosia (London office: 2 Leather Lane, London EC1), who also have sites around Paphos, as well as in Larnaca and Nicosia. A good selection of established homes for re-sale are available through UK specialist agencies and local firms.

Land in Cyprus is measured in units known as donums, one of which is equivalent to about one-third of an acre.

Buying property

A foreign adult or family is allowed to purchase only one freehold villa or apartment or a building plot of about two-thirds of an acre in Cyprus. There are no restrictions on property ownership for those of Cypriot origin.

The Cyprus legal system for property purchase is based on its English counterpart. Locally it is not considered essential to employ a solicitor to handle a property conveyance, but in the author's opinion it is better to be safe than sorry.

All property in Cyprus is registered at the local Land Registry and property purchase procedure is somewhat similar to England and Wales. The first stage is the signing of a preliminary contract, which binds both parties to the transaction on mutually agreed terms. This is subject to the purchaser being able to get a good title to the property and being able to obtain the required permits from the Cyprus government. At this stage a deposit of about 25 per cent is lodged with a notary or lawyer. Searches are then carried out at the Land Registry by the purchaser's legal adviser, to ascertain that the vendor has a good title to the property which can be transferred to the purchaser.

The application by a non-Cypriot to purchase the property, which is submitted to the Council of Ministers at this stage or earlier, is normally a routine matter and costs around £200 sterling. The final contract is only entered into when the searches have proved satisfactory and the permits approved.

Property transfer fees are on a sliding scale, rising from 5 per cent on the first C£10,000 of the purchase price to 8 per cent over C£75,000. Lawyers fees are based on the amount of work involved, plus the cost of the property and are likely to be around £400.

There is a stamp duty to be paid on signing the contract which is 10 cents per C£100 of the purchase price up to C£100,000 and this increases to 20 cents on an excess above C£100,000.

The annual property tax is quite low, for properties under C£100,000 are exempt and thereafter the tax is C£2 per thousand up to about C£250,000, rising still further for higher values. The modest refuse and street lighting charge amounts to about C£30–100 per year, depending on the size of the property.

Mortgages can be arranged in Cyprus with local banks. Most developers have their own schemes. Interest rates are generally 2.5 per cent above the LIBOR rate. Loans are normally granted for between 70 and 80 per cent of the purchase price and are spread over 7 to 12 years.

Foreign currency must be imported into Cyprus by aliens to pay for any property purchased. On resale, repatriation of the original purchase price is allowed immediately and any profit can be exported to a limit of £50,000 per year, beginning in the year following the sale.

Recreation

There are plenty of opportunities for sport and recreation in Cyprus, due to the exceptional climate. Facilities include skiing, sailing, walking, swimming and other sea sports, there are two new golf courses near Paphos, tennis, squash, athletics, bowling, cycling, shooting, fishing, horse racing and riding.

Where to live

A varied choice of locations is available in the southern (Greek) sector of the island, for those seeking a villa or apartment for permanent living or for vacations. There are a number of substantial-sized towns with residential amenities, a variety of quiet villages, some attractive coastal resorts and some pretty mountain hamlets.

Nicosia

Situated almost in the centre of the island, Nicosia has an estimated population of over 150,000 citizens. It is divided into two sections, Greek and Turkish by the so-called 'Green Line' which was instituted following trouble between the Greeks and the Turks which resulted in the invasion of the north of the island by Turkish armed forces in 1974. United Nations soldiers guard the border and maintain the peace between the two factions. This situation does not, however, affect life locally and on the Greek side of the border business is brisk in the city with its wide streets, tree-lined avenues, fine shops, busy offices, hotels and government buildings. Of interest are the city walls built by the Venetians (1567–70), which are now integrated into the life of the metropolis, and the Cyprus Museum which contains the most important collection of Cypriot antiquities and art treasures.

On the Turkish side of the Green Line, business is less prosperous and life is at a slower pace.

Limassol

Population 70,000. The second largest town in Cyprus is Limassol, about 80 km south west of Nicosia and about half way between the island's two airports at Larnaca and Paphos. It is the main port and has two fully equipped marinas. Having expanded considerably over the past decade, it now spreads for over 20 km along the coastline where there are many new hotels on the beach and in the neighbouring hinterland. The shopping facilities are generally regarded as the best in the island. Richard the Lionheart is reputed to have married Berengaria de Navarre at Limassol Castle.

Larnaca

Population around 25,000. This is another town of importance with a large marina, where major hotels and apartment blocks have been built in profusion along the coast road and inland. Many new industries have been established in recent years, particularly in the clothing sector, and the town, the fourth largest in the island, is an important trade centre, with pleasant residential areas. Its international airport has taken the place of the one at Nicosia, which has been unavailable since the Turkish invasion in 1974.

Paphos

Situated almost at the western extremity of the island about 100 miles from Nicosia, the town was formerly outside the mainstream of island life, even though it was at one time the capital of Cyprus. Over the past two decades this region has experienced considerable growth from a fishing village to a major resort with many new hotels and other tourist accommodation. In the vicinity are some fine mosaics dating from Roman times, the Tombs of the Kings, a 13th-century church and strong associations with Aphrodite the goddess of Love.

Ayia Napa

A small fishing village at the eastern end of the south coast which has been transformed over little more than 10 years into a resort of importance with numerous hotel and apartment blocks, restaurants and tourist shopping facilities.

Renting property

In order to protect the tourist industry, a regulation prevents foreigners from letting their property in Cyprus to holiday-makers. However, this rule does not seem to be imposed very vigorously.

Communications

British Airways and Cyprus Airways between them run daily services to Larnaca (flying time about 4½ hours). There are also scheduled fights to Paphos (4 hours). Cyprus Airways serve many

European and Middle East countries. During peak periods there are flights to Cyprus from 15 UK airports.

Telecommunications are excellent, with automatic direct dialling available on a 24-hour basis to over 60 countries.

Health, welfare and education

Cyprus has one of the healthiest climates in the world. Medical treatment costs in government hospitals are low. There are plenty of specialist doctors and surgeons, and private practices for consultation. A new general hospital has been opened at Paphos.

A social security agreement exists between the UK and Cyprus, covering National Insurance and various benefits, including pensions. Details are given in DSS pamphlet SA12. Pensions from UK National Insurance are index linked.

There are many good schools and a college for higher education on the island (see list on pages 67–68).

Climate

	Average daily temperature (°C)	Rainfall Average days	Sea temperature (°C)	Sunshine hours
January	9–18	12	16	169
February	9–19	8	17	197
March	10–20	7	18	255
April	11–21	4	18	285
May	15–27	4	21	355
June	18–30	1	24	379
July	21–35	0.3	26	399
August	21–35	0.4	27	358
September	18–32	1	27	321
October	17–27	3	25	277
November	11–24	6	21	231
December	8–17	11	19	175

FRANCE

General information

Status

Republic

Capital

Paris

Area

551,000 sq km (213,000 sq miles)

Population

55 million (approx)

Location

Latitude 42°N to 51°N; longitude 5°W to 5°E. France is surrounded by mountains and water and its natural boundaries are the Pyrénées and the Alps, the river Rhine, the Channel, the Atlantic and the Mediterranean.

Economy

Taxation

A double taxation agreement exists between France and the UK. Non-residents do not normally pay income tax if they are using a property as a holiday home for personal use only. A non-resident selling a secondary residence in France pays a tax of 33.3 per cent levied on capital gains, but quite generous allowances can reduce the actual assessment substantially. Any tax paid in France can be offset against a UK liability under the double taxation agreement. A wealth tax applies to French assets and property. In 1999 assets not exceeding FF4.7 million are exempt, beyond which the rate is 0.55 per cent up to FF7.64 million and the scale increases to 1.8 per cent for amounts in excess of FF100 million. Married couples and common law couples are assessed jointly. Local rates and occupancy tax are calculated by the local authorities and cover such items as local schools, street lighting, road sweeping etc. Payment is assessed on 1 January annually. VAT is levied at various rates in accordance with EC regulations, currently 20.6 per cent.

Exchange rate

French francs 9.90 = £1.

Exchange control

The purchase of real estate by non-French residents does not now require foreign exchange permission from the French authorities.

Language

French is a comparatively easy language to learn and the effort is well worth while if you live in France for any length of time.

Expatriate community

France still remains defiantly popular among Britons looking to set up home overseas, despite the high supplementary costs of buying a French property and the effects of the recession on property sales on both sides of the Channel. However, vendors in France are often prepared to negotiate on prices and this, along with low interest rates on sterling mortgages and an improved exchange rate, is an encouragement to British buyers. The appeal of the French way of life extends far beyond its own boundaries. France is internationally popular, attracting more than 40 million overseas visitors a year – almost a quarter of them from Britain. For many holidaymakers to France, buying a place of their own is simply the next, logical step. The boom years of 1988 and 1989 may be long over, but many buyers whose ambitions have been checked are merely shelving, rather than abandoning, their plans and may now feel ready again to proceed in view of the improved economy.

· In the past, foreign buyers traditionally headed south – to the Riviera, inland Provence and latterly Dordogne. Now, every nook and cranny of provincial France is explored in the search for that dream home. Reaching those parts has never been simpler. Access is an important consideration in France's favour. Those apparently isolated corners of the country are, in fact, temptingly close thanks to ever-improving communications. France invests heavily in its transport systems. A long-term plan for roads and high-speed railways is regarded as a major force in regional development. Linked to the Channel Tunnel, these networks are bringing not only northern France but the whole country within easier reach for British visitors.

The Channel Tunnel

After a series of high-profile delays, frustrations and financial setbacks, the opening of the Channel Tunnel was the realisation of a centuries-long dream and created the first land connection between Britain and France since the Ice Age. Through-train and shuttle services, for passengers and freight, have transformed the tunnel from a highly complex engineering project into one of the world's most intensively used transport systems.

The shuttle service carries cars, coaches, motor-cycles and lorries on a 35-minute journey between the tunnel terminals at Folkestone and Calais. The terminals have direct access to the M20 in Kent and the A16 near Calais, close to its intersection with the A26.

In Britain, the already heavily congested M25 remains the principal link between the South East and routes to the rest of the country. Cross-Channel traffic is expected to increase significantly, not simply because of the tunnel itself, and this will put even more pressure on the M25. In France, the aim is to provide not only adequate approach roads to the tunnel, but also long-distance routes avoiding the Paris area.

Similarly, while Britain hesitated over the high-speed rail link between London and Folkestone, the French have pressed ahead with construction of TGV Nord Europe, including the line from the tunnel to Paris.

Journey times on the Eurostar passenger through-trains from the Waterloo International Terminal in London are currently 3 hours to Paris and 2 hours and 40 minutes to Brussels (since the opening of the Belgian high-speed rail link in December 1997). There will be further reductions when the British link eventually comes into service. London to Paris will take approximately 2 hours and 30 minutes; London to Brussels will be a journey of 2 hours and 10 minutes.

However, there is still considerable uncertainty surrounding the construction of the high-speed line between London and the Tunnel – including its completion date and the precise route it will follow. Meanwhile, France has Europe's most extensive railway network and the world's fastest passenger trains, and there are plans to extend the TGV network even further. Proposals include the development of a new generation of trains whose maximum speed will be set initially at 300 kph. New track will be designed for speeds up to 350 kph. Tilting TGVs will be introduced, capable of running on existing track at higher speeds than conventional trains. Double-deck TGVs have been introduced on the Paris–Lyon route and the service will be extended to other routes. The double-deck trains, which are being delivered at the rate of one a month, are compatible with the whole TGV network. They can operate at the same speed as other TGVs and can carry 40 per cent more passengers. There are long-term plans for a new tunnel under the Alps, which will eventually link Lyon and Turin.

Thanks to TGV Nord, Eurostar passengers from Britain can connect with other high-speed train services both in France and many other parts of Europe. The Lille Europe station acts as a hub, with the Paris TGV by-pass, the Interconnexion, linking three existing networks (Nord, Sud-Est and Atlantique) and, in due course, TGV Est.

Lyon, too, has a high-speed by-pass, which, with the extension of the line as far as Valence, has cut journey times between the north and south of France by 30 minutes. These will be further improved with the completion of the 300 km an hour TGV Méditerranée to Marseille and Montpellier. The 24.3 billion franc project, due for completion in June 2001, means it will be possible to travel by high-speed train from the Channel to the Mediterranean, a distance of 1,250 km. Paris to the Mediterranean will take only three hours.

The journey from Lille to Marseille will be covered in 4 hours and 25 minutes.

Attractions

Communications within France and to the rest of Europe are excellent, therefore, whichever region you choose for your French home. The sheer variety of property available in France is another factor which guarantees the interest of overseas buyers. Real estate in France remains an attractive proposition. There are estates, country houses of great architectural value and character and restored manor houses, at prices which still compare favourably. The decline in agriculture and the migration to towns and suburbs in France since the Second World War mean thousands of redundant farm buildings and country dwellings have become available. Many of them require complete restoration and have remained on the market, unoccupied, for a number of years. Some are ruins with little or no sanitation. It is still possible to find a tumbledown cottage tucked away in the heart of the French countryside for £10,000, even less, provided you are prepared to spend more money and time making it habitable. Recouping the cost of an expensive renovation, however, could prove difficult, particularly in a buyers' market. Although the French themselves are beginning to show a greater interest in rural properties again, they do not generally share the British taste for out-of-the-way 'character' homes.

Purchasing property

Consider all the options carefully before committing yourself to buy. The importance of taking professional advice cannot be overemphasised. Speak to lawyers, bankers, financial advisers, as well as architects and surveyors, if appropriate. Do as much homework as possible to familiarise yourself with the French system, the terms that will be used and the French professionals you will meet during the course of the transaction. Consult the 'everyday' experts, too, people who have already bought a house or business in France, and who may be only too willing to pass on the benefits of their experiences.

Make sure you ask *yourself* a few straightforward questions, as well. Would you be happier in a cottage that wasn't quite so isolated? Will the bargain *château* cost a small fortune in renovation and upkeep? Have you the skills, time and dedication to repair that dilapidated farmhouse and install mod cons? Be as objective as possible. Put aside the memories of carefree summer holidays in France. Visit your chosen location in the winter when its climate and character are completely different.

There is no need to be intimidated by the French system, for all its bureaucracy and paperwork, provided a number of basic rules are followed. French law provides considerable consumer protection for the home-buyer, but the procedures – legal, financial and fiscal – are as different as the customs, culture and attitudes of the French themselves and should be fully understood to avoid potential pitfalls.

The role of the *notaire* is essential in all property transactions. The French system does not automatically provide your own personal legal representative. Unless you choose otherwise, the *notaire* will be the only legal professional involved. If you are buying a new property (off-plan), the developer will nominate the *notaire*. In theory, the purchaser has the right to choose the *notaire* when the transaction involves existing property. In practice, however, the French agent will probably suggest the *notaire* who handled the previous sale of the property.

The *notaire* is a public officer, controlled by the Ministry of Justice, who will supervise and authenticate the transfer of ownership. Whoever nominates the *notaire*, the *notaire* represents neither the purchaser nor the vendor. Instead, the *notaire's* responsibilities are to the French government: to ensure the law is properly applied and that all fees and taxes due to the state on completion of the deal are paid.

The *notaire* will make certain enquiries and searches on the property with the local authority and the Land Charges Registry, to verify that the property is the vendor's to sell and that there is no outstanding loan against it greater than the current purchase price. In the case of land or farm buildings, the *notaire* will also check that the French agricultural authorities, notably SAFER (the Société d'Aménagement Foncier et d'Etablissement Rural), will not be exercising their right to step in and buy the property instead of you. The *notaire* will not, however, make the exhaustive local searches specifically on your behalf that your solicitor in Britain would. Enquiries relate to the property itself and not to the surrounding area. So you may not be made aware of plans to build a motorway a kilometre away, right in your view of the open countryside.

It is worth carrying out your own enquiries at departmental and local level. Visit the Département de l'Urbanisme in the *mairie* (the town hall). Talk to your prospective neighbours and the patron and regulars at the local café, always an invaluable source of information. In any case, you should go along to the *mairie* to introduce yourself to the mayor. In France, the mayor is a far more influential person than the British counterpart and has greater powers – the authority and responsibility to make many decisions which could affect your property.

Although the *notaire* is not formally your legal representative, ask if you are unsure about anything. If you wish, you may appoint a second *notaire* to supervise the completion of the transaction on your behalf. You might not be popular if you do, however, because the two *notaires* would then share the same fee. Alternatively, you may decide to employ a legal representative of your own, exclusively to defend your interests and to make enquiries and searches on your behalf. In this case, of course, a separate fee for these services would be payable.

When you set out to look for your new home, contact several property agents. Those who are based in Britain will have a network of associate agents in France. Together they will arrange site visits for you, but do not expect the French office to provide detailed printed information about the properties on their books. Instead, they will tend to accompany you on your appointments. Do not be too ambitious about the number of these you can keep in a day. France is a deceptively large country, and even within a single *département* it can take longer than you anticipate to travel from one rural property to another.

Be realistic, too, about the type of property you are looking for. Decide what your priorities are, and then have a good look around. Allow sufficient time to view a number of properties within your price range to appreciate exactly what is available. Choose the dates of your visits to France carefully. Holiday times may suit you, but first make sure that the agency or *notaire's* office will be open.

Consider carefully the precise location of your property. An idyllic quiet spot for a fortnight's vacation may not be so attractive as a permanent residence. That pleasant holiday stroll of a few kilometres to the nearest *boulangerie* could become a chore as a regular matter of necessity. Since the additional costs and fees of purchase are higher in France than in Britain, a mistake at this stage could be not only regrettable but also expensive.

Older properties in parts of south-west France are subject to infestation by wood-boring insects. The *notaire* should be able to advise you whether a property is in an affected area. In some places a survey and any necessary remedial treatment are compulsory on change of ownership when a *certificat parasitaire* is provided.

Surveys are not common practice in French property transactions and can be expensive. Some French banks may not insist on a valuation when deciding on a mortgage application. As we shall discover, however, they will be very interested in the applicant's personal ability to service the loan.

There are professionals in France who will examine a property for you – building experts (*experts immobiliers*) and architects – and there are British surveyors who practise in France. They must have professional indemnity insurance, which should be extended to cover their work across the Channel.

If you are buying an old property or farm building in an isolated area, make sure there is a supply of tap water and electricity as well as room on your own land for the installation of a septic tank. If you wish to have the water supply analysed, contact the *mairie* or the DDASS (Direction Départementale des Affaires Sanitaires et Sociales).

You may decide that a modern apartment, in a coastal resort, perhaps, promises more carefree ownership with fewer concerns about maintenance. In this case, you will encounter the French system of *co-propriété*, under which you will own your apartment outright, rather than on leasehold. Not only will you have the freehold of the apartment itself but also a share of the freehold of the land. The size of your share is determined by the floor area of your flat, which also serves to apportion your contribution towards the general service charges. In France, the co-owners control the management of the property. Major decisions are taken by ballot at an assembly of owners, and each person's voting right is set out, with a lengthy description of the building, in the all-important document, *les règlements de copropriété*. Every apartment block should have one.

Estate agents in France are strictly regulated. They must have a professional qualification and a financial guarantee enabling them to receive your deposit. Without this guarantee, you should pay your deposit to the *notaire*. Agents in France must display details of their professional charter, the sum of their financial guarantee and the name of the organisation which covers it. Professional associations include FNAIM (Fédération Nationale des Agents Immobiliers et Mandataires) and SNPI (Syndicat National des Professionels Immobiliers).

A good agent will assist you throughout your transaction, giving advice, smoothing out any difficulties that may occur, putting you in contact with an architect or builder or helping with planning procedures. Agents must have a mandate from the vendor, authorising them to sell the property and stating the commission arrangements. Responsibility for paying the commission – whether it is the vendor or the purchaser – varies from region to region. In some parts of France the cost is shared between the two parties, although it is becoming more usual for the vendor to pay. French law protects the agent from purchasers and vendors who, having been introduced to each other, attempt to cut the agent out of the proceedings. In such circumstances, the agent would be entitled to the commission and the same amount again.

You could find your home in France through a *notaire*, because, in addition to having legal responsibilities, the *notaire* is permitted to offer properties for sale. The *notaire's* commission, known as the negotiation fee, is fixed in law, but might not be included in the advertised price of a property. It is generally paid by the purchaser.

The agent's fee, on the other hand, is not fixed. It tends to be higher than the *notaire's* and is generally included in the quoted price. Check this is the case, however, and if you negotiate a lower purchase price be clear that the new figure is still inclusive.

When you deal with a British estate agent you should not pay any more commission than if you had gone directly to the French counterpart. British and French agents working together should share the one fee. So establish the price of the property itself, the cost of any fixtures, fittings and additional land that may be included, the commission (and who pays it), the legal fees and taxes due and the monthly repayments and arrangement fee for your mortgage, if applicable.

If you require a loan to purchase the property, find out before you go to France how much you can borrow and how much the loan will cost. You might decide to remortgage your home in Britain and borrow in sterling at UK rates of interest. In this case, you simply change your pounds into francs and buy the French property outright. Alternatively, you could borrow in francs from a French lender against the security of the French home you are buying. Fixed and variable rates can be negotiated and, generally speaking, the repayment term will be 15 or 20 years. In assessing your monthly repayments you should also allow for life, health and invalidity insurance cover on the mortgage.

A French mortgage offer is subject to a compulsory 11-day cooling-off period before you can accept it. This is for your benefit, part of the consumer-protection legislation, but it does hold up the process and you should allow at least ten weeks for your French loan to come through.

Many French banks have specialist teams in Britain to help you with your mortgage application, and a number of British banks and building societies have French offices and French subsidiaries. They can often provide the paperwork for your application in English, loan terms up to 25 years and, using the *French* property as security, the option of a *sterling* mortgage (thus avoiding the necessity of monthly currency conversions for the repayments).

In processing your application, a French bank will make a cash-flow study to assess your ability to repay the loan. They will require full details of your existing financial commitments as well as your income and will not allow your new French mortgage to take your total outgoings above 30 or 35 per cent of your disposable income.

Provided you do not exceed the above restriction, a French bank will normally lend you up to 70 per cent of the basic purchase price. This means that, out of your own resources, you will have to finance not only the balance but also the legal fees, taxes and other expenses. So if these come to an additional 20 per cent, for example, and you take out a loan to cover 70 per cent of the price of the house, you will have to find the equivalent of 50 per cent yourself.

If the property needs renovation or repairs, you can apply for a second loan to help to cover the cost. The bank will require quotations with your application, and your estate agent, surveyor or French builder can advise you. Payments will be made directly to the builders on presentation of invoices. Rates could be slightly higher.

It is advisable to open a French bank account in good time. You can do this in France or Britain, in person or by correspondence (in which case your signature will have to be witnessed by a solicitor and/or confirmed by your UK bank). If you wish to open a resident's account you will have to prove that you have a job in France or means of financial support, and you will have to present some, or all, of the following: passport, proof of residence (a copy of your lease if you are renting, or a certificate of completion of purchase which you obtain from the *notaire*), a letter from your UK bank, and a copy of your *carte de séjour* or application for it.

A French bank account will simplify your payment of fuel, telephone and local tax bills as well as your mortgage commitments. Allow plenty of time when you transfer funds into your French account. It could take longer than expected for the money to be cleared in your account, and if you go overdrawn without arrangement you could be prevented from operating a bank account in France for up to ten years.

You will not be issued with a cheque guarantee card. Cheques can be stopped only if they have been lost or stolen. The *carte bleue* is a charge card, not a credit card, with the amounts debited directly from your account by the bank. You can arrange for pensions to be paid into your bank account in France.

When you have found the property you wish to buy, you will be asked to sign a preliminary contract and to pay a deposit – usually 10 per cent on existing property and 5 per cent if it is new. Make sure you understand the differences between English and French procedures at this stage. There are various types of preliminary contract in France. Be clear about the particular document you are being offered and ensure that it contains all the conditional clauses (*conditions suspensives*) to protect your interests.

There are three main contracts in use for the sale and purchase of existing property. The *promesse de vente* is a unilateral promise by the vendor to sell the property to the purchaser at an agreed price.

Normally, the purchaser has a specified period of time in which to take up the option to buy, and during this time the vendor may not withdraw from the contract or offer the property to anyone else. Although there is no obligation on the purchaser to buy, he or she could still forfeit the deposit if the purchaser decides not to proceed. With the *promesse d'achat*, on the other hand, it is the purchaser who commits him or herself to buy the property and there is no obligation on the vendor to sell at all. On the expiration of the time limit, the contract becomes null and void. Before then, however, the purchaser would lose his or her deposit if the purchaser decided not to proceed. The *compromis de vente* is a bilateral agreement, binding both parties, and this is the most common form used. The purchaser may not have the right to withdraw from the transaction, even on the loss of his or her deposit, unless the contract specifically allows the purchaser to do so.

There are also three main types of contract for the sale of new (off-plan) properties – the *contrat de réservation*, the *vente en l'état futur d'achèvement* and the *vente à terme*. Each provides for the payment of a deposit and stage payments as the building work progresses. The law requires the developer or the developer's agent to produce an architect's certificate confirming that each stage of the work has been completed as specified. When you take out a loan from a French bank on a new property, the funds will be released at intervals to meet those stage payments.

If you wish to buy off-plan you could go to a developer who will sell you a building plot and who has a selection of property designs already approved by the planning authority. Alternatively, you may prefer to act independently. You will have to check that the plot you wish to buy can be developed and then apply to the *mairie* for planning permission for your house (*le permis de construire*).

Any new building in France has to be guaranteed – for ten years on the fabric of the property and two years on the internal installations. These guarantees have to be underwritten by an insurance company to protect the purchaser if the builder subsequently ceases to trade. When you take possession, you will be asked to sign a declaration confirming that everything is in order. If you observe any faults later you must point them out to the developer and claim under the guarantee.

Unless you have found your property from a *notaire*, it will probably be the estate agent who prepares the preliminary contract for you to sign. (However, the details will still have to be recorded by a *notaire*.) Resist all pressure to sign and to hand over your deposit until you understand the agreement fully and are completely happy with it. Allow yourself time to study it carefully. A translation of the document will not be enough. Take professional advice if you are unsure about anything. Consult a lawyer who is well versed in French law and taxation and who can explain all the implications of the contract – what has been omitted as well as the contents.

Whether you are buying a new or an existing property, you should make sure that your contract includes a number of *conditions suspensives*. If any one of these is not fulfilled, you can call off the deal and have your deposit returned. The most important condition, and the one that is mandatory under French consumer protection laws, will safeguard you in the event of your mortgage application being refused. If you need a loan to make the purchase, the contract must state this. If you subsequently fail in your application for finance, you may withdraw from the transaction without penalty. This condition means you can effectively secure a property before you even apply for a loan. However, the preliminary contract will set a date by which you must submit your mortgage application and failure to do so could affect your rights. If, on the other hand, you do not intend to apply for a loan, you must endorse the contract to this effect in your own handwriting. You would then forfeit the law's protection if you found that you did need a mortgage, after all.

Bearing in mind that the preliminary contract is signed before the legal searches are made, you should ensure that a number of other, optional, conditions are included. These should protect you in the event of any detrimental planning proposals or third-party rights coming to light; if the vendor has an outstanding mortgage on the property greater than the current price; if SAFER (see above) decides to exercise its rights of pre-emption on a country property; if you want to make the transaction subject to a satisfactory structural survey. It is always possible to negotiate other conditions as well.

When the *notaire* has completed the enquiries, the *notaire* will draw up the deed of sale, *l'acte de vente*, which contains a full description of the property. Once vendor and purchaser have agreed and signed this document, witnessed by the *notaire*, ownership is transferred. The *notaire* will not hand you the original *acte de vente*, however. Instead, the details will be recorded at the Land Registry, and you must ask the *notaire* if you require a copy (*une expédition*) or a certificate stating that the transaction has been completed (*une attestation*).

The deed is signed in the *notaire's* office, but if you are unable to travel to France, a friend or a member of the *notaire's* staff can sign on your behalf. If you wish to arrange this power of attorney and the purchase is subject to a mortgage, you will have to sign a document before a notary public in the UK. If a loan is not required, a British solicitor can witness the document or the *notaire* may be satisfied simply with your own signature.

The additional costs involved in your transaction will vary between new and old property. Taxes and legal fees on older houses can amount to 8 or 10 per cent of the basic purchase price. To that you may have to add the commission. On new homes, the costs are less – 3 or 4 per cent – but VAT will have already been included in the purchase price.

The costs are made up of stamp duty, Land Registry charges and the *notaire's* fee, as well as transfer duty – about 0.6 per cent on new houses, 7.5 per cent on older ones. The amount payable can vary from département to département. There is a higher rate of transfer duty on agricultural land and commercial buildings.

Personal finances

Local rates, which are lower than the British Council Tax, consist of an annual *taxe foncière* if the property is not let (*taxe professionnelle* if it is) and a *taxe d'habitation*, which is payable by the person occupying the property on 1 January. If you are buying a property off-plan you can apply for a two-year tax holiday before the *taxe foncière has to be paid*.

If you are resident in France for tax purposes, you are liable to French income tax on the whole of your worldwide income. In principle, all non-residents who own a house in France are liable to French income tax on the basis that they receive an income equal to three times the rental value of their property (generally taken to be

5 per cent of the capital value). In practice, however, UK residents owning a property in France can avoid this tax under the Anglo-French double-tax treaty. Where there is no double-tax agreement with France, in the Channel Islands for example, there is no such protection.

British residents who decide to let their property in France must declare the rental income from it both to the British and the French tax authorities. This applies even if the rental is paid in Britain and the money put into a UK bank account. Under the double treaty, the tax will not have to be paid twice. The sum paid to the French Revenue will be credited against the UK tax assessment.

Wealth tax (*impôt de solidarité sur la fortune*) applies to any individual whose assets in France exceed FF4.7 million (in 1999). The tax is payable annually, at 0.55 per cent on the first band above the FF4.7 million threshold, to a maximum of 1.8 per cent on assets over FF100 million.

Non-residents selling secondary homes in France pay capital gains tax at 33.3 per cent. There are allowances for inflation against the original purchase price, purchase costs and major rebuilding and structural repairs where VAT has been paid and the VAT receipts retained. There are also reductions of 5 per cent for every year of ownership after the first two. This means property owned for 22 years is exempt from French capital gains tax. British residents must also declare capital gains on the French property to the UK Inland Revenue, but the tax paid in France will again be offset under the double-tax treaty.

Non-residents of France selling property must also appoint a guarantor to the French Revenue, who will be responsible for any capital gains tax owing. The guarantor could be a bank or a resident of France.

Your property in France will be subject to French inheritance laws and taxes – whatever your nationality, wherever your permanent residence and regardless of your wishes. Many British buyers are surprised by the rigidity of these laws. Most significantly, children are given priority over the surviving spouse, male or female.

It is important to ensure that your will covers your French assets. Where there is no will, the surviving spouse receives merely a quarter of the property. For French residents this applies to the entire estate. A will can offer greater protection for the surviving spouse, but whereas English law allows you to leave your assets to whomever you please, French legislation does not. Children – including adopted or illegitimate children or those from a previous marriage – have a legally reserved share before the surviving spouse is considered. Where there is one child the legal reserve is a half-share in the property; two children receive one-third each; three or more children share three-quarters of the property equally. This is the minimum they must be left. There are particular problems where the children are very young. Legally, it could be difficult if the surviving parent wished or needed to sell the property. If there are no children or grandchildren, the legal reserve will apply to living parents of the deceased, rather than the surviving partner.

Any deliberate attempt to defeat the legal reserve could be treated as a fraud. It cannot be avoided, but its effects can be minimised or postponed by the way in which you structure your property ownership. You should take professional advice to avoid tax disadvantages.

Inheritance tax in France is paid by each individual beneficiary, rather than by the estate. The rate of tax varies according to the relationship between the beneficiary and the deceased. The closer the relationship, the lower the rate. Before any tax is due, there is an allowance, which also varies according to the degree of kinship. Attempting to avoid the reserve of children, therefore, would not only be illegal but would also waste their tax-free allowances.

One solution could be the formation of a *société civile immobilière*, a property-holding company. A husband and wife, for example, would not own the house itself, but shares in the company. These could be divided equally between the two partners, and provided the couple were resident outside France the shares would not be subject to French inheritance rules. Children could still be left a quantity of the shares, with the surviving spouse inheriting a controlling majority.

Alternatively, a husband and wife could have *la clause tontine* included in the conveyance when they buy their property. This has the effect of postponing ownership until one partner dies, when the other becomes the owner of the entire property. However, the clause cannot be added after the purchase, and while both partners are alive the property can be sold only if both agree.

Work and residence permits

EC nationals do not need a work permit in France, although certain professions are restricted and require a relevant French, or compatible, qualification. If you are planning to live in France, you no longer need a *visa de longue durée*, which was previously obtained from a French Consulate General in Britain. Instead, you apply for a *carte de séjour* from the local *préfecture* in France. Since there is freedom of movement between member states of the EC, you are entitled to receive a *carte de séjour*. In theory at least, it is not a question of submitting your application and hoping that it will be granted.

You will need to produce your passport, passport-size photographs, proof of residence in France (a copy of a lease or a title deeds certificate), a contract of employment if applicable, and possibly your birth certificate as well. So-called 'non-economically active persons', for example pensioners or students who will not be earning their living in France, may be asked to prove that they have means of financial support.

Personal effects

Under the free movement of goods, you can take your personal property and household items into France. You no longer have to declare that they have been your property for three months, nor are you restricted from selling them for a year. Televisions and video recorders in France operate off the Secam, rather than the PAL, system. A PAL video tape played on a Secam recorder will show monochrome pictures. You will need to adapt or replace your existing items, and you can buy dual-standard equipment. Satellite and cable television are readily available.

Mains services

Mains water in France is metered, with the price varying from region to region. Contact the water board to have the supply connected or if your property has no existing supply. However, the water board will not dig any channels for pipes on your property and you must arrange this work separately.

Electricity and gas are supplied by EDF (Electricité de France) and Gaz de France, although in the country you will probably need gas in bottles or a tank. Normally, there are three levels of electricity supply for domestic use – 3kW, 6kW and 9kW. The supply you choose will depend on the number and type of appliances you have in your property and are likely to use at the same time. You can request a more powerful supply.

Driving

The speed limit on French roads is 45 km/h in city centres, 50 or 60 km/h in other built-up areas, 90 km/h on ordinary roads, 110 km/h on dual carriageways and 130 km/h on motorways. There are tolls on French motorways (*péages*). *You can pay by cash or credit card.*

If you are stopped for speeding, you could be asked to pay an on-the-spot fine. There are random breath tests, and motorists who are over the legal drink-drive limit face a prison sentence and fine.

Health service

British nationals are entitled to the same health service as the French and should register with the local Social Security office. You can choose your GP. You pay for your treatment or prescription and the doctor or chemist will sign a form enabling you to claim back 65 per cent of the cost. However, you will not be reimbursed if the doctor is not *conventionné, not part of the Social Security system.*

If you are to receive expensive treatment, you can arrange simply to present your Social Security card to the doctor or hospital on the day, instead of having to pay.

It is possible to take out international private medical insurance to cover you in France. Some policies may cover hospital and specialist fees but not GP consultations and treatment. Repatriation can be included.

Education

Children in France go to nursery school from the age of two or three, and there are local authority crèches for babies. From primary education, State or private, there is a national curriculum. State secondary schools are either a *lycée* or a *collège*. The *collège* will take students to the age of 14 or 15, when they will go to a *lycée* and prepare for the *baccalauréat* or a vocational diploma.

Climate

France is more than twice the size of Britain and has coastlines on the Channel, the Bay of Biscay and the Mediterranean, so the climate varies from one region to another. In the south it is temperate, with warm summers and generally mild winters, but in the north there is not much difference from London.

Average daily temperatures (°C)

	Brittany	Normandy	Provence	Côte d'Azur
January	9.3	7.6	12.1	12.2
February	8.6	6.4	11.9	11.9
March	11.1	8.4	14.3	14.3
April	17.1	13.0	18.5	18.5
May	16.0	14.0	20.8	20.8
June	22.7	20.0	26.6	26.6
July	25.1	21.6	28.1	28.1
August	24.1	22.0	28.4	28.4
September	21.1	18.2	25.2	25.2
October	16.5	14.5	22.2	22.2
November	12.1	10.8	16.8	16.8
December	9.3	7.9	14.1	14.1

Conclusion

Buying a French property should not be regarded as the way to make a quick fortune. Prices are too stable and the supply of property too plentiful for that – particularly in rural areas. Resale could be difficult and there is a growing number of British owners looking to sell their homes in France.

The real investment should not be financially motivated, but one of enjoyment and lifestyle. To derive the maximum pleasure from your property in France make friends with your neighbours, take part in the life of your new community and, if you cannot do so already, learn to speak at least a little French!

GERMANY

General information

Status

Federal Republic

Capital

Berlin (Bonn is the administrative centre)

Area

356,505 sq km (137,700 sq miles)

Population

80.5 million (approx)

Location

Latitude 47°N to 54°N; longitude 6°E to 13°E. The Federal Republic of Germany is, in terms of population, size, geography and influence, the dominant country of central northern Europe. Although the climate is generally the same throughout most of the country (continental, influenced by the Atlantic), there are many contrasting environments, ranging from the Alpine south to the flat plains of the north and the river basins of the west. The vegetation also varies considerably, ranging from the Alpine mosses and the thick forests to the agricultural lands. The country is highly urbanised, especially in the Rhineland and the Baltic coast.

Political stability

As the most powerful and probably the most prosperous country in Europe, Germany should have a great future as the leading nation in the new European Union. However, the reunification with East Germany has caused many problems, both political and financial, and relations with some other European countries have deteriorated to a certain extent. As a result the political leaders of Germany will have to work hard to restore the confidence of their neighbouring nations, the recent economic crisis in the Far East has affected exports.

Economy

Cost of living

Living standards, wages and consumption are high compared with the UK, but unemployment is considerable, particularly among workers in the former East Germany, where it reached over 17 per cent last year. The average unemployment figure for the whole of Germany in 1999 is predicted to be over 4 million, and domestic demand for products is likely to be sluggish. Predicted economic growth in 1999 will be only about 1.4 per cent.

Taxation

Direct taxation is very high. Salaried workers pay income tax on a PAYE basis, while the self-employed and others have to declare their income and make regular advance payments in respect of their estimated final tax liability. In addition a solidarity tax supplement is levied as a percentage of income tax. Those who are members of Christian churches pay a voluntary church tax. Social security payments for employees are also high, with contributions for healthcare, accidents, unemployment and pensions. The latter benefit is likely to cause many problems in the coming years as the ratio between contributors and beneficiaries declines.

Currently it is estimated that a married man without children, earning around £30,000 per annum, will pay just over 50 per cent of his wages in direct tax and contributions. Pensions even today can amount to as much as 90 per cent of earnings at the time of retirement.

Exchange rate

Deutsche Mark (DM) 2.95 = £1.

Exchange control

There are no exchange controls in operation.

Language

German. Knowledge of English is widespread.

Expatriate community

It is estimated that there are over 6 million foreigners living in Germany, but probably only about 50 per cent of these are gainfully employed. There is a fair sized British community in many of the larger cities, who have moved there for career or business reasons. Very few UK citizens move to Germany to retire.

Permits

European Union citizens who intend to stay for more than 3 months are allowed to live and work in Germany without a visa but they must have a full UK/EU passport. They are required to register with the Residents Registration Office and the Foreign Nationals Authority and to obtain a residence permit. Those arriving with an E111 health form, who are staying for less than one year, are granted exemption from paying social insurance tax.

Provided they do not intend to stay longer than three months in Germany, or take up employment or establish themselves in a business or profession, nationals of the USA and many other countries do not require a visa to visit Germany. For stays exceeding three months it is advisable to apply for a visa at least six weeks before your proposed arrival in Germany. A good knowledge of the German language is essential for those wishing to work in Germany.

Personal effects

These may be imported free of duty provided they have been in possession of the owner for more than six months. A car may also be brought into Germany without paying duty provided it has been owned for at least a year and is for the personal use of the importer.

Housing

Renting a flat or house is far more popular among Germans for most of their working life, but they may save up money to purchase a small place when they retire.

In big cities with a large working population, it may be difficult to find a home to rent and costs are frequently quite high, furthermore tenants are often responsible for repairs which in the UK are normally undertaken by the landlord. A complete redecoration of the accommodation by the tenant, on completion of the lease is generally expected. The cost of purchasing a home in many parts of Germany is often high. New houses built since the war are generally of excellent quality. For mortgages, a deposit of 30–40 per cent is often required.

Buying property

There are no restrictions on the purchase of real estate by foreign nationals. All purchase contracts must be certified by a notary public and the title only passes to the purchaser on registration in the land register maintained by the district court. The fees for conveyance and certification of the land sale are between 1 and 1.5 per cent of the purchase price. The estate agent involved in the transaction generally expects a commission of 3 per cent of the price obtained from both parties to the transaction.

Where to live

Business and professional people working in Germany will probably need to reside close to one of the larger towns or cities, such as Frankfurt, Hamburg or Berlin where essential services, plus many residential amenities, are within easy reach. However, there are numerous more tranquil regions, especially in the south of the country, in, for instance, the Black Forest area, where a healthy, restful lifestyle can be enjoyed.

Communications

Communications in most parts of Germany are excellent, with plenty of autobahns for speedy journeys. Standards are not yet so high in the former East German sector, but improvements are under way. Travel by air, for both domestic and international flights, is being improved by the formation of new and the expansion of existing carriers, plus the construction of additional terminals at major airports.

Recreation

There are plenty of opportunities for leisure activities in this large country. The Germans are very keen on sport, particularly football, athletics, tennis and motor racing. With much fine open countryside and many mountains, hiking is a popular pastime and so is camping. Facilities for sailing are available on the North and Baltic Seas.

The larger towns have a selection of cinemas, there are often clubs for English-speaking residents and the major London daily newspapers are on sale at some kiosks. Most Germans enjoy eating out and each region has its own specialities of food, wine and beer. There are also many restaurants and cafés which serve menus of other nations.

Driving

Driving is on the right-hand side and there is no requirement to take a German driving test provided you are experienced and in possession of a full British licence. It is possible for foreigners to drive with the driving licence of their home country for a limited period, usually one year, after that it has to be exchanged for a German licence, for which a fee has to be paid. Before applying for a German licence, it is necessary to attend a short course on first aid, as drivers are legally obliged to give help in case of an accident, and to carry a first aid kit.

Third party insurance is obligatory and usually more expensive than in the UK. The level of vehicle tax depends on the size of the car's engine. The equivalent of the MOT Test is much more strict in Germany.

Speed limits are marginally higher and on the autobahns an upper limit of 130km/hour is only 'advised'.

Education

Compulsory education for children begins at the age of six and continues for nine or 10 years' full-time school attendance. Thereafter pupils are usually required to attend a vocational school for one day per week until the age of 18. All state schools are free. In addition, there are about 300 private fee paying schools, many with boarding facilities. There is also a wide range of universities, polytechnics and private colleges.

Health services

A high standard of medical treatment is available and Germany has more hospital beds per 10,000 population than any other EU country. All foreign nationals employed in Germany are subject to the same costly health insurance scheme as German citizens.

Details of European Community rights are given in DSS pamphlet SA29.

Climate

Germany lies on the western edge of the European-Asiatic continent. The climate is mainly maritime in nature, but occasionally continental climatic conditions impose intense hot and cold periods. Mostly, the climate is comparable with that of the UK.

Average monthly temperatures (°C)

	Berlin	Frankfurt	Hamburg	Munich
January	−1.3	0.7	0.3	−0.6
February	0.1	2.2	1.0	0.2
March	3.4	5.3	3.5	3.8
April	7.9	9.3	7.5	7.8
May	13.2	14.3	12.3	12.9
June	16.2	17.3	15.4	15.9
July	18.0	18.7	17.1	17.8
August	16.7	17.7	16.3	17.0
September	13.5	14.4	13.6	13.5
October	8.4	9.4	8.8	8.3
November	3.5	4.7	4.3	3.1
December	0.7	1.9	1.6	0.0

GIBRALTAR

General information

Status

British Crown Colony

Capital

Gibraltar

Area

5.5 sq km (2.5sq miles)

Population

30,000 (approx)

Location

Latitude 36°N; longitude 5°W. The British colony of Gibraltar lies on the southern tip of Spain where the Mediterranean Sea and the Atlantic Ocean meet. It is dominated by a 430 m-high block of limestone and is itself an isthmus.

The population density is the second largest in Europe.

Political stability

Gibraltar has a large measure of internal self-government, under the Constitution enacted in 1969, which provides for a Westminsterstyle parliamentary system, with the Governor retaining responsibility for external affairs, defence and internal security. There are 15 elected members in the House of Assembly, plus a Speaker and two ex-officio members.

Under the provisions of the Treaty of Rome, relating to European dependent territories, Gibraltar joined the EU in 1973, but by agreement it is excluded from the administration of VAT, the

Common Agricultural Policy, Common Customs Tariff and harmonisation of turnover taxes.

A substantial demand exists for Gibraltar's right to self-determination.

Economy

Despite all the problems in the past, there is a spirit of quiet optimism in Gibraltar now that an offshore finance centre has been established which provides a variety of services, including trusts, tax-exempt companies, insurance and collective investment schemes, and employment. Furthermore, the European Union has partly funded a massive face-lift to the establishments in Main Street, the location of the principal shopping facilities. The Rock's image has been improved by the completion of a re-vamped cruise ship passenger terminal which serves about 100 liners per annum and by a new-look airport terminal. The 'frontier' customs post with Spain has also been improved. These facilities should help to impress the five million tourists who visit the Rock every year. Many of them are day trippers, but their purchases are a welcome addition to local incomes.

Currency

Gibraltar pound notes and coins are issued, but UK coinage is also legal tender.

Cost of living

The rocky terrain is not suitable for food production and there is little scope for primary production, so the inhabitants rely heavily on the port for their prosperity. Resourceful local entrepreneurs trade in the world markets and import goods from the most competitive sources, so prices are quite reasonable. Cheap agricultural goods, imported from Spain, keep down living costs. Cigarettes and drink are also cheap.

Taxation

Income tax is levied on employees under PAYE. After certain allowances the rate is 20 per cent on the first £1,500 and rises progressively until it is 50 per cent on sums over £19,500. Estate duty is levied on property in Gibraltar at the rate of 5 per cent on estates between £20,001 and £40,000, rising to 25 per cent on portions over £100,000. Local property rates are 62p in the pound on the net annual value, payable in four equal quarterly instalments. Employees' contributions for social insurance, inclusive of old age pension and unemployment contributions are around £17.87 per week. Gibraltar has no tax treaties with other countries, but a Gibraltar resident in receipt of income from the UK is entitled to a tax credit on the lower of the Gibraltar or UK tax paid.

There are no wealth taxes or capital gains tax in Gibraltar. Exempt companies can be registered for a fee of £225 annually. Once granted, exemption is guaranteed for at least 25 years and the companies do not have to pay Gibraltar income tax.

A favourable tax position is available to certain 'High Net Worth Individuals', who can acquire residential property in Gibraltar, which must be available for their exclusive use for not less than seven months in any tax year. They must reside in that property for at least 30 days per tax year. On fulfilling these conditions they become resident for tax purposes in Gibraltar, but are taxed only on a fixed amount of assessable income. The minimum tax sum payable each year is £10,000. Qualifying estates are not subject to Estate Duty or other capital taxes in Gibraltar. A fee of £500 is payable when applying to qualify as a High Net Worth Individual.

Gibraltar is now important in offshore finance with an expanding finance centre offering a variety of services, including tax exempt companies, trusts, collective investment schemes and insurance.

Exchange rate

G£1 = £1.

Exchange control

There are no exchange controls.

Language

English is the official language; Spanish is widely spoken.

Expatriate community

There are about 4,000 British expatriates, many of whom are devoted to yachting, naval and marine pastimes.

Security

The 4 km-long isthmus, which has only one point of exit apart from the sea, means that Gibraltar is safe from many undesirables.

Residence and work permits

All visitors to Gibraltar must be in possession of a valid passport or identity card, but EU and Commonwealth citizens do not require a visa. EU nationals can apply for a residence permit which will be issued for a period not less than five years on satisfying the Principle Immigration Office that they are self-employed or have a job offer, and this employment is expected to last for at least 12 months. If employment is for less than a year, then the residency permit will be limited to the length of the employment. An EU citizen coming to look for employment in Gibraltar is granted six months to find a job. When work has been found, the Immigration Department will issue a certificate of residence for the duration of the contract; if this is for more than a year, the certificate of residence will be for five years.

Non-EU nationals do not have automatic rights of residence and must find gainful employment, but the employer must satisfy the Employment Department that there is no Gibraltarian or EU national, who satisfies the job requirement and is available and willing to do the work.

Personal effects

No duty is payable on personal effects.

Housing and development

The Gibraltar government encourages private sector development to try to achieve economic self-sufficiency. They have been quite successful in this respect with land reclamation projects, construction of finance and commercial centres and also the extension of public services. Tourism is also expanding and real economic growth is averaging around 10 per cent annually.

Although sites are scarce, some significant housing schemes have been launched, including Queensway Quay, by internationally known Taylor Woodrow. A new development by the same firm, known as Cormorant Wharf, is set around a private marina, within easy walking distance of the town centre. This offers garden flats, penthouses and apartments, all with sea views. For details fax: (Int. 350) 75529.

There are more than a dozen estate agents active in Gibraltar, some of whom can offer flats in established apartment blocks. Recent offerings have included three-bedroom units priced between £60,000 and £75,000.

Buying property

Gibraltar law and the procedure for acquiring property closely follow the practice in England. It is very desirable to employ a solicitor and there are a number of firms in Gibraltar and the UK who specialise in the conveyance of local property. Stamp duty amounts to 1.26 per cent of the purchase price, there are modest land registry and land title registration fees. Lawyers' fees are according to a scale which works out at between 0.5 and 1 per cent depending on the size of the transaction.

Where to live

As property on the market is very scarce, and the Rock is so small, it is difficult to give guidance on where to live.

Communications

GB Airways is the flag carrier, with daily scheduled flights from Gatwick (2½ hours) and weekly flights from Manchester. Flights are offered by various other operators including Monarch airlines, who have flights from Luton.

Tangier just across the Straits can be reached by the Bland ferry in about 2½ hours, and in 1 hour by jet catamaran.

International direct dialling and telex make worldwide communications simple.

Recreation

Existing amenities include three beaches, two cinemas, a casino, crazy golf and scenic tours. Sights include the caves, the apes on Upper Rock, Moorish Castle, Trafalgar Cemetery and Europa Point lighthouse. A large area of the Upper Rock, including the apes' den and St Michael's cave, has been designated an official nature reserve.

For other hobbies, a trip over the border into Spain is necessary where extensive golfing, tennis and hiking opportunities exist, as well as numerous social activities.

Gibraltar Broadcasting Station operates its own radio and TV services which can also be heard or viewed along some parts of the Spanish Costa del Sol. Reception of BBC World Service is good.

Health services

The Gibraltar National Health Service provides free treatment to all who make social security contributions. EU nationals are granted free emergency treatment if they are short-term visitors, but if they are based or working in Gibraltar they must contribute to the social security fund. The weekly contribution for an employed adult is £17.87.

Private medical facilities are offered by the International Health Clinic at Marina Bay and private health care insurance is advisable.

Climate

As can be seen from the table below, the climate of Gibraltar is fairly mild and sunny. Winds in the summer vary from dry westerlies to humid easterlies. The 'Levanter' is a local phenomenon caused by warm air forced up by the cliffs, which then condenses as its temperature reduces and this causes a dense blanket of cloud to form around the top of the Rock.

	Monthly rainfall (mm)	Average daily temperature (°C)	Average daily sunshine hours
January	15.4	13.6	6.05
February	64.9	13.7	6.69
March	108.7	13.8	5.35
April	12.6	16.9	5.89
May	79.8	17.1	8.98
June	6.7	20.1	9.78
July	–	24.1	10.46
August	1.7	24.3	9.25
September	0.2	23.5	9.16
October	14.7	18.9	7.12
November	15.2	16.4	4.45
December	14.4	14.5	3.94

GREECE

General information

Status

Republic

Capital

Athens

Area

131,990 sq km (51,245 sq miles)

Population

9.7 million (approx)

Location

Latitude 31°N to 41°N; longitude 36°W to 39°W. Greece occupies the southern part of the Balkan peninsula and also has many attractive islands both large and small. The principal one is Crete, while Rhodes and Corfu are also very well known. Four-fifths of the mainland is mountainous and there are at least 20 mountains over 2,000 m with a permanent snow line. Another striking characteristic is the huge areas of woodland in Greece, with 89 million hectares covering almost half of the country. Also, no part of Greece is more than 100 km away from the coast. Athens has many historic associations and is visited by millions of international tourists every year.

Political stability

As with a number of Mediterranean countries, steady democracy has triumphed over its oppressors. In the case of Greece, the military junta that was running the country in an excessively brutal fashion collapsed in 1974 in a bloodless coup and was replaced by a democratic government. Greece has been a full member of the European Community since 1981, and the EU has contributed very substantial sums for infrastructure improvements. Greece, like the UK, has not yet joined the common European currency (euro).

Economy

Cost of living

Inflation is still a problem in Greece. There is also considerable unemployment. Tourism remains an important sector in the economy. Currently living standards in Greece are appreciably lower than in most other EU nations. Essentials such as food, especially from the markets, are good value for money. This, however, is not the case with luxury items.

Taxation

Personal taxation is calculated on the worldwide income of residents (usually people living more than six months of a year in

Greece). A personal allowance and a wife's allowance is granted, and income tax rises from 5 to 40 per cent. A pay-as-you-earn system exists for those in employment; otherwise tax is payable in three equal instalments, but a 5 per cent reduction is granted to those who pay all their tax on the date the first payment is due. VAT is levied at 18 per cent with a reduced rate of 8 per cent on basics including food. A reduced rate of 4 per cent is levied on books and printed matter. There is no general capital gains tax and dividend tax has been abolished. There is now an annual property tax payable by owners of the more expensive homes.

Exchange rate

Drachmas 489 = £1.

Exchange control

In operation, but relaxed for EU citizens. Have the currency importation recorded on an official import document as this simplifies the re-export of the currency when the property is sold.

Language

A basic understanding of the fundamentals of Modern Greek is advisable, although a knowledge of English is often found in tourist areas.

Expatriate community

Greece has become more popular during the last few years. Many people have chosen to retire there and over 3,000 expatriates are in employment.

Security

Internally, it is prudent to take standard precautions against theft and burglary by installing security equipment.

Residence permits

British subjects can enter Greece without a permit, but with a passport, for periods of up to three months, but they must register with the local police within eight days of their arrival. A temporary residence permit, valid for six months, is issued for stays of between three and 12 months. Thereafter, residence permits are renewed for a five year period. Registration and applications for these permits are made to The Aliens Department if you are living in Athens, or to the local police station if you reside elsewhere in Greece.

Work permits

Under the European Union rules, work permits are no longer required.

Personal effects

No duties are payable as long as a certificate has been acquired from the Greek Embassy and a five-year residence permit has been issued in Greece. Those going to work in Greece are also allowed to import a car duty free.

Housing

Although there has been quite a lot of interest in the purchase of homes in Greece during the past two decades, there are only a few specialist agencies able to offer a service to prospective purchasers in the UK.

Greece has introduced legislation allowing EU citizens to acquire rights on properties – like the Greeks – in most of Greece.

Buying property

As with the purchase of real estate in other countries, it is essential to employ a lawyer to handle any property transaction in Greece. This can be a local firm or a specialist solicitor in England with a qualified colleague in Greece.

Having reached an acceptable agreement on terms etc, a preliminary sale agreement is signed by both parties in the presence of a Notary Public. This document contains all the details about the property, the price, completion date and a penalty clause, should either party withdraw from the transaction. A deposit (perhaps 10 per cent of the purchase price) will be paid (preferably to a stakeholder) and the purchaser's lawyer will check the validity of the title, and that the property is registered at the local Property Registry Office. In the case of a new property, a check is made that proper planning permission has been obtained by the builder. The sale takes place when the sale contract is signed by both parties in the presence of the Notary Public and the balance of the purchase price is paid to the vendor.

The fees payable include a Property Transfer Tax of about 9 to 13 per cent of the purchase price, the Notary Public's fee of just 1.5 per cent and the lawyer's fee which may amount to between 1 and 1.5 per cent. The purchaser's lawyer deposits a copy of the Sale Contract at the local Land Registry, so that the change of ownership can be officially recorded.

There is an annual property tax to be paid by the owner. The islands are popular with British holidaymakers and property buyers. Locations such as the Cyclades group (Naxos, Kea and Paros for example), also Crete, Corfu and Skiathos are well known. However, a new area that is attracting interest is the Mani region, which lies south of Kalamata in the south-west of the country. Spectacular scenery can be found amid the mountains and along the coast, where there are also some fine beaches. The area has not been over-developed and current planning policies are aimed at preserving the natural beauty of this part of Greece. A typical small development near the sea is being offered at Riglia (48 kilometres from Kalamata). This comprises four two-bedroom villas built of local stone in an orchard setting. The properties have a veranda with sea views and are priced at £59,000 freehold.

On Kefalonia, one of the Ionian Islands, Metaxata Villas is a high-class development in an attractive location with sea and mountain views, yet within 15 minutes drive of the island's main town of Argostoli. Here a range of apartments is being built at prices from £39,000, as well as two-, three- and four-bedroom villas which will cost from £122,000. The UK selling agent is Brian A French & Associates (tel: 0171 284 0114).

Communications

British Airways and Olympic Airways have scheduled flights from Gatwick, Heathrow and provincial airports to Athens and other destinations in Greece. Charter flights are also available to many destinations, particularly in summer.

Despite the fact that Greece is perhaps a little isolated from western Europe, road and rail links are good.

Recreation

The legacy of the past 5,000 years of Greek civilisation is probably one of the greatest attractions in Greece today. Unique examples of architecture and sculpture exist in abundance, with perhaps the most impressive relic being the Parthenon which stands, together with other masterpieces, on the rock of the Acropolis in Athens, and receives about 1.5 million visitors per year. Greek culture extends into theatre, dancing and festivals.

Greek cuisine is generally very good but limited, and eating out is both popular and cheap.

Modern leisure facilities such as swimming pools and tennis courts are quite plentiful, especially in the popular resorts. Also, because of the number of islands and the large amount of coastline, water-based pursuits such as sailing, water-skiing and wind-surfing are popular.

Many of Greece's recreational facilities are very much orientated to the tourists but, because of the pleasant climate all year round, the tourist trade is not as seasonal as in some countries and so the facilities are maintained at the highest level throughout the year.

Health services

For short visits, take form E111 with you to ensure urgent free medical treatment within the Greek national health system. Those working in Greece must obtain a medical booklet from the local IKA (health service) office, which must be produced on all visits to hospital or a doctor. The local health service is barely adequate for the demand, so private medical insurance is advisable.

Education

There is free and compulsory education for children between the ages of 6–15. The first six years are spent at primary school and the last three years at lower secondary school. Books and transportation are provided free.

Climate

The term generally associated with the Greek weather is that of an 'olive climate'. The fundamental characteristic of it is the smooth transition from one season to the next. A short spring with moderate temperatures, followed by a long, hot summer and then a pleasant autumn with average temperatures above those in spring, lead finally to a usually mild and sunny winter. There are about 3,000 hours of sunshine each year, rain in summer is an unknown phenomenon and the cooling north-west winds blow. Rainfall varies throughout the country, from about 1,500 mm per annum to less than a third of that in the south.

REPUBLIC OF IRELAND

General information

Status

Republic

Capital

Dublin

Area

70,282 sq km (27,165 sq miles)

Population

3,480,000

Location

Latitude 52°N to 55°N; longitude 5°W to 10°W. The Irish Republic, comprising about 80 per cent of the island of Ireland, lies on the extreme west of the European sub-continent and is separated from England, Wales and Scotland by the Irish Sea. The capital is Dublin, on the east coast, and here the majority of manufacturing enterprises are located, as well as the main trading centres and the major communication arteries. Elsewhere there is only limited urbanisation because large areas are devoted to farming and open space.

Political stability

Political instability has been a problem in the Republic of Ireland for many decades, and for the last 30 years there has been sectarian violence in Northern Ireland and elsewhere. However there now seems to be a solution to the problems following a deal struck at the Stormont talks in April 1998. After months of intense negotiations under the Chairmanship of US Senator George Mitchell, a 69-page document was produced which appears to be acceptable to the main parties. Only time will tell if everyone's hopes are realised in respect of the new deal.

Economy

In recent years there has been a considerable improvement in the Republic of Ireland's economic situation. Gross national product has grown by an average of 5 per cent annually, compared with 1.55 per cent in the rest of the EU, and this has taken place during a period when the rest of Europe has slowed down. Unemployment is now at its lowest level for a decade, and below the EU average. Inflation is low. Membership of the EU has produced substantial financial benefits to Ireland.

Taxation

Income tax starts at 24 per cent on incomes up to £14,000 for a single person after a personal allowance of £4,200. For taxable incomes above £14,000 the rate is 46 per cent. Married couples have a personal allowance of £8,400. They pay 24 per cent on taxable incomes up to £28,000 and 46 per cent thereafter.

Householders pay annual charges for water supplies and refuse collections which vary according to district. Social security contributions amount to about 8 per cent of taxable income. VAT is levied at various rates ranging from 0 to 21 per cent.

Cost of living

is about the same as in the UK. House prices nationwide increased by about 30 per cent during 1998, but in Dublin the rises were much greater. The average price of a second-hand home in the capital is now over £150,000.

Exchange rate

Punts (IR£) 1.19 = £1.

Exchange controls

There are no restrictions on importing money into Ireland.

Language

Everybody speaks the Irish version of English, with Gaelic as a second tongue for many. Knowledge of Gaelic is essential for all top government employees, and is a qualification for many posts.

Expatriate community

Partly because of traditional links with the UK and partly because of geographical proximity, there are a large number of Britons who live permanently in Ireland.

Security

Ireland does have a problem with house-breakers and petty thieves, so it is worth while installing burglar alarms – preferably those linked to the *Garda* (police station) or a security company.

Residence and work permits

Citizens from countries in the European Union are able to live and work in Ireland without restriction but must have a full UK/UE passport to work in Ireland.

Personal effects

These can be imported duty free by people wanting to set up permanent residence if the items have been owned for over six months. Normally, importation should be within six months of arrival.

Where to live

Boom conditions exist close to the capital and the average price of a second-hand house in Dublin is now in excess of £150,000. Five years ago, a starter home could have been purchased for about £55,000. With a shortage of sites (it is estimated that only about 2,000 acres of suitable land exist for the development of new homes in and around the capital) house builders are now constructing far more apartments.

In Greater Dublin, 293 units are to be built at Clondalkin; 123 houses at Tallaght and 304 houses at Lucan. Further afield at Wicklow town, 72 two-storey town houses are being offered at prices from £114,000 and another site at Aughrim, Co Wicklow offers four house types from £82,000. In the south west at Killaloe, Co Tipperary, three-, four- and five-bedroom houses on the shores of Lough Deg cost from £68,495.

For established property, there are numerous estate agents throughout the country. Their professional body is the Irish Auctioneers and Valuers Association, 38 Merion Square, Dublin 2, (tel: 01 61 1794).

Property Ireland, a monthly newspaper, contains a wide selection of homes for sale. It can be obtained from _Property Ireland,_ Unit 5, Woodpark, Sallynoggin, Co Dublin. The following national news-papers contain regular property sections: _Irish Times_ (Thursdays); _Irish Independent_ (Fridays); _Examiner_ (Saturdays); _Sunday Business Post_ and _Sunday Tribune._

Buying property

Property purchase procedure is similar to the UK, and completion normally takes place six to eight weeks after the signing of a contract. The scale for stamp duty on second-hand residential properties ranges from nil on properties costing under IR£5,000, and rises to 6 per cent on homes which sell for over IR£60,000. For property costing £150,000–£160,000, the rate is 7 per cent; for the band between £160,000–£170,000 it is 8 per cent; and for property above £170,000 it is 9 per cent. No stamp duty is payable on new residential properties with a floor area of less than 125 square metres. There is also a land registration fee. Solicitors' fees are about 2 per cent including VAT.

Mortgages are available through local banks and building societies. At the time of going to press the interest rate was approximately 6–6.5 per cent and dropping.

Communications

Air

The national airline is Aer Lingus, which provides flights from London to Dublin, Cork, Shannon and Sligo. British Airways and a number of other companies also have services to selected airports in Ireland. The flight time from London to Dublin is approximately one hour.

Sea

Irish Ferries Ltd provide car and passenger ferry services from Pembroke to Rosslare and from Holyhead to Dublin. Stena Line have the shortest sea crossing to southern Ireland via their Fishguard to Rosslare ferry. They also provide ferries from Holyhead to Dun Laoghaire and a catamaran service from Holyhead to Dublin.

Recreation

With an abundance of open countryside there are plenty of opportunities for horse riding, walking, climbing and camping. Water-based activities such as fishing, boating and canoeing can be enjoyed on the River Shannon and on the lakes and coast. Golf courses are abundant and other popular sports include rugby, Gaelic football and hurling. For horse-racing enthusiasts there are around 30 courses throughout the country and some of the Irish classics are world famous. The many lakes and mountains and an attractive, extensive coastline are particularly favoured by tourists, who are very important to the nation's economy.

Education

This is compulsory for 6–15-year-olds.

Health services

In Ireland medical standards are high and, subject to income limits, free medical care for those on a very low income can be obtained in public hospitals and from some medical practitioners. BUPA, PPP and WPA have interfund agreements with Irish medical insurance companies. British government retirement pensions can be paid in Ireland.

Climate

The climate tends to be cool, damp and changeable. The western part of Ireland is the wettest. May and June have the most sunshine, while July and August are the warmest months. The average temperature in January and February is between 4° and 7°C.

ISRAEL

General information

Status

Parliamentary democracy

Capital

Jerusalem

Area

27,817 sq km (10,840 sq miles)

Population

4,882,000

Location

Latitude 30°N to 33°N; longitude 35°E. Israel, the land of the Bible and historic homeland of the Jewish people, is situated in the Middle East, along the eastern coastline of the Mediterranean. The geographical diversity of Israel is quite remarkable for such a small country, as it has mountains and plains, fertile fields and barren deserts, seacoast and rocky uplands. In Galilee in the north, forested highlands merge with green valleys. Sand dunes and citrus groves mark the coastal plain bordering the Mediterranean. Deserts stretching southwards through Negev and Arava meet the tropical waters of the Gulf of Eilat on the Red Sea.

Political stability

The State of Israel was created in 1948. A system of strict proportional representation is used in the elections to the Knesset (the Israeli Parliament) and all governments have been the result of coalition agreements.

Israel's short history has been a stormy one. The country has fought five wars with its Arab neighbours. The founding of the State caused a refugee problem when 600,000 Palestinians fled to surrounding countries and 800,000 Jews fled Arab countries and were settled in Israel. Arabs are full citizens of the State and both Jews and Arabs have to co-exist in Israel.

The coalition government cannot rely on majority support, mainly because of the consequences of a proportional representation system that allows undue weight and influence to political extremists and religious zealots. This being the case, it means that governments progress slowly and carefully, sometimes having to fudge important yet unpopular policies.

Economy
Costs of living

Israel lacks the natural resources necessary to back up its rapid economic growth. Infrastructural growth, welfare services and massive defence expenditure have put a huge strain on the economy. The economic plan introduced in 1984 has helped to reduce inflation from 445 per cent a decade ago to the 1997 figure of 10.4 per cent. Economic stability is much improved and there has been an improvement in Israel's foreign reserves. Immigrants can expect to have a high standard of living, mainly because of the strength of their home currencies. Israeli produce is of the highest standard and is reasonably priced. Petrol costs much the same as in the UK.

Taxation

Special compensations for new immigrants do exist in terms of tax regulations. All savings are tax free for the first 20 years of residence. VAT at 17.5 per cent is charged on all goods and services (except in duty-free Eilat).

Exchange rate

Shekels 5.7 = £1.

Exchange control

It is possible to bring into Israel an unlimited amount of foreign currency, travellers' cheques and Israeli shekels. There are restrictions on what can be taken out, and a tax is payable on departure.

Language

The official languages are Hebrew and Arabic. English is widely spoken.

Expatriate community

Since the creation of Israel in 1948, immigration (especially by Jews) has been extensive. Eastern European, North American, Asian and African migrants have all flocked to the country. There has also been considerable migration from Britain with almost 20,000 British Jews having made the journey. Clearly, then, Israel's society is very cosmopolitan.

In 1990 the population increased by 5.7 per cent as a result of the immigration of Jews from the former Soviet Union and Ethiopia and other countries in Eastern Europe and South America. This immigration continues unabated.

Security

For many years security has been a primary issue for the government. The result is that the country has one of the best equipped and most rigorously trained armies in the world.

Residence permits

All applications must be made to the Ministry of the Interior. An initial tourist visa of three months' duration may be extended by the Ministry, on consideration of the application, and payment of a nominal fee.

Work permits

It is necessary for the potential employer to make an application for a work permit on your behalf to the Ministry of the Interior.

Personal effects

No duties are payable on household goods.

Housing

Housing in Israel varies from the Arab-style villas of simple design and the red-tile roofed houses of the early settlers, to ultra-modern seaside cottages built to exacting architectural specifications. Most Israelis, however, live in apartment blocks, ranging from one-room studios to those with four bedrooms. Many of these flats are in fact rented, as this is cheap compared with buying property.

Where to live

This is very much a personal choice. Some people choose big cities, others the quieter country villages. Some move to the coast whereas others prefer to live inland.

Communications

Air

Twenty-four international airlines operate flights to Israel's Ben-Gurion international airport, which is 18 km from Tel Aviv and 50 km from Jerusalem. International charter flights also operate, as well as many internal services.

Sea

Shipping lines offer regular sailings from Europe and arrive at Haifa port.

Road

Over 1,500 km of new roads have been built during the past decade and previously existing roads have also been improved.

Telecommunications

Israel is fully integrated into international communications systems by means of underwater cables and communications satellites.

Recreation

Being a warm Mediterranean nation, all kinds of outdoor activities are popular. Facilities provided by the municipalities such as swimming pools and tennis courts are generally good, as are those in the tourist coastal regions. Spectator sports such as football and especially basketball are popular too.

Israeli cuisine is regarded as very good, although non-kosher food is a little harder to get. Therefore, those with a taste for pork or shellfish, or dairy produce with meat meals, will have to search for a private restaurant to cater for them (not hotels or large restaurants which sell only kosher food).

Israel is, of course, the Holy Land, and so is scattered with monuments and architecture celebrating that fact. Museums, theatre and cinema are also popular.

Driving

It is possible to drive in Israel on a valid UK licence. International traffic signs are used and the signposts are in English.

Insurance is quite expensive, with compulsory third party cover costing about £100 and fully comprehensive over £500. The maximum no claims bonus is only 30 per cent, which possibly reflects the quality of Israeli driving.

Seat belts are compulsory in the front seats.

Health services

The Ministry of Health is responsible for all health services in Israel. It prepares health legislation and oversees its implementation, controls medical standards and supervises the planning and construction of hospitals. The cost of medical treatment is quite high though, so health insurance is advisable. There are no vaccination requirements for visitors

A social security agreement does exist between the UK and Israel. Details are given in DSS pamphlet SA14.

Climate

Israel's climate is characterised by hot, dry summers from April through to October and wet winters from November to March. The rainfall, in general, is higher in the north and west of the country than in the south and east.

Average monthly temperatures (°C)

	Tel Aviv	Haifa	Eilat
January	9.4–18.3	7.6–17.4	9.6–21.3
February	8.7–18.8	8.5–17.8	10.8–22.8
March	10.1–20.3	8.3–21.3	13.4–26.3
April	12.4–22.3	12.6–25.5	17.1–30.7
May	17.3–25.0	14.5–24.6	20.6–34.8
June	19.3–28.3	17.7–27.6	24.1–37.1
July	21.0–30.2	20.0–29.9	25.3–39.9
August	22.1–30.1	21.2–30.0	26.0–39.9
September	20.3–31.4	19.7–29.6	23.7–36.4
October	15.0–28.8	15.0–28.8	20.4–33.3
November	12.2–24.5	12.2–24.5	16.0–28.3
December	8.8–19.0	8.8–19.0	10.6–23.3

ITALY

General information

Status

Republic

Capital

Rome

Area

301,247 sq km (116,303 sq miles)

Population

56,400,000

Location

Latitude 36°N to 47°N; longitude 6°E to 18°E. Geographically, Italy lies in the temperate and hot temperate zone. The climate is influenced by both the Mediterranean Sea that virtually surrounds it and to a lesser extent the continent to the north. Another feature of Italy is the startling length of its coastline, and there can be little doubt that this, more than anything else, has had the most profound influence on Italy's development. The vegetation varies greatly, depending on the climatic and geological factors: in the north there are considerable areas of woodland and productive land, whereas in the south scrubland tends to predominate. The main population centres are mostly in the central northern region. A number of islands form part of the country including Sardinia, Elba and the most well known, Sicily.

Political stability

The Italian people are not generally renowned for their inner calmness and stability. For most of this century, they have been beset by political problems which have been difficult to resolve. This is due in part to the election of a succession of governments without a workable majority, and the electoral system appears to favour coalition governments which are fragile. Nevertheless, Italy's growing standing in world affairs has been impressive and is probably partly due to the nation's membership of the European Union and NATO.

Economy

Cost of living

Italy's post-war industrial development has been considerable and has brought prosperity to many people, particularly in the central and northern regions, for Italy is very much a divided nation in terms of wealth and living standards, and the south is far less affluent and successful. Prices in Italy are about the same as in the UK although some goods, especially market produce and local wine, are cheap. Top-quality goods, such as clothes, china, glassware and fine furniture, are very expensive. Inflation stands at about 2.5 per cent.

Taxation

Under Italian law each individual is responsible for reporting his or her financial affairs to the local tax authorities. Personal income tax (IRPEF) is charged on income from all sources and ranges from 10 per cent on incomes up to 6 million lire, rising progressively to 50 per cent on incomes over 600 million lire. Thus it is higher than in Britain, but a double taxation agreement exists between Italy and the UK.

A Council Tax known as ICI (Imposta Comunale sugli Immobili) is payable by all individuals or companies (resident or non-resident) who own a property in Italy. It is paid in two instalments (June and December) at a rate of between 0.04 and 0.07 per cent of the property's statutory value, the actual rate being decided by each local council (*comune*). The tax is administered and collected by the *comune* and where it is not paid on time penalties are imposed.

Capital gains tax on properties (INVIM) will continue to be payable on gains accrued before 1 January 1993 when a property is sold, up to the year 2003.

An inheritance tax varies according to the relationship of the beneficiaries. A capital gains tax is based on the increase in value of real property when it is sold or on transfer of ownership because of death.

VAT ranges from 19–38 per cent.

Exchange rate

Lira 2,922 = £1.

Exchange control

Exchange control legislation has been liberalised in view of Italy's membership of the EU.

Language

Knowledge of Italian is very useful, as English is spoken only in the more popular tourist regions.

Expatriate community

A growing number of British people take up residence in Italy every year. There are expatriate diplomatic communities in Rome and Naples. British business executives are especially active in the northern cities.

Security

Petty crime and muggings do occur in popular resorts but this is no more a problem in Italy than elsewhere.

Residence permits

British citizens, like all other EU nationals, have free entry into Italy. They must obtain a residence permit within seven days of arrival, which is generally valid for two years and renewable. For full-time permanent residence, a certificate of residence is needed to make the applicant subject to Italian laws and taxes.

Work permits

These are not necessary for EU nationals, but a worker's registration card is required.

Personal effects

They may be imported free of duty by holders of a certificate of residence.

Housing

Unlike many other Mediterranean countries, there are few developments aimed at attracting foreign nationals, and so it may be necessary to seek a place on the open market. In general, land is not cheap, but bargains are sometimes available for houses of varying size, age and quality.

When seeking a house, it is wise to show no undue interest should a property be offered that meets your requirements, as keenness is often met by a price increase. It is best to leave it to the selling agent to settle matters later on. It is always advisable to deal with reputable firms. Personal contacts, say, in a bar, are less desirable, because if a deal is ever finalised, under Italian law the contact is entitled to a commission as a result of the introduction.

All Italian estate agents must have a licence to trade, issued by the local town hall, and must pass oral and written exams.

Buying a property

Before signing any document for the purchase of a property it is advisable to make enquiries both at the local Land Registry (Ufficio Tecnico Erariale) and at the Deeds Registry (Conservatoria dei Registri Immobiliari) as well as at the local municipality (*comune*) to ensure that the vendor has a registered title to the property and that the chain of title is unbroken. Make sure also that there are no mortgages or charges against the property and that planning permissions have been obtained, building regulations complied with, municipal taxes paid and, if the property includes agricultural land, that there are no pre-emptive rights of adjoining landowners.

It is essential to employ a local surveyor (*geometra*) who will be prepared to carry out most of these searches. He can also oversee or plan any structural work required.

The first formal legally binding step is the signature of a contract (*contratto preliminare or compromesso*) often drawn up by the vendor or agent and not necessarily by their lawyer. This is a legally binding contract to purchase on the terms stated, and a deposit of between 10 and 30 per cent is payable. This is forfeited if the purchaser does not conclude the deal; if the vendor reneges he or she has to compensate the proposed purchaser by the return of twice the deposit. In either circumstance it may be possible for further damages to be claimed by the disappointed party.

The final deed for the formal transfer of ownership in the property is the conveyance or transfer (*atto di compravendita*) by the vendor to the purchaser which involves the services of a notary (*notaio*) who oversees the deal and ensures that the transfer takes place according to law. This is a public official who does not act for either of the parties. The notary's duties are to draw up the deed, see to the payment of any capital gains tax and outstanding penalties for town planning irregularities and then to register the document, both for the purpose of the title being brought up to date and for the raising of a tax assessment.

A certified copy, issued by the notary of this conveyance document, is evidence of title and contains the names of the two parties to the transaction, a description of the property with map references, boundaries, price, receipt for the purchase money, details of rights of way, and other easements and warranties that the vendor will be the legal owner, that the property is sold with vacant possession and that it is not subject to any charges.

To advise you personally and guide you through the transaction it is advisable to employ your own lawyer (*avvocato*) as well as the surveyor (*geometra*) referred to.

It is, of course, particularly important to remember that the documents you sign will be in Italian and that you should consult advisers who are able to explain their contents in correct and intelligible English.

There are a number of costs to be borne during and after the transaction – roughly, about 10 per cent of the purchase price should cover taxes and registration fees. Under-declaration of the purchase price in the final deed used to be common in order to reduce the vendor's capital gains tax (INVIM) and the purchaser's transfer costs, which led to haggling with the Revenue. But for some years now an official solution to this problem has been found which still permits the conveyance to contain, in many cases, a figure less than the real price paid, provided that it agrees with or exceeds the official value to be derived from the local Land Registry (*Catasto*). Such official value is based on a notional annual rent known as *rendita catastale*, which is revised upwards from time to time.

When a property is purchased from a professional builder the purchaser normally pays VAT in addition to a registration tax.

Of course, you must also budget for the costs and fees payable to your *avvocato*, your *geometra* and possibly your interpreters and translators as required.

During 1999 it is expected that the Italian Government will announce some improvement in the tax burden on citizens who rent or own 'first homes', as well as a reduction in the tax based on the rateable value of residential property.

Mortgages are available and the Abbey National Bank has a branch office at Via G Fara 27, 20124, Milan. At the time of going to press they were offering variable rate loans in lira of up to 85 per cent of the purchase price for residential homes and 75 per cent for holiday homes, the term of the loan being between 3 and 20 years. A survey fee of 0.2 per cent of the value of the property is charged.

Where to live

Tuscany and Umbria have appealed to British buyers as the locations for holiday and retirement homes over the past decade, when the Italian property market was in the doldrums. With sterling still strong against the lira interest in this region continues, although property prices are increasing. Recent offerings have included a 15th-century farmhouse with four bedrooms, guest cottages and staff apartment, in the heart of Tuscany, for which the asking price was £750,000. A more modest two-bedroom farmhouse near Lucca, and accessible to Pisa, was on the market for around £65,000. In Umbria Italian specialist Brian A French (established 1972) has recently offered a selection of homes in the province of Perugia, including a 19th-century farmhouse built of hand-made bricks and set in a large mature garden. At £76,000 it is habitable, but could be improved.

The area near Lake Como in northern Italy, where many Italians have second homes and which is in close proximity to other European countries, attracts some British buyers. Other locations of interest include Liguria, particularly near seaside resorts such as Alassio, while much further south in Calabria, reasonably priced homes can be found near the coast. Off the north-west coast the island of Elba is a popular destination for Italian families as it has not suffered from extensive development for foreign tourists. A small block of one-bedroom apartments with beach frontage at Naregno was on the market recently at £83,500 per apartment. The islands of Sicily and Sardinia are also of interest to some foreigners.

Communications

Air

Italy has very good internal and external air services. There are some 26 airports, 15 of which are international and have services from Britain, the main ones being Rome, Milan, Bologna, Venice, Pisa, Florence and Naples. Flying time from London and Manchester is between 2 and 3 hours. There are now daily flights from London to Florence.

Rail

The Italian State Railway has a network of over 16,000 km of track and carries over 1 million people every day. The railways form an integral part of the commuter services.

Sea

Italy's islands are linked to the mainland by comprehensive ferry services.

Road

An autostrada network, totalling 5,910 km, is the country's main artery, but tolls are charged. In general, Italian roads are good and often very spectacular.

Recreation

Italy has a great deal to offer new settlers, with a vivid history and unrivalled classical traditions and superb monuments, yet an up-to-date outlook. Italy was, of course, the birthplace of the Renaissance and consequently it is impossible even to try to list the marvellous examples of art and architecture to be found in many of the great Italian cities such as Florence, Rome and Venice. Suffice to say that anyone who appreciates fine art and beauty will appreciate Italy.

More modern arts are also very much alive and well, in the form of cinema and theatre. Equally popular is opera, which is not centralised in the main centres but performed throughout the nation in many small towns.

Sports facilities such as gymnasiums, swimming pools, golf courses and tennis courts exist in abundance. Skiing in the northern Alpine region is popular too. The most favoured spectator sport is undoubtedly football, and Italian clubs such as Juventus, Roma and Inter Milan are recognised as having some of the world's best players.

Italians enjoy eating out and plenty of good restaurants are to be found. Every region has its own speciality dish. Several different styles of eating house exist, including the *ristorante* (conventional restaurant), the *trattoria* (family-owned cheaper restaurant), the *rosticceria* (hot food) and *pizzeria* (pizzas).

Driving

It is not necessary to retake your driving test in Italy, as a British licence may be converted into an Italian one which lasts for ten years. It is also possible to drive on British number plates for the first year, after which the car must be re-registered in Italy and undergo a roadworthiness test. In Italy, road tax is based on the car's engine size. The general rules of the road are much the same as elsewhere in mainland Europe. The traffic police have a reputation for applying the law to the letter and are inclined to impose on-the-spot fines. Maintenance costs are roughly the same as in Britain.

Education

Schooling is compulsory for the 6–14 age group.

Health services

The public health service in Italy is not highly regarded, but private hospitals, many run by the Church, are efficient. Consequently, most foreigners have private medical insurance.

Full details of social security rights can be obtained from the DSS.

Climate

The geographical aspects, such as the influence of the Alps in the north and the Mediterranean in the south, make for an interesting climatic pattern.

	Rome average		*The Alps average*		*The Lakes average*		*Adriatic Coast average*	
	temp (°C)	*ppt* (*mm*)	*temp* (°C)	*ppt* (*mm*)	*temp* (°C)	*ppt* (*mm*)	*temp* (°C)	*ppt* (*mm*)
January	7.4	74	−2.3	51	6.0	74	6.7	11
February	8.0	87	−1.3	447	7.0	218	9.1	43
March	11.5	79	1.8	82	9.2	91	10.3	35
April	14.4	62	5.2	138	13.3	47	13.5	42
May	18.4	57	9.1	132	16.5	105	17.7	62
June	22.9	39	13.5	128	19.7	88	21.8	66
July	25.7	6	15.8	148	23.7	12	24.3	95
August	25.5	23	15.4	117	24.3	117	23.4	9
September	22.4	66	12.7	115	18.5	35	20.0	43
October	17.7	123	7.6	119	9.8	20	10.5	132
November	13.4	121	2.8	116	8.4	79	9.8	54
December	8.9	93	−1.6	59	7.3	70	5.7	12

temp = temperature   ppt = precipitation

MALTA

General information

Status

Republic

Capital

Valletta

Area

320 sq km (122 sq miles)

Population

360,000

Location

Latitude 35°N; longitude 14°E. Malta, and its two sister islands, Gozo and Comino, are about half the size of the Isle of Wight. It is situated in the middle of the Mediterranean, about 90 km from Sicily and 290 km from the North African coast.

Political stability

Malta actively encourages foreign residents and, moreover, in recent years has established itself as an important financial centre. Stability and continuity is assured since recent legislation relating to these issues was passed through Parliament, without division and with the full blessing of the opposition. The policy of the recently elected Labour government seems to be similar to that of the previous nationalist administration.

Economy

Cost of living

In general, prices compare favourably with the UK, especially for food and essential services. Inflation is low (less than 3 per cent) and the economy of the island continues to prosper. Unemployment is modest (average 3.5 per cent) and there is a shortage of skilled labour in some of the new industries.

The Maltese currency is strong and Malta is considered to be one of the top countries in Europe for foreign currency reserves.

The Government's plans to improve the island's residential amenities are progressing well and already many roads have been improved. New water and drainage schemes are being installed and telephone systems modernised. A large new liner terminal is to be constructed and a free port has been established in the south of the main island. Many hotels are being upgraded and extended.

Among substantial new residential developments is Portomaso, a waterfront scheme in the fashionable district of St Julians, which is on the northern coast. It will overlook a magnificent new yacht marina and will include high quality apartments with one to four bedrooms and spacious private terraces. Some units will have their own private swimming pools. A tree-lined promenade extends around the marina and there will be extensive underground parking. The development also incorporates shops, restaurants and a new five star Hilton hotel. St Julians is a prime residential district within easy reach of Valletta, the island's capital. Further details can be obtained from Cassar & Cooper Real Estate, St Annes Court, Tigne Sea Front, Sliema, Malta. This agency is also handling the sale of Sunblessed Horizons Retirement Developments on Malta's sister island of Gozo (see page 122) and has an extensive register of established villas and flats for sale in many parts of Malta.

Another well-established local estate agent (formed in 1969) is Frank Salt Ltd (2 Paceville Avenue, Paceville, Malta). They are selling four large new developments in Malta. Two of these are on scenic sites and the other two include marinas. The firm also has a wide selection of established properties for sale in Malta and Gozo. They predict that the Government's proposed new conditions for foreign residents will make the purchase of residential property in both islands an even more attractive proposition.

Taxation

Married couples submitting one tax return together are exempt from tax on joint income up to approximately £7,125, thereafter the rate is 15 per cent on income between £7,125 and £9,900; 20 per cent on £9,900 to £12,560, 25 per cent on £12,560 to £15,200; 30 per cent on £15,200 and £17,900 and 35 per cent on anything above £17,900. Single people are exempt from tax on income up to £5,340 and then there is a range of rates up to 35 per cent, with the top rate being paid on incomes in excess of £14,200. The income bands quoted above are approximate.

A double taxation agreement exists between Malta and Britain (as well as between most other Western countries).

For special taxation arrangements for permit holders, see 'Residence Qualifications' on the next page.

Exchange rate

Maltese liri 0.62 = £1. Sterling sums mentioned below are based on this exchange rate.

Exchange control

There are no restrictions on transferring abroad the proceeds of the sale of a property in Malta after the payment of capital gains tax on the net profit. However, if the property sold has been the owner's principal residence in Malta for at least three years, then capital gains tax is not charged.

Language

The national language is Maltese, but English is spoken almost universally. Maltese and English are joint official languages.

Expatriate community

Evidence of the century and a half of British rule in Malta is still to be found in many shapes and forms. The substantial resident British community of more than 3,000, combined with a further 3,000 who own holiday property there, maintains the link with the past.

The links between the UK and Malta are still apparent and this, combined with the friendly and hospitable attitude of the Maltese, makes for a pleasant atmosphere.

Security

Standard precautions against theft and burglary are advisable.

Residence qualifications

Holders of permanent residence permits with substantial capital and incomes are granted special financial concessions. To qualify they are required to have capital of at least LM150,000, which can be held anywhere in the world, or an annual income of LM10,000 of which at least LM6,000, plus LM1,000 per dependent, must be remitted to Malta each year. The rate of income tax is then only 15 per cent, with a minimum of LM1,000. Any unspent income or capital in excess of the minimum can be repatriated. People in this category are permitted to purchase a flat costing a minimum of LM20,000 or a house costing at least LM30,000. Alternatively a residential property may be rented, provided the minimum rent is at least LM1,200 per annum. The Government announced at the end of 1998 that these minimum property purchase prices may be increased in the near future.

One car can be imported without paying any customs duty; also all household and personal goods.

Expatriates are not allowed to be employed or to engage in business without the authority of the Maltese government. Tourists may visit the island at any time, provided that each sojourn does not exceed three months.

Temporary residents staying for periods in excess of three months can apply to the immigration authorities to renew the entry visa once a year. This is a simple formality and many British people live in Malta on this basis. They are not entitled to the taxation advantages for permanent residents, but are normally subject to local tax conditions if their stay exceeds six months in one continuous period and then only on income remitted to Malta. Proof needs to be provided, however, that they have sufficient income to live in the island without becoming a financial burden to the government.

Property can be used as a permanent or holiday residence by the purchaser or immediate family only, but guests can be accommodated when the owner or a member of the family is staying in the property. Funds for property purchase must originate from outside Malta.

Personal effects

Once a residence permit is acquired, no duties are payable on personal effects. Exemption from Customs duty is granted on household and personal effects and also on a car imported within six months of arrival in Malta. Pets can be imported from the UK with a quarantine period of only three weeks.

Housing

A wide range of modern and well-established villas and apartments is available for sale all over the island. Expatriates are limited in that they can own only one property, which must be of a value exceeding LM15,000 (if renovating an old property, this can be the total amount including building costs), in order to prevent speculation on the property market at the expense of the local residents. In general, residential property is available at a reasonable price. However, prices are rising owing to the greater expectations of local owners and strong local demand. The popularity of Gozo is growing quite fast.

Buying property

A notary public is employed to draw up a preliminary agreement, which contains the basic data about the transaction, and this is signed by both parties. The purchaser pays a deposit, which is normally 10 per cent. Searches are then carried out by the notary to ascertain if there are any defects in the title or liabilities which were not known when the preliminary contract was signed. If there are any problems, the purchaser can withdraw from the contract and recover the deposit paid. The searches do not cover future development plans for the area; these have to be checked with the Planning Authority. A permit to acquire a property by a foreigner is required from the Ministry of Finance. This is a formality, provided the applicant does not already own a property in the Maltese Islands – a foreigner may only own one property at a time.

Finally, the notary or estate agent will provide the purchaser with a full statement of account and request that the necessary foreign funds be imported, preferably by telegraphic transfer. The Central Bank of Malta requires evidence that these funds have come from outside Malta and the notary will take the bank credit note, together with the Ministry of Finance permit, to the Central Bank for endorsement. Then the final deed can be signed by both parties simultaneously and the balance of the purchase price plus fees are paid.

Deeds prepared by the notary are bound every six months and submitted to a judge or magistrate for checking. They are then taken to the notarial archives and a second set is kept at the notary's office, where it can be inspected by anyone.

Foreigners may rent property free of restrictions except where the lease is for more than 16 years, when an application to the government is necessary.

It is possible to borrow money for house purchase at rates of interest that are currently up to 9 per cent. Loans are generally granted over a maximum of 10 years. Purchasing costs are: 10 per cent for stamp duty; 1 per cent for the notary; a Ministry of Finance fee of about LM100; search and registration fees of between LM25 and LM70. Local authority rates are not charged. There is no VAT or other tax on property.

Where to live

The capital of Malta is Valletta, a fascinating city with many fine old buildings and an excellent shopping centre. Many local families and non-islanders, however, prefer to live in nearby Sliema and its suburb of St Julians. Popular inland towns include Rabat, Mdina and Mosta and there are some attractive resorts further afield at St Pauls Bay, Marsaslokk and Mellieha. Malta is quite a small island with a good road system, so everywhere is within about half an hour's drive.

The sister island of Gozo, to the north, is less well known, but offers much peace and seclusion. It can be reached within half an hour via the ferry from Cirkewwa and is well worth a visit. Farming is an important occupation and the many green fields are a pleasure to see. To conserve the sparse soil in the valleys, many of the villages have been built on the summit of the rocky hills. The capital is Victoria.

The other island in the group is tiny Comino, which has just one hotel and facilities for water sports.

Inspection flights

Winter fares are from £190 return for a minimum three-day visit. Details from the Association of Estate Agents in Malta, The Whispers, Ross Street, Paceville, Malta.

Communications

There are regular daily flights to Malta operated by Air Malta, and also package tours and 'flight only' offers.

Letting property

Non-Maltese owners of property with swimming pools are now allowed to let holiday homes provided that they apply for a licence, which costs about £950 per annum. Villas with these facilities command rentals of around £65–£135 per day in the high season. Licence applications must be submitted through a Maltese managing agent.

Recreation

Facilities exist for golf, football, water sports, horse racing, hockey, cycling, athletics, fishing and netball. Indoors there are opportunities for billiards, snooker, ten-pin bowling and table tennis. Non-sporting pursuits include the cinema and the theatre; there are local television and radio programmes; 700 years of historical development provide a fine heritage of remarkable architecture. All British national newspapers are available daily. TV includes cable/satellite, BBC, CNN, Sky, Euronews, etc.

Driving

At times, standards are a little erratic. Cars drive on the left, officially. International driving licences are accepted.

Health services

The climate is good, and the hygienic conditions help the Maltese to enjoy a high standard of health.

A health agreement between the UK and Malta is beneficial to British people living in the island. Permanent residents are exempt from hospital charges; holders of temporary residence permits pay greatly reduced hospital charges.

Climate

The climate is warm and healthy, with mild, moist winters and hot, dry summers, as the following table shows:

	Average daily temperatures (°C)	Monthly rainfall (mm)	Sea temperature (°C)	Sunshine hours
January	9.5–15.0	88.2	14.5	5.3
February	9.4–15.4	61.4	14.5	6.3
March	10.2–16.7	44.0	14.5	7.3
April	11.8–18.7	27.5	16.1	8.3
May	14.9–23.0	9.7	18.4	10.0
June	18.6–27.4	3.4	21.1	11.2
July	21.0–32.2	0.9	24.5	12.1
August	21.8–30.6	9.3	25.6	11.3
September	20.2–27.0	44.4	25.0	8.9
October	17.1–23.7	117.9	22.2	7.3
November	13.8–19.9	75.5	19.5	6.3
December	11.1–16.7	96.0	16.7	5.2

PORTUGAL AND MADEIRA

General information

Status

Republic

Capital

Lisbon

Area

92,000 sq km (32,225 sq miles)

Population

10,299,000

Location

Latitude 37°N; longitude 6°W. Situated on the south-western tip of the European mainland, Portugal has very obvious attractions. The environment is still fairly unspoilt and there are perfect beaches. Being on the Atlantic coast means that greenery flourishes, whereas elsewhere on equal longitudes scrub and thorn prevail. Therefore, Portugal is subjected to the warmth befitting its proximity to the equator and the cooling influence of the Atlantic, which together combine to provide ideal conditions.

Political stability

A bloodless revolution in 1974 overthrew nearly 50 years of virtual dictatorship but the present régime appears to have adequate control. Portugal's stability was enhanced by entry into the European Community.

Economy

Cost of living. Portugal is one of the cheapest countries in the EU for living costs. The country enjoys many of the advantages of membership of the EU and has reaped further benefits from the abandonment of restrictions between member countries. Local produce, particularly fruit and vegetables, is of good quality and reasonably priced. Most Portuguese wine can be enjoyed far more cheaply than in Britain, and meals in restaurants compare favourably with London and other large cities.

It is considered that a couple, owning their own home in the south of Portugal, can live quite comfortably on an income of £10,000 per annum.

Hambros Bank (Gibraltar) Ltd has opened a branch at Loulé, Algarve.

Taxation

Income tax is self-assessed annually. Returns and payment have to be made by the end of May each year and you will be given a fiscal number. Rates are 15 per cent on the first £7,000–£18,000 of taxable income and 40 per cent thereafter.

People living in Portugal for over 183 days in any one year are treated as resident and are liable to Portuguese income tax on their whole-world income. Non-residents pay tax only on any income they receive in Portugal. A double taxation agreement exists between Britain and Portugal.

Death duties are payable on transfer of a property following death or by gift. The rates charged vary from 0 per cent to 50 per cent, depending on the relationship.

There is an inheritance tax, but non-residents are not liable for capital gains tax.

The municipal tax is between 0.70 and 1.3 per cent of the value of the building. The rate for land is lower at 0.8 per cent. This is an annual tax, but urban homes for permanent occupation, where the price is under $10 million, are exempt for ten years. VAT is 5 per cent for basic items and 16 per cent at standard rate.

Exchange rate

Escudos (written $): $302 = £1.

Exchange controls

Non-residents can bring unlimited foreign currency into the country, including travellers' cheques and escudos in notes or coins.

Language

Portuguese is spoken and some knowledge of it would be useful. However, English is fairly common in tourist areas, especially where there is a substantial expatriate community.

Expatriate community

The southern coastline (Algarve) attracts a variety of European citizens, particularly from the UK, Germany and Scandinavia. The business community is settled around Lisbon and Oporto. A growing number of British citizens are choosing the Estoril/Cascais area, and also the largely unspoilt coast near Oporto and the west coast close to Obidos lagoon, as the location for holiday homes.

The Association of Foreign Property Owners in Portugal was formed on the Algarve in 1987 to help expatriate property owners and residents to understand and comply with Portuguese legislation. This non-commercial, non-political organisation is properly constituted under Portuguese law.

Services available to members include help and advice on purchasing residential property, guidance on the completion of official Portuguese forms, recommendations of trustworthy legal and financial consultants, access to household, motor and health insurance on special terms and general advice on dealing with any problems which might arise.

A newsletter is published regularly and seminars are held from time to time to discuss a variety of general interest matters.

Over 3,000 members now belong to the Association, whose offices are at Rua Infante D. Henrique No. 222° Portimao. Details of subscriptions can be obtained from AFPOP, Apartado 728, 8500 Portimao, Algarve, Portugal (tel 010 351 82 458509; fax 010 351 82 458277).

Security

It is a good idea to install a security system to protect your property from undesirables, particularly if the house is to be closed for long periods.

Residence and work permits

EU nationals may enter Portugal for up to three months to seek work or establish a business. Those intending to live or work in Portugal for more than three months require a residence permit, application being made to the nearest Foreigners' Department of the Portuguese Ministry of Internal Affairs. These are generally valid for five years, but may need renewing after two. An identity card must always be carried and application forms for this document can be obtained from any British Consulate Office in Portugal. The forms are then submitted to the local parish council. Registration with the nearest British Consulate Office is advised.

If you spend fewer than 183 days in Portugal in a year you are normally classed as 'new'.

Education

State education is free, but parents may be charged for books and stationery. Primary education commences at age six and lasts for four years, secondary education is only compulsory until the age of 15. Further education includes technical colleges and universities, and here tuition fees may be charged.

Personal effects

These may be imported free of duty so long as they have been in the owner's possession for more than 12 months.

Housing

Many villa and apartment estates have been built on the Algarve in recent years and in resorts close to Lisbon and there are new and established homes in the Oporto area. Old properties for modernisation come on the market quite frequently.

Portugal has prepared new planning regulations for development in the country to solve some of the problems created by uncontrolled development over the past two decades.

Building zones, agricultural and green zones have been specified and some new building is restricted.

Mowlem, the British builder, is constructing Alto Golf and Country Club on the Algarve which includes luxury residential properties and Jones Portugal has fine villas and apartments near Portimao, also on the Algarve.

Buying property

Check with the local tax department to make sure that the existing owner has paid the rates up to date. Sometimes these can be several years in arrears, and as rates are attributed to the property not to an individual, a new owner could be liable for outstanding debts. Have a search done at the Land Registry to ensure that the property is correctly described in the records and that it is free of charges and does not have any encumbrances, such as rights of way etc. Obtain from the Town Hall a Usage Licence which for residential property is a Habitation Licence.

Once all the vital preliminaries have been completed a promissory contract (*contrato promessa de compra e venda*) of purchase and sale is prepared. This gives information on the property, the price to be paid, inventory of contents (if any), date of completion, date of possession and any other details to be agreed between both parties. A deposit of 10 per cent or more is paid by the purchaser which is forfeited if the buyer defaults. Should the seller renege, he or she forfeits twice the amount of the deposit to the buyer.

The document is signed by both parties before a Portuguese Notary and a transfer tax known as SISA may be payable by the purchaser. The terms of this tax change quite frequently. Currently it is 8 or 10 per cent depending on the value of the property. There is a sliding scale for lower priced homes. Thereafter there is a sliding scale which rises to ten per cent on sales exceeding 30.9 million escudos. On new property from a builder, VAT is payable on the purchase price of the property instead of SISA.

The final deed of conveyance (*escritura*) signed before the notary in Portugal, gives the purchaser a proper title to the residence, and the change of ownership is recorded at the Local Land Registry.

Notarial and Registration fees generally amount to about 2.5 per cent of the purchase price, while the charges made by the *advogado* (your solicitor) are generally between 1 and 2 per cent. If you use Portuguese estate agents to buy or sell property make sure they are licensed by the Mediador Autorizado. Mortgages are usually available from British or Portuguese Banks.

It is essential to obtain permission from the Bank of Portugal when importing funds into Portugal to pay for the purchase of a property. Known as *Boletim de Autorizacao de Capitals Privados* (Licence to Import Personal Funds), the application must be accompanied by substantial details about the transaction and the amount to be imported, the purchase price, estate agent's commission (if any), legal fees, surveyor's and architect's charges, as well as Land Registry fees. The permit may take up to one month to be issued, but it is vital, as without it it may not be possible to resell the property at a later date.

If you do not live permanently in Portugal it is desirable that you appoint a fiscal representative in Portugal to whom the tax department can send all correspondence regarding your tax affairs. This representative must be resident in Portugal and can be your tax adviser, a friend or a lawyer.

Inspection flights

Cheap flights to inspect property are available via charter services throughout the year.

Communications

There are daily flights from the UK to Lisbon and Faro by British Airways and Portuguese Airlines (TAP). To Madeira, there is a twice-weekly service from Heathrow to Funchal. Internal flights (including Madeira and the Azores) are run by TAP. Lisbon airport has been modernised and its capacity increased.

Train services are available via Paris (journey time approximately 24 hours Paris–Lisbon).

Recreation

Spectator sports are a very popular form of leisure in Portugal, especially football and also the traditional bullfight (more merciful in character than the Spanish version). Golf is a popular pastime with a number of good courses within reach of Lisbon and many along the Algarve. Horse riding, water sports and camping are among other enjoyable pursuits.

Eating out is common, with restaurants plentiful and open until late. The food is possibly as good as anywhere in Europe.

As far as the arts are concerned, Portugal has its own theatre tradition, abundant museums and galleries, fine orchestras and beautiful and arresting architecture. The cinema is popular and films are often dubbed into English.

There are also many clubs and societies for expatriates' use. The Algarve region has a Lions Club and also a Lioness Club, an archaeological association, and meetings of the Rotarians and the British Legion. Bridge tournaments are held in some hotels and bingo has been legalised. Other clubs and associations elsewhere include the Royal British Club, the Charity Bridge Association and the Royal

Society of St George (or David or Andrew). The British Council in Lisbon also helps to organise exhibitions, lectures, films and concerts.

Driving

Foreign-registered cars may enter Portugal for a period of up to six months on production of the registration document. A Green Card (from your insurance company) is now required by law.

It is advisable to carry a spare parts kit and obtain GB stickers while the car is still registered in Britain. British driving licences are valid. Carrying petrol in cans is forbidden.

Portugal uses the international road sign system. The rule of the road is to keep to the right. Traffic approaching from the right must be given priority, except when entering a public road from a private driveway or a side road with a stop sign. The speed limits are roughly the same as elsewhere on the mainland of Europe, ranging from 50 to 120 km/h.

Health services

There are many English-speaking doctors in Portugal and a British hospital in Lisbon. Free emergency out-patient treatment is available to any Briton who produces form E111 and a British passport. For permanent residents, private health insurance is advisable.

As a member of the EU, Portugal is covered by the terms of the reciprocal agreement with the Department of Social Security. For details see DSS pamphlet SA29.

Hospital treatment and essential medicines are free under the Portuguese Health Service.

Climate

Portugal is regarded by many as having one of the most pleasant climates in Europe. Throughout the year the temperature is warm without ever being sweltering. The proximity of the country to the Atlantic means that the air is freshened by the sea breezes that bring with them the moisture that allows vegetation other than scrub to flourish. The average temperatures in the two most popular areas for migration are as follows:

	Average temperatures (°C)	
	Algarve	*Lisbon/Estoril*
January	12	12
February	13	12
March	14	14
April	16	16
May	18	17
June	21	20
July	24	21
August	24	22
September	22	21
October	19	18
November	16	15
December	13	12

Where to live

The three regions most preferred by expatriates for permanent residence or a holiday home are the Algarve coast in the deep south of the country, the towns close to Lisbon such as Cascais and Estoril, and the Costa Verde, near Oporto.

The Algarve

The Algarve is favoured with a wide range of sandy beaches stretching from the border with Spain as far west as Cape St Vincent.

The capital of the region is Faro, and the conversion of the local airstrip into an international airport speeded up the development of the whole coast as it became accessible to most northern European countries in about 2½ hours' flying time. A new terminal has improved facilities for passengers considerably. Faro has a population of about 50,000 and is a good shopping centre. It has a small harbour and some pleasant municipal gardens, several museums and interesting churches.

The eastern end of the Algarve towards the Spanish border is less developed. Here there are some fine beaches and quite attractive hinterland. Substantial EU-funded infrastructure projects and a newly completed motorway have improved the area and its accessibility. One of the towns to benefit is Tavira which is within an hour's drive of Faro and only 10 miles from Spain. The town has a Roman bridge, fishing harbour and attractive seventeenth-century buildings. Nearby is a fine 27-hole championship golf course and other amenities. There are a number of low density developments and land, and building costs are less than elsewhere on the Algarve.

West of Faro the coastline becomes more indented with rocky coves, islets and sandy beaches which are reminiscent of the Cornish coastline. The town of note nearest to Faro is Almansil, a regional shopping centre, and on the coast are three major resort towns, namely Quinta do Lago, Vale do Lobo and Quarteira. Facilities include golf courses, tennis clubs, hotels and a wide range of villas and apartments used either for summer holidays or permanent living.

Further west along the coast is the well-known resort of Albufeira, originally a fishing town, with a large open-air market. The beaches are popular, with unusual rock formations; above, on the clifftop, the winding streets have a variety of well-established and recently built properties. Many retail establishments, restaurants and bars serve the local population and also the considerable number of holiday-makers who visit the town every summer. From nearly every vantage point, there are views of the sea.

The next major town on the inland road is Lagoa (not to be confused with the port of Lagos, further to the west). As the wine capital of the province, Lagoa is considered to be important as an agricultural market town.

Portimao is a large fishing port at the mouth of the river Arcade, but its popular residential suburb is Praia da Rocha which has a large sandy beach, interesting cliffs and attractive rock formations. This is a family resort with a wide choice of new properties and hotels.

The last large town going westwards along the coast is Lagos, which has a variety of entertainment and shopping opportunities. At one time Lagos was the capital of the Algarve. Small resorts of interest from the residential point of view near Lagos include Praia da Luz, a true family resort, and also Burgau and Salema. This part of the coastline is memorable for the many rugged, tiny coves where the sand is regularly washed clean by the Atlantic waves.

The Lisbon area

Lisbon is a fine city located near the mouth of the river Tejo. It has many grand buildings, and the huge variety of commercial establishments makes it an ideal centre for sightseeing. This is not perhaps a place where many British people decide to spend their retirement years.

Of greater interest in this respect is Estoril, about 24 km west of Lisbon, known for most of this century as a cosmopolitan town because it provided shelter for many former administrators and even kings from bygone European states. The town has a good beach on the Atlantic and is well known for entertainment activities which include a large casino, night clubs, restaurants, exhibition halls and theatres. Modern apartment blocks vie with Victorian villas to attract those who want to live near the facilities.

Nearby Cascais is a fishing port and also the home of many well-to-do people from various nations.

A few miles inland is the ancient hill town of Sintra where Portuguese kings made their summer home from the fourteenth century. There are many fascinating buildings to be visited and sites to be seen.

Costa Verde

This is the northern sea coast of Portugal (the green coast) and lies between the frontier with Spain in the north and the mouth of the river Douro in the south.

It is not an area where many foreigners have settled for retirement, but it does attract tourists looking for somewhere different.

Oporto is the main centre of habitation and this town can be reached by domestic flights from Lisbon in a flying time of about 40 minutes. There are also rail and coach services from the capital.

As the second largest city in Portugal, it is also well known for having given its name to the famous wine – port – and British expatriates there tend to be connected with the trade.

Located at the mouth of the river Douro, this mainly working city does not necessarily impress at first sight but with time and effort many attractions can be discovered. There are numerous museums and a good selection of hotels, plus leisure amenities.

Among coastal resorts is Espinho, south of Oporto, which has a long sandy beach.

To the north of Oporto lies a large fishing port known as Póvoa da Varzim, an excellent seaside resort with good facilities for tourists; further north still lies Ofir which has a long stretch of white sand backed by pinewoods, while a few kilometres inland is Barcelos, which is well known for the large open-air market held on Thursday each week.

Another seaside resort is Viana do Castelo, 71 km from Oporto. Located near the mouth of the river Lima, the town has various hotels and good shopping.

The Anglo-Portuguese Society, Canning House, 2 Belgrave Square, London SW1X 8PJ (tel: 0171 245 9738) publishes a newsletter for members and arranges meetings and events in Great Britain to inform people about Portugal.

Central Portugal – Beira Litoral

The inland section of this old province is not well known to British expatriates or vacationists, but it has already been discovered by a few enterprising European families, who have bought residential properties in some attractive locations at reasonable prices.

On the coast there are two quite well-known resorts, namely Figueira da Foz (15,000 inhabitants), which has an enormous beach and is situated in the south of region, and Aveiro (population about 25,000) which is some 60 km to the north. This coastline is known as the Costa de Prata.

The main inland centre of habitation is Coimbra (40,000 inhabitants), which was Portugal's capital between 1143 and 1255. It is an important city of learning, having been a centre of university education continuously since 1537. It also offers good facilities and shopping amenities for the surrounding villages.

East of Coimbra there is mountainous country, rising to the heights of Serra do Acor and valleys where the principal river, the Alva, flows rapidly.

One of the villages in this area which is attracting some attention from foreigners is Arganil. Here are hotels and restaurants, and there is a tourist office in the town hall. A few kilometres to the south-west lies Gois, founded in the 17th century, which has a number of interesting monuments and an old bridge decorated with Hispano-Arabic tiles. Local amenities are quite good and include a health centre.

Small farms in the area are occasionally available for restoration, as well as former stately homes which can be converted into tourist hotels. Retirement homes in or near country villages are also available, at reasonable prices.

Madeira

This Atlantic island which belongs to Portugal lies about 1,000 km south-west of Lisbon, but much closer to the African coast. It is 56 km long by 21 km wide and the terrain is very mountainous because of its volcanic origins. The coastline is largely steep cliffs so there are few beaches, but inland greenery and colourful flowers are to be seen everywhere.

About one-third of the island's population of 300,000 lives in Funchal, the capital, and the rest are scattered in towns, villages and hamlets in the countryside.

Funchal is built on a hillside overlooking the bay and harbour. The main hotels are located in or on the perimeter of the town and the central zone is packed with buildings ancient and modern containing the major shopping premises and administrative headquarters.

Outside the immediate vicinity of Funchal, property prices tend to be lower, and the construction of a new motorway to the West of the island is encouraging foreign residents to purchase homes in the country area, rather than in Funchal and developers are seeking suitable sites for new homes.

The quiet holiday island of Porto Santo has some fine sandy beaches. It lies 40 km north-east of Madeira and has a population of 3,000. A local airport has regular flights to Madeira and also to Lisbon.

All procedures and taxes in the mainland of Portugal apply to Madeira.

Average temperatures range from 16°C in January to March, to 22°C in August and September.

Azores

Located in the middle of the Atlantic, about two hours' flying time west of Portugal, the Azores comprise nine islands with a total of about 2,350 sq km. They are all of volcanic origin and each has an individual landscape, but every one benefits from lush vegetation, hills and valleys and blue seas.

The 254,000 residents enjoy a temperate maritime climate, for the locality is at the centre of an anticyclone zone and bathed by a branch of the Gulf Stream. The largest island is São Miguel which has good facilities for visitors; services are also available on the islands of Terceira, Faial and Pico, all of which have airports.

SPAIN

General information

Status

Kingdom

Capital

Madrid

Area

510,000 sq km (197,000 sq miles)

Population

39,887,000

Location

Latitude 36°N to 43°N; longitude 8°W to 6°E. The popular image of Spain is that of Benidorm or Torremolinos, one of high-rise hotels, crowded streets and an endless nightlife. Yet there is far more to Spain than the commercialism of the popular holiday resorts. Blessed by an idyllic climate and at times breathtaking countryside, there is a different Spain which has been popular for many years among those looking for their place in the sun. Sun, of course, is one of the main attractions of the Iberian peninsula, but Spain's appeal is not limited to its climate.

Residence and work permits

Foreigners are allowed to visit Spain as tourists for up to 90 days on the production of their passport at the point of entry. Formerly the law did not limit the number of visits in any one year and as a result some foreign residents used to leave Spain for a brief period towards the end of their 90 days and then return almost immediately, have their passport stamped and so commence a further 90-day period of 'tourism'.

The authorities are now much more strict in this respect and are only prepared to give one 90-day extension, which is known as a *permanencia* and means a *temporary* stay. This is obtained at a police station and some evidence of the applicant's ability to finance the continued stay in Spain is required.

Those who are going to remain in Spain for any length of time as property owners or tenants need a residence permit. These can now be obtained from a local police station immediately on arrival in Spain.

Retired citizens from EU countries who wish to live permanently in Spain can now obtain a residence permit on arrival, from the local *comisaria* (police station) by presenting their passport and proof of sufficient income on which to live (pension, investments etc). Also required are proof of medical insurance through their own country's Social Security system or private medical insurance, and four passport size photos. The completed application form requesting a residence permit has to be accompanied by the above documentation and a fee of 700 pesetas in the form of Spanish State

Paper which is obtainable from official tobacco shops. Normal residence permits are renewed after one year for five years, and thereafter a permanent permit may be granted.

Along with the residence permit a tax identification number (NIE) will be issued, as anyone who resides in Spain for more than 183 days is liable to pay Spanish income tax. EU citizens working in Spain require an EU registration card, which is issued initially for one year and renewed for a period of five years.

EU citizens require work permits but have the same opportunity of employment in Spain under similar conditions to those of a Spaniard. The words 'non-discrimination' and 'equal treatment' mean that Spanish labour authorities can no longer insist that employers considering the employment of EU nationals advertise the job first at the Spanish employment office and give preference to any qualified Spanish applicant. The employer thus has a free choice who he or she employs.

Work or residence permits cannot be refused to any member of the family of any EU worker. Children under the age of 21 and spouses who are dependent on the worker have full rights to reside and obtain employment in Spain. Children of EU workers have the same rights to trade-school education and apprenticeship schemes run by the state, as Spanish nationals.

The regulations require any EU foreigner seeking work in another EU country to obtain from the State Employment Office similar treatment to its own nationals looking for work. Furthermore, when a foreigner loses a job through no fault of his or her own, unemployment pay may be claimed in the same way as a local worker. Of course, it will be necessary for EU workers to be registered by employers with the Spanish Social Security system and to have appropriate contributions and income tax deducted from pay.

Qualifications of foreign professional people, such as doctors, dentists, architects, lawyers, etc, are gradually being recognised in Spain, enabling them to practise locally.

EU citizens with a residence permit are able to vote in municipal elections by registering their names at the local town hall where they live.

Personal effects

No customs duty or VAT are imposed on household goods and clothing imported for personal use, by EU citizens. Those EU citizens taking up official residence in Spain are also permitted, under certain conditions, to bring in a car free of import duty and IVA (VAT).

Housing

Spanish pueblo-style developments have been of substantial interest to overseas buyers in recent years. This is a high-density method grouping terraced houses with pedestrianised precincts. Those with larger sums to invest tend to purchase detached villas, especially if they are going to live in them for substantial periods of the year, as they offer much more privacy.

Apartments continue to be popular, especially for those seeking a holiday home, but as those overlooking the sea are now scarce and expensive, for reasonably priced apartments it may be necessary to examine the possibility of units being built a short distance inland.

Both developers and agents have improved their methods of presentation and marketing by using more sophisticated displays, models and specialised exhibitions. Inspection tours are also offered, but generally these are now of a more personalised nature and the previous practice of taking a dozen or more prospective buyers on a weekend visit to Spain, and keeping them so busy that they had time to see only the properties being offered by the agent or developer, has now gone out of fashion.

The improvement in the UK residential property market has had a significant effect on the demand for holiday and retirement homes in Spain. Most of the long established estate agents and builders involved in selling property along the Mediterranean coast of the Iberian peninsular are enjoying an upsurge in interest from prospective UK based buyers, who are being encouraged by the return of the 'feel good' factor, plus the beneficial exchange rate for the peseta, currently at about 235 to the pound sterling.

Currently the selection of established villas and apartments is good along the Costa del Sol and Costa Blanca and in addition there are a number of new developments being offered. These include schemes by well-known names such as Taylor Woodrow who have five developments on the Costa del Sol, including a prestige site with golf course near Marbella, as well as developments in the Balearic Islands (two on Menorca and eight sites in Majorca). Barratt International Resorts offer sites on the Costa del Sol, Banner Homes have an apartment scheme near Marbella and Marriott Vacation Club also have apartments in the same resort. A number of local Spanish developers are also active along the coasts. There is no doubt that now is a very favourable time to acquire a home in Spain.

The future

A less well-known region likely to create the interest of those seeking a holiday or retirement home during the next decade is the Costa de la Luz, between Cadiz and Huelva, on the Atlantic coast. Here the terrain is varied and there are attractive beaches, mountainous regions and fertile plains close to the border with Portugal. Access is quite easy via Gibraltar Airport.

The Costa de Azahar, and also the Costa Dorada, have scope for future expansion, while the islands of La Palma, Fuerteventura and Gomera in the Canary group, which lie off the coast of Morocco in the Atlantic, could become more popular.

Political stability and economy

Spain is still suffering somewhat from the recession and unemployment is high, but as an active member of the EU events should improve.

The depreciated value of the peseta will undoubtedly encourage more families from the UK to spend their vacations in Spain during 1999, where they will be able to enjoy some of the improvements carried out in major coastal resorts in recent years. The arrival of more tourists will also be welcome news for both business and the government.

Cost of living

There is not much difference these days between living costs in Spain compared with the UK, but certain local produce, including wines and spirits, can be found at advantageous prices. Inflation is currently under 3 per cent.

Taxation

Both residents and tourists who live in Spain for more than 183 days per year are subject to income tax. After allowances, rates range from 20 per cent to 56 per cent according to taxable income. But there is a double taxation agreement between Spain and the UK. Residents in Spain are taxed on their worldwide assets, after allowances.

The calculation of property taxes is based on the *valor catastral* (official assessed value) allocated to each property. These values were originally quite low, but as a result of the country's economic growth, they are being recalculated, and are now approaching the real value of the property.

Spanish tax on capital assets must be paid by non-residents. This is calculated at two tenths of 1 per cent of the *valor catastral* up to 25 million pesetas and a slightly higher figure for sums in excess of this. Non-residents who do not let their property, and only use it for a few weeks per year, pay tax at 25 per cent on an imaginary income for the annual period of use. This is based on 2 per cent of the *valor catastral*.

Local rates

Property owners pay an annual real-estate tax known as *Impuesto de bienes Inmuebles* (IBI), based on the official value *(valor catastral)* of the property. This varies according to location, and size of the home. The owner must pay the amount due between 15 September and 15 November, even if no notification is received and late payments incur penalties.

Plus valia is another local tax. This is based on the theoretical increase in value of the land since the last sale. With apartments or pueblo-style town houses on new urbanisations, the increase is likely to be very small as only small areas of land are involved. The tax should be paid by the vendor but is often passed on to the purchaser. The theoretical increase is calculated by reference to indices of value maintained by the local authorities regarding land in their area.

Tax on property profits

Non-residents who sell their property at a profit must pay 35 per cent tax on the profit after allowing for a tapering relief of 10.52 per cent per year of ownership. To ensure that this is done anyone purchasing a property from a non-resident must pay 5 per cent of the purchase price over to the tax ministry. Where the vendor has made a loss on the transaction or the amount deposited is in excess of the computed figure, a refund is eventually made to the vendor. After owning a property for 10 years or more, no capital gains tax is payable, but the deposit is still payable and is then returned.

Non-residents of Spain, who own only one Spanish dwelling-place – an apartment or house – no longer need to have a fiscal representative who is living in Spain, but they do require a fiscal identification number and have to submit an income tax return each year. A simplified tax return form has been introduced recently.

General rates

These may be payable to the local authority and have been modest in the past, but are being increased. The rate is generally about 0.4 per cent of the rateable value. In most places no rate demand is issued, so it is necessary to check the figure due annually at the town hall. A surcharge of 20 per cent can be imposed when payment is made after a fixed settlement date. Some authorities also make a fairly modest charge for refuse collection and sewage disposal.

Purchasers of new property from a developer pay VAT at 7 per cent on the declared value but only 4.5 per cent in the Canary Islands. Property bought privately incurs a stamp duty of 6 per cent. If you have a computer and are connected to the Internet, you can consult the *Boletin Oficial del Estado* which lists all the recent Spanish laws on taxation and other subjects. The website is http://www.boe.es.

Exchange rate

Pesetas 251 = £1.

Exchange control

Since early in 1992 foreign exchange restrictions have been abandoned. Everyone is permitted to have bank accounts in any foreign currencies either in Spain or abroad and can bring in any foreign currency and change it for pesetas and can exchange pesetas for any foreign currency.

The normal rate for VAT is 16 per cent. Some necessities are taxed at 7 per cent and for certain luxury goods the rate is 33 per cent. Specified items are exempt from VAT.

Language

A knowledge of Spanish would be very useful although many Spaniards do speak English, especially in the tourist regions.

Expatriate community

There are more British people than any other expatriate nationality living in the country, but there are also substantial numbers of residents from Germany, Holland, Belgium, Scandinavia, the United States and Russia.

Security

As in most countries it is wise to take precautions against theft from buildings by installing adequate security systems. Street crime and muggings can be a problem in popular resorts during the summer.

Buying property

It is advisable, when buying property in Spain, to take all the professional help and advice available.

When working through estate agents, it is sensible to ascertain their reputation and experience. In Spain the title 'estate agent' should be used only by individuals of Spanish nationality who are qualified by examination and registered. However, some licensed estate agents are little more than sleeping partners in foreign (British) firms, having few qualms about the firm's reputation. Consequently, some lapses in professional standards do occur.

Although builders and developers are not required to comply with such standards, again it is advisable to check their respectability and financial soundness.

The legal process is often lengthy and it is essential to employ a solicitor. There are a considerable number of British firms of solicitors with special departments to handle overseas conveyancing, and some of these are listed under International Lawyers in Appendix 3. These firms often have arrangements with a Spanish solicitor (*abogado*) who undertakes the necessary work in Spain. It is certainly an advantage to have legal advice available in the UK to resolve any language problems and for advice to be available in England whenever it is needed.

Compared with procedures in the UK the conveyance of residential property in Spain is somewhat different. Having found a suitable property, a deposit (usually 10 per cent of the agreed price) is paid by the purchaser to the vendor's legal adviser or agent and a private contract is prepared, by the *abogado* which gives details of the purchaser and vendor, describes the property, the purchase price, completion date, method of payment, proposed date of possession and details of any extras agreed to purchase. Once this document is signed by both parties and the deposit has been paid, a binding contract exists.

A search is then carried out at the Land Registry to make sure that the property is legally owned by the vendor and that there are no charges or mortgages registered against the property. Other vital information that requires checking includes the boundaries of the property, compliance with building restrictions if any, and confirmation that the land has been zoned for development.

The transfer of ownership deed *(escritura)* is then prepared and signed in the presence of a Notario (Notary) who is a public official responsible for ensuring that the requirements of the law are carried out in connection with the preparation and signing of the *escritura*. The balance of the purchase price is paid on or before the *escritura* is signed.

Next the *escritura* is taken to the local Land Registry *(Registro de la Propiedad)* for tax assessment and recording of the new owner's name in the Registry of Properties. When the *escritura* is returned, bearing the stamps of the Registry, the property is finally yours and registration protects your ownership.

For many years there was a frequently used custom of understating the full sale and purchase price in the records to reduce the tax liability. This is a very unwise practice as the authorities are now much better informed about property values, and the penalties are severe if they discover any infringement of the rules.

A sum equivalent to about 10 per cent of the cost of the property should cover the purchase expenses. These will include 6 per cent transfer tax on the declared price of an established property or 7 per cent VAT (4.5 per cent in the Canary Islands) on a new residence purchased from a developer, plus 0.5 per cent legal documented acts tax and land registry fees. There is a scale fee for the preparation and legalisation of the *escritura* by the notary and your own abogado or solicitor will probably charge a fee of about 1 per cent of the purchase price plus disbursements.

Consumer protection law

The purchase or rental of residential property is now subject to certain regulations. These require the provision of complete and precise information about the product being offered. They also require vendors to draft contracts in clear and simple terms and strengthen the principles of good faith and equal and balanced obligations in contracts of purchase and sale.

Furthermore, developers must produce on request the name and registered office of the vendor and a general plan of the property location, plus a description and plan of the public utility services, and safety measures in the event of fire. A description of the building and grounds, together with the size of the property, is required, as well as the construction and insulating materials used in the building. Other data which must be issued include land registry details, total purchase price and payment method, copies of licences and building permissions, statutes of the Community of Owners (where applicable), and information on the payment of taxes and rates levied on the property.

The total purchase price will include agent's fees and VAT unless otherwise stated; in the case of delays in construction or completion, an interest payment will have to be established in the contract.

The law also regulates the contents of sales literature, which has sometimes caused confusion in the past.

Severe fines will be imposed for contravention of these requirements.

Mortgages

Abbey National (Gibraltar) Ltd offer mortgages on residential property in the south of Spain, the islands of Tenerife and Majorca, and also real estate along Portugal's Algarve coast.

They have extensive knowledge of legal and surveying procedures around the Iberian peninsular and provide a fast service at competitive rates of interest to those buying holiday or retirement homes in these localities. Abbey National's offices are at 237 Main Street, Gibraltar.

Jyske Bank Gibraltar Ltd, 76 Main Street, Gibraltar, also offer mortgage facilities in Spain.

Community of Owners

In Spain, the Law of Horizontal Ownership requires that in property with communal facilities such as shared gardens, swimming pools, tennis courts or public entrance halls and passages, and in blocks of apartments or pueblo-style villa schemes and others, it is the owners who decide how their development is to be maintained and managed day by day. Thus the Community is run according to the decisions approved by the majority of owners, yet the rights of minorities have to be protected.

Each Community of Owners must have its own regulations which are known in Spain as the *estatutos* (statutes) and these should describe in detail the parts which are jointly owned by all the members and those that belong entirely to individual owners.

The proportionate share of the common property belonging to each owner should also be stated and so should many other matters of importance to the general well-being of all the parties concerned.

Before making any purchase in this type of scheme it is vital that every prospective owner should be fully aware of the obligations involved, so reading the appropriate documents is essential.

Every owner is required to pay his or her appropriate share of the Community expenses and, under article 9 of the Law of Horizontal Ownership, owners are required to:

1. maintain the property, fittings and installations in satisfactory repair so that no damage or danger will occur to the other owners;
2. care for all installations in the individual's property which are for the benefit of other owners; this includes water pipes, mains drainage and electrical writing;
3. allow work to be carried out in the property as is necessary to provide new services for other owners;
4. obey Community rules and regulations contained in the statutes or imposed as the result of resolutions passed at general meetings of members;
5. pay promptly the appropriate share of the general expenses.

In accordance with the law, a chairman of the Community must be elected every year. Known as the *Presidente*, this person represents all the owners and is also responsible for ensuring that the Community's affairs are conducted in accordance with the law and in the interests of everyone.

If an administrator is not appointed to handle day-to-day affairs then the *Presidente* undertakes the tasks of an administrator. The latter need not be an owner, but the *Presidente* must own a property in the development.

An administrator's duties include ensuring the affairs of the Community are run satisfactorily and that services are adequately maintained. He or she also deals with the maintenance and repairs of the buildings and other joint property belonging to the Community, prepares an annual budget for approval by the owners and, if no treasurer has been appointed, collects owners' annual contributions and also keeps adequate records of meetings.

An Annual General Meeting of the Community must be held at least once a year, and notice in writing has to be sent to every owner not less than six days before the appointed day.

A general meeting can be called by the chairman at any time of the year, or by a group of owners representing at least 25 per cent of the total of owners.

Matters to be dealt with at the AGM include election or re-election of the officers, approval of the Community's accounts for the previous year and a quotation of expected expenses for the next year, and to fix owners' contributions towards these expenses.

Voting at meetings is undertaken on a majority basis by the members or their proxy. Voting is based on the size of the property owned by the voting member, but the total of those attending a meeting must hold at least 50 per cent of community property to pass a valid resolution.

Minorities are protected by the rule that states that a group of owners who between them own at least 25 per cent can apply within one month to a judge for a decision where they consider their rights have been prejudiced by a resolution.

A resolution can be declared invalid by a judge on the application of just one owner, where it is contrary to the laws of Spain or if it is against the Community's own regulations.

Where to live

The choice of where to live is extensive. The weather is perhaps one of the most important deciding factors and, with an equitable climate for almost the whole of the year, the Costa del Sol, between Nerja to the east of Málaga and the frontier with Gibraltar, is one of the most popular regions.

Costa del Sol

Much of the 160 km of coastline has been heavily developed with high-rise hotel and apartment buildings during the past three decades, and towns like Torremolinos, Marbella, Estepona and Fuengirola have been expanded almost beyond recognition.

The long stretches of sandy beach tend to be overcrowded in the summer with package tour holiday-makers, who patronise the many vacation attractions, such as the 30 or more golf courses between Málaga and Gibraltar, tennis clubs, swimming pools, nightspots, casino and an extensive range of bars and restaurants offering a worldwide choice of food. For permanent residence most expatriates prefer to seek out some of the small towns and villages largely unknown to the hordes of European tourists who descend on the coast in the peak holiday months between June and September.

Salobrina to the east of Málaga is an attractive town built on a hill. It has white painted walls and is crowned by a fine castle overlooking the sea. A town house in one of the narrow streets leading to the summit could provide a retirement home for a couple prepared to mix with local people away from the tourist traps.

Calahonda is a fishing community of interest on the road beyond Motril, a little industrial town with a port.

In the hinterland, mountain villages including Algarrobo and Competa which are deep in the Sierra Almigara are now more accessible with the completion of a new road, and the area claims to be one of the warmest parts of Spain in winter. Velez-Málaga is an inland town hardly touched by tourism – it was founded by the Phoenicians in about 600 BC.

All these locations are readily accessible to the coast, although some of the mountain roads are a little uneven.

West of Málaga, the province's capital which has a population of 400,000, the coast has been commandeered for the benefit of vacationists and there are few peaceful locations. Carvajal, near the fishing village of Los Boliches, still enjoys some serenity; Carteya, a small village with Roman ruins near San Roque, is favoured by some foreigners.

Sotogrande, a luxury urbanisation with golf courses and marina, has been developed over the past two decades. It is easily accessible from Gibraltar.

At Fuengirola, the Municipality has opened a Foreigners' Office in the town hall to assist foreigners in their dealings with local authorities and on tax matters, etc.

Mijas, a popular village 8 km from Fuengirola, was formerly a pretty centre of habitation but has recently been spoilt following exploitation by developers.

Mountain villages of note behind Spain's most popular coastline include Jimena de la Frontera and Casares where many old rural houses have been modernised for permanent living by foreigners. Other places to consider are Benahavís, Istán, Monda, Ojén and Coín which is a market town serving the farming community in the neighbourhood.

During the years of the tourist market's deepest depression in the early 1990s, important centres such as Marbella became somewhat dreary and unkempt, but more recently the municipalities have encouraged huge investments of time and money to improve local facilities and infrastructure. Dubious establishments and areas associated with drugs have been closed down, new shopping centres have been opened, the centre of Marbella now features plenty of flowers and trees, plus controlled car parking areas, and the main coastal carriageway is much safer for pedestrians, with plenty of underpasses to reach the beaches. Furthermore the new motorway to Cadiz, funded by the EC, has done much to reduce heavy lorry traffic in the centre of Marbella and neighbouring towns. So there are now first-class facilities along the coast for residents and visitors.

Costa de la Luz

This little-known territory lies close to Gibraltar and stretches westwards beyond Cadiz to the boundary with Portugal.

Because of the distance from Málaga airport this coast has not really been discovered by the 'international set', although Spaniards from Madrid and elsewhere have enjoyed holidays here for many years. This beautiful coast, washed by the Atlantic, is expected to become more popular for permanent settlement and holidays, as it is very accessible via Gibraltar airport.

Tarifa, on the border of the Costa de la Luz, is the southernmost town in Spain. This residential resort has a population of 21,000 and enjoys excellent views to Africa, just eight miles across the water.

The major city is Cadiz and within easy reach is the nature reserve and national park of Donana, about 76,000 hectares, by the mouth of the river Guadalquivir. Inland is the city of Seville (population 600,000) with its many cultural attractions. It is Spain's only inland port and ships of 15,000 tons can still navigate the Guadalquivir for some 100 km from the estuary to the city.

Between Tarifa and Cadiz, the attractive little coastal village of Zahara de los Atunes, is worth a visit.

Costa Almería and Costa Calida

Almería is a large commercial town (population 200,000) adjacent to a stark hilly hinterland and extensive areas of open land which were formerly unproductive. Because of the warm climate it has recently been possible to produce profitable early vegetable and fruit crops, such as tomatoes, avocados and melons, under plastic sheeting. This produce is transported to England and parts of northern Europe in the winter when crops are not available from other sources.

This prosperity, together with an expanding tourist trade, has attracted investment in residential property, particularly in places such as Mojácar, Adra, Almeriamar, Aguadulce and Roquetas de Mar.

The coast of Murcia province is known as the Costa Calida. The largest town is Cartagena, which has important military and naval installations. It is also a manufacturing and shopping town.

The largest resort is La Manga, a strip of land with the Mediterranean on one side and the Mar Menor, a shallow inland sea, on the other. Highly geared to tourism, this town is very busy in the summer but almost empty for the rest of the year. Further east along the coast are Mazarrón and Aguillas, which have many good beaches.

The town of Murcia is situated in the hills about 32 km from the sea.

Costa Blanca

The exact dimensions of the Costa Blanca are in dispute among experts. Some say the region starts at Denia and continues westwards 480 km as far as Cape Gata, beyond Cartagena. We have described Murcia and Almería under their own headings; so information on the Costa Blanca is confined to the territory from Denia to east of the Mar Menor.

The capital is Alicante, a fine city and harbour with an international airport on its perimeter. It has every possible residential amenity, with a first-class shopping centre, some of Spain's best restaurants, an impressive cathedral, museums, sporting facilities, and a full range of schools; in fact, an ideal place to reside if you want to live amid the hustle and bustle of a big city.

To the east of Alicante the coast is littered with resorts, large and small, where Britons and many other Europeans have taken up residence in large numbers during the past 25 years.

There has been considerable building activity in towns such as Calpe, which has many multi-storey blocks of apartments, Moraira, a pleasant seaside town with a marina where private villas predominate, and Jávea, where there are both luxury villas and multi-storey blocks of apartments, but few new hotels have been constructed, and the town is almost wholly residential.

Other small towns worth considering as the location for a permanent home include Villajoyosa, an ancient port; Altea, where the beaches are mainly pebbles and the old village is reached via 257 steps; Santa Pola, a small port where the restaurants are famed for serving some of the best seafood in the area.

Benidorm, the Blackpool of Spain's southern coast, should be avoided if you are seeking a quiet, peaceful life away from the masses, but it does have two fine sandy beaches.

Inland, Elche is renowned for its thousands of date palms which thrive throughout the city. These grow mainly in groves which are watered by a tenth-century irrigation system.

Locations away from the coast include Jijona, home of Spain's nougat manufacturing industry, Alcoy, where a variety of sweets are made, Guadalest, home of the 'eagle's nest' fortress built by the Moors over a thousand years ago, Jalón, a centre for the wine industry, and Gata, best known for cane and basket work.

Costa del Azahar

The Costa del Azahar has 112 km of coastline stretching from Vinaroz in the north to Almena in the south where it adjoins the province of Valencia. Known as the Orange Blossom Coast, because of the extensive plantations of this delicious fruit, the landscape is quite wild in places. There are many fine sandy beaches and coves, which are particularly safe for bathers and for the enjoyment of many kinds of water-sports. This part of Spain is not well known to international tourists, yet the residential facilities are good so it is an area well worth considering for property purchase.

The main town is Castellon de la Plana, a port and the provincial capital. Other towns of note include Peniscola, Benicasim, Las Fuentes, Almazora, Nules and Chilches. There is an excellent network of roads, and some fine scenery inland.

Costa Dorada

The 'golden coast' includes the provinces of Barcelona and Tarragona. The two main cities after which the provinces were named are substantial industrial and commercial centres with large populations. Resorts include Sitges, Comarruga, Salou, Cambrils, Ampolla and San Carlos de Rapita.

Costa Brava

Just over the border with France the Costa Brava is the nearest coast for motorists from Britain. It can be reached via autoroutes all the way from Calais and is therefore popular with those who do not wish to fly to Spain.

The summer climate is not quite as warm as in the south and winters are generally cooler, but the average number of hours of sunshine in July exceeds 300.

Major resorts include Blanes, Lloret de Mar, Tossa de Mar, San Feliù, Palamos, Llafranch, Aiguablava, Estartit, La Escala, Rosas and Port Bou.

Gerona, the capital of the Costa Brava, is full of monuments to the past, for it was founded at the confluence of the rivers Ter and Onar several centuries BC. Ten bridges and an entire square cross the water and at the centre of the city is the old cathedral which dates back to the eleventh century.

Although there are a number of well-organised holiday resorts with high-rise buildings, the coastline has not been entirely spoilt by the ravages of summer visitors.

To the north of Palamos, there are pleasant small populated areas such as La Foscal, Sa Riera, Sa Tuna and Aiguablava where villas can be found in small numbers, many with sea views.

Just inland, the town of Bagur is endowed with attractive small mansions huddled amid woodland and palm trees. These are owned mainly by wealthy Spanish families from Barcelona and other large cities, who prefer to nurture their families in country surroundings or near the sea rather than burden them with the problems of city living.

Occasionally this type of property comes on the open market to be snapped up by ambitious foreigners who delight in living in an aristocratic style. Prices are high for this type of home.

Also away from the coast are Pals (not to be confused with the beach resort Playa de Pals – 6 km away) and Peratallada, once heavily fortified and where archaeologists unearthed in 1946 an entire Iberian city of the fifth to fourth centuries BC.

Northern Spain

The Cantabrian coast is far less well known to most Europeans compared to the Mediterranean Costas, but it is a region of considerable beauty. All along the coast, which is on the Bay of Biscay, there is an abundance of open green and wooded countryside, with mountains projecting into the sea. There are many fine sandy beaches which alternate with cliffs and a mixture of fishing villages, some of which have yachting harbours. Inland there are some historical villages in the valleys and tiny hamlets amid forests and meadows.

The province of Vizcaya is among the smallest in Spain, but has one of the highest per-capita incomes in the country, emanating from the industrial tradition of the city of Bilbao on the left bank of the River Nervion. Surrounded by mountains, Bilbao was founded around the year 1300; it has grown into a huge industrial complex, yet still has a protected old city where the more important shops are located, also a Gothic cathedral, ancient market and some parks.

To the east of the city, other places of interest include Guernica, the seat of regional authorities and government since the Middle Ages and the fishing villages of Lekeittio and Ondarroa, both of which have fine sandy beaches.

The adjoining province of Guipuzcoa, also to the east, stretches up to the border with France. Its most important town is San Sebastian, a resort of about 170,000 inhabitants, which is very popular with Spanish city dwellers for summer holidays. The modern town has wide boulevards and elegant tree-lined avenues, while the picturesque old quarter is grouped close to the fishing port and River Uremea. Much of the town is near the superb sandy beach of La Concha, which curves elegantly around the bay. San Sebastian is certainly well worth considering as a place of residence for those requiring a home in the north of Spain and there is a good selection of modern and well-established homes for sale.

The Balearic Islands

Majorca

The largest island in this group is Majorca (in Spanish, Mallorca) with an area of 3,640 sq km (1,405 sq miles), about the size of Cornwall. Located in the Mediterranean over 150 km off the Valencia mainland, this island is heavily involved in mass tourism and attracts around 3 million visitors each year.

The majority of facilities and hotels for holiday-makers are located around the bay of Palma in places such as Magaluf, El Arenal, Illetas, Ca'n Pastilla, Palma Nova and Cala Mayor. Many high-rise apartments have been built overlooking the sea between Santa Ponsa and Paguera, while on the east coast much development has taken place at Cala Figuera, Cala d'Or, Porto Cristo, Cala Millor and Cala Bona.

Close to the north-west is a range of hills. The town of Soller is surrounded by citrus fruit groves and almond trees, and Valldemosa is the home of a former Carthusian monastery.

The centre of the island is flat and fertile, with two main towns: Inca, where there is a leather factory, and Manacor, centre of the island's artificial pearl industry.

Pollensa, Alcúdia and Ca'n Picafort in the north are favourite residential districts for foreigners who want to live well away from the centres of intense activity.

Minorca

The second largest island in the group is Minorca, which measures about 50 by 20 km and has a permanent population of 50,000. It is about 40 km from Majorca and is quite different in character. Occupied for long periods by the British in the eighteenth century, the island has many souvenirs of the former garrison, including Georgian architecture and sash windows.

Far less dependent on tourists to earn a living, the islanders manufacture a wide range of leather goods (particularly shoes), distil gin to English recipes and produce fashion goods.

Mahón, the capital, is a tidy town with a main square, several principal streets and a host of narrow lanes. It adjoins a 6 km-long natural harbour, claimed to be the finest deep-water anchorage in the world after Pearl Harbor.

Many new estates have been built in recent years for local people and new residents from Britain and elsewhere. These are mainly located on the south and east coasts at Santo Tomas, Son Bou, Calan Porter, Binibeca, Villa Carlos and El Grao. On the north coast there are settlements at Fornells and Cala Morell.

The main town on the west coast is Ciudadela, the former capital. It has a picturesque harbour. Very little development has taken place in this region and deserted beaches are frequently discovered.

Minorca enjoys a temperate summer climate, but does suffer from cool winds at times during the winter.

Ibiza

The third largest of the Balearic Islands, with an area of 570 sq km, is located about 40 km west of Majorca. It is nearer to the coast of North Africa than to the Catalan city of Barcelona.

A relatively mild climate is enjoyed throughout the year with an average of 300 sunshine days per annum. In the peak summer month of August temperatures reach 26°C, and in the winter the average temperature is 12°C.

Ibiza town, the capital, has a permanent population of 23,000 people. There is a modern town with shops near the harbour, but the fascinating part is Dalt Vila – the old town whose narrow cobbled thoroughfares climb steeply to the summit, where the cathedral and fortress have superb views over the town and across the sea.

The other principal towns are quite small, with populations of around 10,000 people. These comprise San Antonio Abad and Santa Eulalia del Rio. They have both surrendered to tourism and are not ideal for residential purposes. Small resorts which attract prospective home owners include Cala Longa and Roca Lisa.

The Canary Islands

To encourage economic diversification, the Spanish Government has created a Zona Especial (ZEC) for the Canary Islands. This allows considerable tax benefits to those setting up business operations in the islands, including a corporation tax of just 1 per cent for trading companies registered within ZEC.

Tenerife

The largest island is Tenerife which is almost in the centre of this group of seven inhabited islands. A long-time favourite with northern Europeans keen to escape from the winter rigours of their homeland, Tenerife has the highest mountain (Teide) in Spain, a long coastline with sandy beaches in parts and a climate described by some as 'eternal spring'. Average air temperatures range from 16°C, in February to 24°C in August. Most of the rain falls between November and February, but cloud can accumulate over Teide occasionally to hide the sun from towns in the north.

The capital is Santa Cruz, a busy commercial and industrial town, also a port, but not much favoured for property ownership by foreigners.

Puerto de la Cruz on the opposite side of the island has all the facilities desired by vacationists. The lower part of the town adjoins the sea. Sandy beaches are rare but a huge lido has been built on the promenade to accommodate sun and sea enthusiasts. In the higher part of Puerto are some of the best hotels, also apartment blocks, a casino and the Botanical Gardens.

The expatriate community resides mainly on the outskirts and in the nearby Orotava valley where a considerable number of villas have been built among banana plantations and on hillsides.

Some years ago a new international airport was built in the south of the island and to make it accessible a fine new road was constructed.

The improved communications have been largely responsible for an entirely new holiday community built at Playa de las Americas and for the expansion of Los Cristianos village. Huge new hotels and apartment blocks and a yacht marina have been completed. Property prices have increased substantially over the last two years and a studio apartment can now cost around £30,000.

The climate in this corner of Tenerife is warmer than elsewhere and the average number of sunshine hours is greater; hence the popularity with the international community.

Further north-west, on the coast, Los Gigantes and Puerto de Santiago are also expanding.

Gran Canaria

Gran Canaria is well known worldwide because of its capital, Las Palmas, but it is in fact only the third largest of the islands.

Popular with British people in the first third of this century as a place for rest or retirement, the island has not maintained its attractions in post-war years compared with Tenerife. Although a number of holiday packages are offered by tour operators, there is a lack of organisations in Britain selling residential property in Gran Canaria.

With a population totalling over a quarter of a million people, Las Palmas is the largest city in the Canaries. It is a major commercial centre, a seaport and a cosmopolitan resort all at the same time. Major attractions include Santa Catalina Park, described as a huge outdoor café, Las Canteras, a 3 km-long beach of fine sand, the Canary Village featuring local folklore, and the Garden City with palatial residences and more modest houses all set in gardens with colourful blooms all year round.

Like Tenerife, Gran Canaria has some new resorts in the south, such as Playa de San Agustin and Playa del Ingles which are connected with the north by a good road. Tall hotels, blocks of flats, squat villas, pools and self-service food parlours are there in abundance.

A little further west beyond Maspalomas, some urbanisations have been built around Puerto Rico.

Fuerteventura

The second largest island has an area of 2,000 sq km and is growing in popularity with tourists for it offers a variety of sandy beaches.

Of the total population, which is around 20,000 people, over 7,000 reside in the capital, Puerto del Rosario, which is expanding steadily. It enjoys useful facilities and a harbour.

The nearest beach is Playa Blanca which is close to the airport. On the north coast, Corraliejo was a small fishing port, but is growing in popularity because the bleached sand and the azure sea are so inviting for holiday-makers.

The southern strip of the island is known as Jandia. Along both sides of the peninsula are many more beaches.

Lanzarote

This island (800 sq km) has enjoyed boom conditions over the past two decades, with many new developments both private and commercial.

The capital, Arrecife, has only modest attractions but the shopping facilities are adequate and the international airport is nearby.

On the north-west coast, the Fire Mountains are spectacular and reminiscent of a lunar landscape. More than 300 extinct volcanic cones still exist and in parts volcanic fires glow a few feet below the surface.

In the north, the land is sufficiently fertile to grow crops such as onions, tomatoes and vines with the aid of volcanic ash piled around the plants. This absorbs moisture from the night air and supplies water to the plants.

Costa Teguise, a few kilometres north-east of Arrecife, is a large urbanisation owned by an international company which installed all the necessary services and roads some years ago and the land is now being developed, with apartments and villas being built. A nine-hole golf course is in operation and this is irrigated daily with part of the output from a desalination plant.

Only a ten minute drive from the airport is the island's main tourist resort. It has a six kilometre-long sandy beach and a fine range of residential and tourist amenities.

The other islands

In order of size the remaining inhabited islands in the Canaries are as follows:

La Palma

(725 sq km) population 80,000. A green island where a small colony of foreigners have made their home, with a mountain peak nearly 8,000 feet above sea level. Volcanic activity on the southern tip of the island occurred as recently as 1971. The capital and port, Santa Cruz de la Palma, is an attractive, clean place with new offices and flats blending quite well with traditional architecture.

Due to the frequency of bright, clear skies, La Palma has been chosen as the site for the astrophysics complex.

Gomera

(378 sq km). Located offshore from Los Cristianos, the port in the south of Tenerife, Gomera has a peak nearly 5,000 feet above sea level in the centre of the island. The capital, San Sebastian, was the place where Christopher Colombus left the known world in September 1492 on his voyage of discovery to America.

Gomera attracts the attention of the day tourists who come on the car ferry from Tenerife, which takes about 1½ to 2 hours or hydrofoil, which is quicker.

Occupation of residential property by foreigners is gradually taking place.

El Hierro

(277 sq km). This little known island is the most westerly in the Canary Group. It has attractive landscapes, fertile land and tree clad mountains along the peaks of which there are a thousand volcanic craters. The main town is Valverde in the north east corner of the island. Here the irregularity of its landscape creates steep streets and twisting labyrinths of lanes. The green valley from which it gets its name is full of gardens and orchards plus some picturesque country homes. Tourism is still in its infancy.

Inspection flights

As there are frequent charter and scheduled flights, few firms dealing in property in Spain have inspection flights on a regular basis.

Recreation

Spain has been Europe's sunshine playground for many years and so it is hardly surprising that there is a vast range of leisure activities.

Sport is popular in Spain. As well as the traditional bullfight, football and cycling attract a large and enthusiastic following. For some, one of Spain's main attractions is golf; the many courses in such a perfect setting are hugely popular. Also, other facilities such as tennis courts and swimming pools are plentiful. Contrary to many people's image of Spain, there is still a great deal of stunning countryside left, and this encourages many to take up walking and camping.

In contrast, the main resorts and cities provide a large array of entertainment, varying from cinemas, theatres and nightclubs to shops. In parts of the country, the traditional culture is very strong and can be observed in the form of crafts and dancers. Food is also taken very seriously and restaurants are plentiful and good value.

The size and nature of the British expatriate community has encouraged the growth of clubs specifically for them. These include the British Society, the Rotary Club, the British Legion, the British Association of Marbella, the English Speaking Group of Marbella, the International Music Society, theatre groups, clubs for bridge, dancing, gardening and flower arranging, the Malaga Cricket Association, and bowling and numerous golf clubs.

English language television is now available along part of the Costa del Sol in addition to TV from Gibraltar.

Communications

Air

Excellent selection of scheduled flights via Iberia, British Airways and other European airlines, plus a wide range of charter flights at competitive prices.

Rail

The nation is well served by an efficient rail service, and regular trains to and from France make for an adequate international service.

Road

Good trans-Pyrenean road communications have vastly improved the journey by road (via the cross-Channel ferries or Channel Tunnel) from the UK. Now motorways have been constructed in the north and south of the country.

Commuter services in Spain are frequent, if a little crowded.

Sea

There are car ferry services from Portsmouth or Plymouth to Bilbao and Santander using ships of over 30,000 tons.

Driving

There are some good roads in tourist areas and around the large cities, but some of the country and mountain roads are rather primitive. Traffic drives on the right-hand side of the road and passes on the left. All traffic approaching from the right has right of way. The wearing of seat belts is compulsory and those who do not comply will be fined heavily. Third party insurance is compulsory and a Spanish bail bond is advisable, as, if you injure a pedestrian or damage another vehicle, you can be gaoled while the accident is being investigated. You must always carry your driving licence. An international or European driving licence is required.

Driving licences

EU citizens holding a Spanish residence permit, who have an EU Driving Licence issued in their country of origin, can now continue to use this licence when driving a car in Spain, but must take their EU licence to the local Spanish Provincial Traffic Office for vetting and registration. Furthermore they are required to undergo a Spanish medical examination every 10 years, if under the age of 45, every five years if between the ages of 45–70, and annually if over 70 years.

Education

Education is compulsory for children aged 6–16 years. Those who do not obtain a place at secondary school receive youth training.

Health services

In general, public hospitals and medical practices are good although perhaps not quite UK standard. Private health insurance is worth while, to cover such things as post-operative or geriatric care. An agreement with BUPA exists also. A new tax of 4 per cent has been imposed on private medical insurance policies arranged in Spain.

Private medical facilities for the elderly are gradually expanding. For instance, Interpares is a sheltered housing scheme near Malaga, where the residents are mostly over 65 years of age and come from many different countries, yet live together in a friendly community (see pages 121–22).

Climate

Spain's climate varies from the temperate in the north to hot and dry in the south and inland. Those who can, desert Madrid in the hottest months.

| | Madrid | | Barcelona | | Palma | |
	Temperature (°C)	Rainfall (mm)	Temperature (°C)	Rainfall (mm)	Temperature (°C)	Rainfall (mm)
January	−4–14	39	6–13	31	2–18	39
February	−3–17	34	7–14	39	2–19	34
March	0–22	43	9–16	48	3–21	51
April	2–25	48	11–18	43	6–23	32
May	4–29	47	14–21	54	9–27	29
June	9–23	27	14–25	47	13–31	17
July	12–36	11	21–28	27	16–33	3
August	12–35	15	21–28	49	16–33	25
September	8–31	32	19–25	76	14–31	55
October	3–24	53	15–21	86	9–27	77
November	0–18	47	11–16	52	6–22	47
December	−2–14	48	8–13	45	3–19	40

SWITZERLAND

General information

Status

Confederation

Capital

Berne

Area

41,288 sq km (15,945 sq miles)

Population

6,200,000

Location

Latitude 46°N to 47.5°N; longitude 6°E to 10.5°E. Switzerland is situated in the central Alpine region of Europe and borders Italy to the south, Austria and Liechtenstein to the east, Germany to the north and France to the west. The south of the country is dominated by the Alps, which reach an altitude of more than 4000 m, and the north-west by the Jura range. In between this spectacular yet unproductive land lies the hilly 'middle land' where the majority of the towns and villages are situated.

Political stability

There can be little doubt that Switzerland is the most politically stable nation in Europe, if not the world. It is a federal state made up of 26 cantons, which in turn are split into some 3,000 communes. This is the basis of a unique political structure in which direct democracy is paramount. In terms of international relations, Switzerland has remained neutral since the Congress of Vienna in

1815. In economic matters changes may be on the way during the next decade, for the country is currently outside the EU but in EFTA.

Economy

Cost of living

The Swiss franc has dropped considerably in value against sterling and other world currencies during the past three years, but the rate of exchange against sterling is beginning to improve again. Food is expensive when compared with elsewhere but the quality is good. The Swiss are renowned for the production of certain luxury items such as music boxes, lace, chocolates, ladies' fashions and, of course, watches, and while some of these are expensive, they are of the highest quality. Inflation is about 2 per cent, unemployment is around 4 per cent.

Taxation

Tax sovereignty is vested in the Swiss Confederation and in the 26 cantons, all of which grant taxing powers to their communes as well. This means that there are 26 different cantonal tax laws as well as federal tax legislation, and that taxes are levied by three separate authorities: federal, cantonal and communal.

There are no standard rates of income tax or capital tax, as these are normally levied at progressive rates. Federal withholding tax (*impôt anticipé*) and federal stamp duties are levied at flat rates. Taxes from 0.5 per cent per annum of the value of any property owned are payable to the commune, canton and Swiss government. In the Swiss tax system, the accent is on cantonal and communal taxes which form the bulk of the total tax revenue.

VAT is chargeable at two rates: 6.5 and 2 per cent.

Exchange rate

Swiss francs 2.40 = £1.

Exchange control

There are no restrictions on the import and export of currency.

Language

There are four national languages in Switzerland: German, spoken by 65 per cent of the population in northern, eastern and central areas; French, spoken by about 18 per cent mainly in the west; Italian, spoken by about 10 per cent of the population in the southern Alps; Rhaeto-Romanic, spoken by less than 6 per cent in certain villages in the canton of Grisons. Knowledge of English is widespread, especially in the tourist areas.

Expatriate community

A cosmopolitan population is one of the hallmark of Switzerland. About 15 per cent of the total population is made up of foreigners, and the country has been favoured by British expatriates for many years.

Security

All Swiss males are conscripted into the army for military training and so the country has a powerful militia, well able to defend the interests of the federation, should the need arise.

Residence permits

Tourists are not allowed to stay in Switzerland for more than six months in any one year. Residence rights are not granted automatically to those who own property in the country. Applications are considered from those who have adequate finances to support themselves and are of retirement age, having ceased all business activity, or suffer from poor health (needing mountain air). Those who have a job or own their own business in Switzerland are also considered.

Work permit

Before an alien can acquire a work permit, a valid passport, an assurance of a residence permit and an employment contract are required.

Personal effects

No duties are payable.

Housing

At first glance, it may appear that Swiss property prices are very much higher than in comparable countries, but one must not forget that, to the Swiss, it is unthinkable that anything should be built that is not up to the highest standards of quality and craftsmanship. This standard can be recognised in the new chalets and apartments which all have superior finishes, fitted kitchens, sanitaryware, double superior glazing, and joinery work of the best quality. Furthermore they are generally spacious homes compared with those built in some neighbouring countries.

It is attention to detail that leaves nothing to chance. Usually separate laundry rooms and ski stores will be included in the price. Apartment buildings may also contain a sauna or a swimming pool and will usually be managed by a highly efficient concierge.

For many years government policy has been to limit the number of residential properties being purchased by foreigners, in order to protect the interests of their own nationals. In the past each canton has had its own rules, which were changed frequently, often at quite short notice. Now all areas of Switzerland are subject to authorisations for foreigners to buy property and these permits are granted in areas which encourage tourism, such as the larger resorts and nearby villages. Cities such as Geneva, Lucerne, St Gallen etc are completely excluded.

All foreigners are subject to these restrictions except those domiciled in Switzerland and having a Type C residence permit.

Foreigners are not allowed to own more than one property. Husband and wife cannot buy two properties separately, but children aged over 20 have the right to buy one property individually.

There are certain resale restrictions on foreigners who own residential property in Switzerland. For instance, in the canton of Valais foreigners may sell their property immediately to a Swiss national, but must wait for five years to elapse before selling to another foreigner. Properties in the cantons of Vaud and Fribourg may be sold by foreigners to any nationality at any time, while in the German speaking cantons foreigners have to wait 10 years before they are allowed to sell their property. These regulations are changed from time to time, so it is worth checking the current situation before placing an apartment or chalet on the market.

The selection of properties available in some tourist areas varies. Prices range from about £30,000 for a small apartment, while chalets can be purchased from approximately £100,000 depending on location and size. Resale properties are sometimes cheaper than new ones and may include some furniture.

Mortgages are obtainable for up to 80 to 90 per cent, depending on the purchaser's personal circumstances. All mortgages can be paid off in part or in full at any time during the term, without penalty, subject to 6 months' notice.

Buying property

The legal formalities are handled by a public official known as a notary, who acts for both buyer and seller. The notary registers the change of ownership at the Central Land Registry at Berne, which normally approves the transaction within three months on average. Any mortgage arrangements which are required should be made before the authorisation application is made by the notary, as it is entered in the deed of purchase which is ultimately signed by both parties.

The legal fees, taxes and registration fees payable by the purchaser normally total between 2.3 per cent and 5 per cent of the purchase price.

A notary can be granted power of attorney to sign all documents on behalf of the purchaser.

Where to live

Zürich is the largest city with a population of 360,000. It is the main financial centre and one fifth of the country's workforce is employed in the canton.

Inspection flights

Scheduled flights only, not specifically for property inspection.

Communications

Air

Excellent services from Heathrow, Gatwick and Manchester to Basle, Berne, Geneva and Zürich international airports, via Swissair and British Airways. Also reasonably priced economy services (GO and EasyJet) from Luton, Stansted and London City. In the winter there is also a service from Heathrow to Sion. Flying time is between 1½ and 2 hours.

Rail

The Swiss Federal Railway network is about 5,000 km in all, having over 1,800 stations and being fully electrified. The rail service is integrated closely with other modes of transport to provide a close-knit and efficient facility, which includes direct links to international airports, a wide range of postal, coach and boat services, and mountain railways and cable cars. All this means that the internal communications network in Switzerland is of the highest standard.

Road

The network is about 69,000 km long, with the national motorways stretching to about 1,800 km.

Recreation

The Swiss environment is ideally suited to the pursuit of a number of outdoor activities. Obviously, the Alpine regions have some of the finest winter sports facilities in the world, including skiing, skating and curling. The mountainous environment provides wonderful climbing, and hiking and camping are also very popular. The Swiss life-style necessitates quality facilities and so tennis courts, swimming pools and golf courses exist in abundance. The Swiss lakes provide plenty of opportunity for water sports and fishing.

Some of the most popular areas of Switzerland are the health resorts and spas. The clean air and pleasant climate make spas a blessing both for the sick and for those merely seeking relaxation.

Nor is the cultural side of Swiss life lacking in any way. Music and theatre are thriving, the successes ranging from traditional yodelling to modern jazz concerts. Also, throughout the year, many festivals and celebrations occur based primarily on old folk traditions. All this, combined with fine examples of art and architecture in the larger towns, makes Switzerland an enjoyable and fulfilling place.

There is no lack of good restaurants offering exemplary cuisine of many different types. Traditional Swiss food is not of any distinct type, but eating houses do specialise in the local delicacy.

Driving

The rules of the road differ little in Switzerland from elsewhere in mainland Europe. The minimum age for driving is 18 years. Drivers and front seat passengers must wear seat belts and children under 12 must travel in the rear of the car. Vehicle lights in heavy rain must be switched on, and dipped headlights are compulsory in road tunnels. All laws concerning speed, lights and seat belts are strictly enforced by the police, who are authorised to collect fines on the spot.

Health services

Health insurance is not compulsory, but as there is no national health scheme it is advisable, as treatment may be expensive. Such insurance is necessary for all members of the family and not just the breadwinner or head of the house.

A social security agreement does exist between the DSS and the Swiss authorities and details are given in DSS pamphlet SA6.

Climate

The climatic conditions of Switzerland vary considerably and perhaps no country in Europe combines within so small an area such marked climatic contrasts. In the northern plateau, surrounded by mountains, the climate is mild and refreshing. South of the Alps the climate is warmer, coming as it does under the influence of Mediterranean weather. The Valais area is noted for its dryness. Summer brings warm weather but at high altitudes it is often quite cold at night.

	Geneva			*Zürich*		
	Average temp (°C)	*Average ppt (mm)*	*Sun (hours)*	*Average temp (°C)*	*Average ppt (mm)*	*Sun (hours)*
January	3	60	54	2	66	46
February	4	57	98	4	60	79
March	8	66	149	8	69	149
April	12	63	206	12	90	173
May	17	69	243	18	114	207
June	21	87	269	21	150	220
July	22	72	297	22	150	238
August	22	105	266	22	141	219
September	18	99	198	18	165	166
October	13	87	131	13	81	108
November	6	93	61	6	72	51
December	4	81	44	2	72	37

temp = temperature
ppt = precipitation

TURKEY

General information

Status

Republic

Capital

Ankara

Area

780,000 sq km (296,380 sq miles)

Population

60 million

Location

Latitude 36°N to 42°N; longitude 26°E to 44°E. Turkey stands both in Europe and Asia, so it has two cultures. To the west of the Bosphorus, which connects the Black Sea and the Aegean, is the European part; to the east, Asian Turkey comprises much high table land and mountains. Ankara is in the centre of the Anatolian peninsula in Asia, while Istanbul, the largest city, is in Europe and has suburbs in Asia.

Political stability

Surrounded by Russia, Iran, Iraq, Syria and Greece and having occupied northern Cyprus illegally since 1974, Turkey remains an important bridge between eastern and western continents. Increasing links with the west, associate membership of the EU, membership of NATO and the Council of Europe, combined with expanding tourism, should help to increase stability.

However, a campaign against tourism by Kurdish groups has resulted in attacks on tourists in parts of Turkey. As a result the

British Foreign Office has advised citizens to avoid travelling in south-east Turkey if possible, until the security situation improves.

Economy

Inflation and the constant depreciation of the Turkish lira against many international currencies is of considerable concern. In the summer of 1999 the pound sterling purchased around 626,110 Turkish lira, compared with under 400,000 at the same period a year earlier.

Taxation

There is a double taxation agreement with the UK. Income tax ranges between 25 and 55 per cent. VAT is 15 per cent, but subject to change on luxury items.

Exchange control

In operation in a limited way.

Language

The Turkish language belongs to the Ural-Altaic group and is spoken by about 150 million people in the world. It is written in Latin characters. More and more Turks, especially among the young generation, are studying foreign languages. Turks who have daily contact with foreigners (in shops, hotels, hospitals etc) know at least one of the major European languages.

Expatriate community

The expatriate community is gradually expanding and a number of British citizens now own holiday or retirement homes.

Residence permits

Applications for residence permits should be made to the local Foreign Affairs Division of the Security Department of the Ministry of Internal Affairs.

Work permits

Applications should be made to the Under-Secretariat of the Treasury for the General Directorate of Foreign Investment by the company for whom the employee will work.

Personal effects

No duties are payable on personal effects imported by permanent residents but may be charged on electronic goods.

Housing

There are a few estate agents in the UK who market homes in Turkey. Information may also be obtained from the Turkish Tourist Office or from a personal visit to Turkey.

Buying property

The Turkish Civil Code requires that the sale transaction for residential property must be signed at the Land Registry where the property exists. The Registrar then issues the title deeds showing the property is registered in the name of the purchaser. A UK lawyer should be brought into the transaction who could instruct an associate Turkish lawyer to enable documentation to be signed by virtue of a Power of Attorney, prepared by the lawyer. The assistance of a lawyer at every stage is vital, because any deficiency in the procedure causes serious consequences. On signing a purchase contract, a deposit is paid and the balance is due on completion. Mortgages can be arranged to purchase property in Turkey. According to the Law of Village and Law of Military Forbidden Zones and Security Zones, foreign citizens may not own immovable properties in some villages, military and security zones. It is important to ensure that the property being purchased is not in such a village or zone, at a very early stage.

The amount of dues and taxes payable is 4.8 per cent of the amount declared to the Land Registry from both buyer and seller. It is the practice in Turkey (as in some other European countries), to underdeclare the purchase price, but legal advice should be sought before the underdeclaration is formalised. Notary fees are between 0.7 and 1.4 per cent. The annual property tax is generally 0.4 per cent of the declared value.

With the Turkish lira substantially depreciated, property prices seem to be reasonable. For example it is possible to buy new two-bedroom villas at Yalikavak with shared pools on the Bodrum Peninsula at prices from £55,000 to £69,000.

Where to live

Although Turkey has a wide variety of environments and cultures, Europeans seem to prefer to live in resorts on the Aegean and Mediterranean coasts. Among the most popular towns with British people are Antalya, Bodrum and Izmir.

Antalya is located on what is known as the Turquoise Coast, so named because of the alleged colour of the sea in this area, where swimming is possible almost all the year. The coastline has many attractive beaches, yet in places the mountains tumble straight into the sea. Wet winters and hot summers encourage the growth of a wide variety of Mediterranean plants. Banana plantations, citrus groves and ornamental palms are also found in abundance.

Antalya, which enjoys spectacular views over the Bey Mountains, is an ancient town with a history which goes back to the second century BC. It has many historic buildings, but now most of the 200,000 inhabitants live in modern apartment blocks. However, the old town has been successfully restored, and there is a yacht marina for boating enthusiasts.

About 290 km further west, opposite the Greek island of Kos, lies the expanding resort of Bodrum, which is quite well known to British tourists. Again the town's origins date back thousands of years and there are some impressive monuments to the past including a fine amphitheatre and a castle. Today this is a prosperous town with a yacht marina, extensive shopping facilities and some pleasant beaches. The town centre is well built up, but there are numerous villages along the coast of the peninsula where there are new developments of homes and other residential amenities.

Izmir is Turkey's third largest town, having over 2 million inhabitants and being the second port after Istanbul, so it is a place of importance. Much of the town centre is relatively modern, for a horrific fire destroyed the heart of Izmir in 1922 and there is little of historic interest in the central area. Modern buildings and large new apartment blocks abound and there is a good shopping area, some excellent hotels and a wide range of restaurants.

Inspection flights

These are arranged individually by selling agents.

Recreation

There is a wide variety of pursuits available in Turkey including yachting, hunting and fishing, skiing and mountaineering, as well as sampling the different cultures. The traditions (both religious and folk) and a rich heritage of monuments and museums are of interest. Shopping in the markets and bazaars is also very popular, where traditional crafts such as carpets, ceramics, copper and brassware can be purchased.

Communications

Air

Regular flights to Istanbul and Ankara by Turkish Airlines and British Airways, which take about 4 hours. A new airport at Bodrum is now open.

Sea

Passenger services from Italy, Greece and Cyprus.

Road

From London, Istanbul is about 3000 km. The journey can be made either all the way by road or part way by car ferry from Italy.

Telephone, postal and broadcasting facilities are adequate and western newspapers are available daily.

Driving

Vehicles can be brought into Turkey for up to three months by registering them on the owner's passport.

Speed limits are enforced at 50 km/h in built-up areas and 90 km/h elsewhere.

Health services

Many Turkish doctors and dentists have received training abroad and do command a foreign language. There are also some foreign operated hospitals in Istanbul.

A social security agreement between the UK and Turkey exists to protect entitlement to benefits, details of which are available in the Contributions Agency's pamphlet SA22.

Climate

	January	*April*	*July*	*October*
		Temperature (°C)		
Marmara region	7	16	28	19
Aegean region	9	20	30	21
Mediterranean	11	22	32	23
Black Sea region	8	16	27	18
Central Anatolia	4	15	30	18
Eastern Anatolia	–9	6	20	12

$\boxed{23}$ Countries Across the Oceans

AUSTRALIA

General information

Status

Independent state

Capital

Canberra

Area

7,686,884 sq km (2,967,909 sq miles)

Population

Approximately 18.6 million

Location

Latitude 10°S to 43°S; longitude 113°E to 153°E. Australia is the only continent entirely occupied by one nation with one central government. It is the world's smallest continent in both population and size (except Antarctica) although it is 25 times larger than Great Britain. It is also the most remote continent, which has meant that the flora and fauna have developed in a unique way.

Political stability

The method of government is based on the British parliamentary system. There are three tiers of administration: Commonwealth, state and local government. Voting for those of age is compulsory for both federal and state elections.

Important factors of Australian heritage are a democratic government, a free press, respect for individuals and an independent judiciary.

Constitutional links are still maintained with Britain and allegiance is given to Queen Elizabeth II, who is formally Queen of Australia, but Australia may be declared a republic within a few years.

Economy

Food and meals in restaurants in the big cities tend to be a little more expensive than in the UK, but a bit cheaper in the more rural districts. Clothes, shoes, furniture and large household equipment are generally more expensive, but the depreciated value of the Australian dollar against the pound sterling will benefit visitors in certain ways.

Inflation reached a low point at just under two per cent during the final months of 1998 and it will probably hover around two to three per cent in 1999. Unemployment is still high in some areas and on a national level averages over 8 per cent of the working population. It is not expected to drop much below 8 per cent in the foreseeable future.

The Olympic Games are to be held in Sydney in the year 2000 and there is a building boom in the city preparing for the great event. Tourism is expanding rapidly and may exceed two million visitors by the turn of the century. In spite of the problems in Asia, Australia looks to the future with a strong economy and low inflation. Revenue from tourism is expected to reach A$22 billion a year by the turn of the century.

Taxation

Taxes are levied at Federal and local government levels. Other taxes such as on petrol, stamp duty and payroll taxes are levied by state governments, while local governments/councils receive the real estate taxes. Income Tax is one of the chief sources of revenue. This is collected under a PAYE scheme from salary and wage earners.

A self-assessment system generally applies. On incomes between A$1 and A$5,400 the tax rate is nil. Between A$5,401 and A$20,700 the marginal tax rate is 20 per cent. There are three further tax rates – 34 per cent between A$20,701 and A$38,000 – 43 per cent between A$38,001 and A$50,000 – over A$50,000 the marginal tax rate is 47 per cent. These rates exclude the Medicare levy of 1.5 per cent. Under the Government's Family Tax Initiative, assistance is provided to families with at least one child. These provide increases in tax free thresholds and further assistance is provided to single income families, including sole parents.

The tax year runs from 1 July to 30 June each year and returns have to be submitted to the tax office by 31 October. Every resident must have a tax file number. There is a double taxation agreement with Britain.

There is a sales tax on many goods. Other taxes include capital gains (the taxpayer's principal residence is usually exempt) and fringe benefits tax, payable by employers on items such as company cars used for private purposes, and low interest loans, etc.

There is a wide range of Social Security benefits available.

Exchange rate

Australian dollars (A$) 2.40 = £1.

Exchange control

There are no restrictions on currency imports.

Language

English is spoken everywhere, with some local variations on pronunciation and phrases.

Expatriate community

Since the Second World War, about 5.7 million migrants from over 120 countries have settled in Australia. After New Zealand Britain remains the largest source of immigrants (mainly because of the Commonwealth connection) but there have been substantial arrivals from China, South Africa, Bosnia and the Far East.

Citizens' rights

After a period of two years' permanent residence migrants can, if they wish, become Australian citizens, whereupon they must enrol as electors and vote in elections. They may apply for an Australian passport, register as an Australian citizen any child born abroad and will have the right to be protected overseas under Australian diplomatic arrangements. Furthermore, they have the right to stand for parliament, apply for appointment to a public office and to enlist in defence forces and government jobs requiring citizenship.

Security

In international relations, Australia's geographical position helps to make it one of the most secure of nations. Nevertheless, a powerful military force is ready to repel any potential aggressors. Internally, Australia faces problems typical of an advanced capitalist nation, with one especially worrying aspect being the menace of drugs.

Residence permits

For many years the Australian Government has encouraged migrants from various parts of the world and in 1998/99 the published migration programme totals 68,000 new permanent residents (excluding those admitted under the humanitarian programme), which is the same figure as in the previous year. There is special emphasis on the family stream, those with selected skills (IT skills are in great demand), business skills and independents.

In a recent report it was stated that at the beginning of 1999 there was a high level of job optimism, with more job vacancies in New

South Wales and Western Australia than in any year since 1995. However, new migrants still have to fulfil the strict requirements imposed on them by the Australian Department of Immigration.

In recent years there has been much tinkering with the rules and regulations affecting the emigration policy and in the main the winners have been educated young skilled migrants in professions and jobs where there are vacancies in Australia.

A points system is operated to decide if an individual or family is eligible for emigration under the Skilled Australia Linked visa class applicants and Independent migrants. Points are awarded under headings such as age, skills and qualifications, language (ability to communicate effectively in English), family relationship, citizenship, sponsor and location factor. The total points to qualify does vary from time to time. Health and character tests are also required.

New Zealanders are the only citizens who can work and live in Australia without the approval of the immigration authorities, and the numbers doing so have more than doubled over the past decade.

After New Zealand, the UK provides a greater number of migrants than any other country. Application for migration kits with full details are obtainable from the Australian High Commission Offices, Australia House, Strand, London WC2. Quite substantial non-returnable Visa application fees are charged by the Australian Government.

More business migrants are being sought from around the world. These will mainly comprise the owners of successful small business, who can transfer their skills to Australia and establish new firms capable of employing local people. There is an application fee of £1,230 for business skills migration.

Young people between the ages of 18 and 30, who hold a British, Irish, Dutch or Canadian passport and who live in the UK or Ireland can obtain a once-only Working Holiday Visa at a cost of £60. This allows them to remain in Australia for a maximum of one year and they are expected to be able to prove that they have sufficient funds to support themselves during this period. They are allowed to take temporary jobs to supplement their funds and can travel extensively in Australia during their stay. The AUSWAT (Australia Work & Travel) Organisation has been established to assist these young people. The services they offer (for a fee of £295) include assistance with obtaining the necessary visa, pre-departure information, a meet and greet service at Sydney and 3 night's hostel accommodation on arrival, a job directory listing employers willing to offer temporary jobs to participants, budget flight information, a postal address for incoming mail and 24-hour emergency support while in Australia. Full details about AUSWAT can be obtained by telephoning 0171 478 2022.

Work permits

On applying to the Australian Consulate, details of work skills and professional experience are required so that it may be decided whether the immigrant's skill is of use to Australia.

Visa applications for vacations

Except for citizens of Australia and New Zealand, everyone requires an entry visa for holidays and short stays of up to three months. These are now much easier to obtain via the newly introduced Electronic Travel Authority which can be issued by Travel Agents and certain airlines.

Personal effects

Personal effects and household goods owned for at least one year may be imported free of duty.

Housing

About 70 per cent of all homes in Australia are owner-occupied. The average design is often single-storey with three bedrooms. Construction is generally brick, weatherboard, fibre cement or brick veneer. The last-mentioned is most popular and has an inner frame structure of timber lined with plasterboard. This is ideal for the Australian climate and costs less than a full brick home. Prices vary substantially in different parts of the country and are beginning to rise, but are lower than for similar homes in Britain.

Three bedrooms, lounge/dining room, kitchen, bathroom, toilet and laundry room is an average house in Australia. The term 'home units' is commonly used to describe apartments, where the purchaser can obtain the equivalent of a freehold title. They are found mainly in the inner-city areas, where sites are scarce and expensive.

New house prices vary considerably in different parts of the country. For example, Sydney is heavily developed, so most new homes are being built in the outer metropolitan areas, where three-bedroom brick-veneer houses including land cost around £73,000 and four-bedroom homes from about £120,000. In Melbourne, three-bedroom brick-veneer houses range from £52,000. In Brisbane, from £75,000 is the price range for a four-bedroom lowset brick-veneer unit with concrete tile roof and car port. In a beachside suburb of Adelaide, about £50,000 is required for a three-bedroom brick house. In Perth a four-bedroom unit can be acquired for £58,000. Finally, at Canberra the cost of a new three-bedroom house is from £50,000. Apartments are available in some towns and cities at lower prices.

The Financial & Migrant Information Service of the Commonwealth Bank of Australia, 85 Queen Victoria Street, London EC4V 4HD, produces an excellent cost of living and housing survey every year.

Banks, building societies and government housing authorities provide the bulk of housing finance. Purchasers are expected to have a deposit of about 20 per cent of the purchase price. Total repayments are normally limited to about 30 per cent of the applicant's combined annual gross basic income. Interest rates are approximately 6.25–6.80 per cent and the maximum term is 30 years.

Stamp duty varies between states. First-time buyers purchasing a property costing about £75,000 pay 2.5 per cent in Sydney, 3.5 per cent in Melbourne and about 2.3 per cent in Perth, 2.6 per cent in Brisbane, 3.2 per cent in Adelaide and 2.5 per cent in Canberra. Legal fees also vary from one part of the country to another, but are generally around 1 to 2 per cent.

Many families living in the cities have a second home in the country or by the sea for holidays and weekends.

Education

Except at private establishments, tuition fees are not charged at primary or high schools, but parents are expected to pay for certain items including uniforms, fares, textbooks and writing materials, arts and crafts materials, library and sports facilities and excursions. At primary level, which is co-educational, schooling generally lasts six or seven years.

Where to live

In such an enormous continent, the choice of residential zones is vast. The suburbs of Sydney, New South Wales, are an excellent base for permanent residents, for the comprehensive facilities of the cosmopolitan city are close at hand. Brisbane's Gold Coast in Queensland is popular for retirement and holidays, while Melbourne, Victoria, has its devotees who seek a more traditional way of life. The coastal cities in the south are popular with expatriates from Europe. Adelaide has a population of over 1 million – about 85 per cent of the state population.

Animals

An import permit must be obtained in advance of shipment for cats and dogs. This costs £20 and takes up to four weeks to obtain. Applications are made to the Australian Quarantine Inspection Service in the destination state. An Export Health Certificate has to be obtained from an approved veterinary surgeon before shipment and the animals are inspected at Heathrow airport by an Australian approved vet and then sealed in kennels before dispatch. All cats and dogs must have up-to-date vaccinations and on arrival they are placed in quarantine for 30 days.

Inspection flights

None, but flights from the UK can now be purchased for about £460 during the off-peak season.

Communications

Transport and communications present enormous challenges for Australia because of the vastness of the country and the sparse population in most inland areas.

Air

Twenty-seven international airlines including Qantas, the national airline, operate to and from Australia. Domestic airlines carry over 10 million passengers a year. Regular charter flights from London offer lower fares than schedule services.

Rail

The railways are mainly government owned and operated. Much of the 39,000 km of track is used by freight, but over 300 million passenger journeys are also made, mostly on the frequent and cheap commuter lines.

Road

There are over 822,000 km of road in Australia, used by more than 3.6 million motor vehicles. The trans-continental routes are used especially by the trucking industry but most towns and cities have excellent networks that are heavily used by commuters each morning and evening.

Telecommunications

The established postal, telephone and fax systems make use of the most modern equipment and are generally very good for such a large country so isolated from the rest of the world.

Recreation

About 6 million Australians take part in sport, which includes tennis, cricket, surfing, the various forms of football and swimming, and a wide range of newer sports which are rapidly increasing in popularity. Recent Australian successes, especially in sailing, golf, squash and cricket, have prompted a surge in the popularity of these sports.

The climate lends itself to the pursuit of many outdoor activities including bushwalking, fishing and boating. The fine beaches, wondrous underwater scenery and ideal coastal waters are also a rich source of pleasure.

Club life, run by sporting or social organisations, forms the main source of nightlife. Membership entitles one to use the sports facilities, too. Bars are usually male preserves, with heavy drinking taking precedence.

Entertainment and cultural pastimes are good. The theatre and especially the cinema have gained international reputations. Television includes home-produced 'soaps', many of which are seen in the UK, and also British 'serials' including *Coronation Street*. Sydney Opera House and Australian opera singers are world famous.

Driving

Short-term visitors may drive on a British licence or international driving permit, but long-term or new residents must take another test soon after arrival. Regulations for the driving test vary slightly from state to state as do the regulations on vehicle safety and speed limits. Details are obtainable from the Agent General's Office.

Health and social security services

The Medicare Health Scheme guarantees all Australians 85 per cent of their medical costs, as well as access without charge to any public hospital in-patient and out-patient facility. The scheme is financed by a 1.5 per cent levy (recently increased to 2.5 per cent for families without private health insurance, who are earning over A$100,000 per annum). Short-term visitors have to pay the full cost of treatment and private cover is strongly advised. Pharmaceutical charges are being increased to A$20 per prescription, but there are reduced rates for pensioners, etc.

Australia claims to have one of the best social security payment systems in the world. Most people can claim some sort of payment from the Government, even those in full-time employment, especially if they have children. In addition to family payments, other allowances include pensions of various sorts, bereavement allowance and those out of work can get a jobsearch or newstart allowance, providing they are actively looking for work. There are also sickness, mature age and widow allowances, plus rent assistance. Newly arrived migrants normally have to wait about six months before claiming any allowances, but this may be extended to two years in the future.

Climate

Australia's climate ranges from tropical in the north to temperate in the south. The surrounding oceans moderate the extremes of climate, giving the coastal areas a very pleasant weather pattern. It is important to remember that summer lasts from December to February and winter from June to August.

	Average daily sunshine (hrs)	*Annual ppt (mm)*	*Average temp for hottest month (°C)*	*Average temp for coolest month (°C)*
Adelaide	6.9	531	23.0	11.1
Brisbane	7.5	1,157	25.0	14.9
Canberra	7.2	639	20.3	5.4
Darwin	8.5	1,536	29.6	25.1
Hobart	5.9	633	16.7	7.9
Melbourne	5.7	661	19.9	9.5
Perth	7.9	879	23.7	13.2
Sydney	6.7	1,215	22.0	11.8

temp = temperature
ppt = precipitation

CANADA

General information

Status

Commonwealth nation

Capital

Ottawa

Area

10,010,000 sq km (3,850,000 sq miles)

Population

25,354,064

Location

Latitude 48°N to 70°N; longitude 60°W to 140°W. Canada, with the longest coastline in the world, is about the same size as the whole of Europe and is the second largest country in the world. In this vast area are some of the world's largest lakes, huge prairies, massive mountain ranges and broad expanses of tundra. The north of the country is very cold as it stretches right up to and beyond the Arctic Circle. The majority of the population live within 500 km of the border with the United States.

Political stability

By many people, Canada is regarded as the epitome of a stable and strong democracy, with a well-developed party political system. A poll among readers of a Canadian magazine found that despite their varied backgrounds, Canadians are generally a happy lot, quite optimistic about their future and largely in agreement on a number of fundamental issues. According to a United Nations report, Canada is among the best countries in the world in which to live. From personal experience this does seem to be true. The country plays a leading role in world affairs and is a well respected member of the Western Alliance.

The thorny problem of independence for Quebec desired by French-speaking Canadians who feel their culture is being forgotten by the English speaking majority, is still unresolved. A second referendum on the subject in 1995 was marginally rejected and it seems that some voters have grown tired of the issue.

The vast majority of citizens now seem to prefer that the country's leaders should reach a sensible understanding with the faction, whereby Quebec should retain its unique character, while maintaining the equality of the 10 provinces of the country.

Economy

Cost of living

As one of the most financially stable countries in the world, Canada enjoys high standards of living for most sectors of the population. Wages are substantial and inflation is minimal. Living costs are about the same as in the UK, but heavy fuel bills in the winter must be expected. Gross domestic product is increasing, but is still below the figure achieved in the summer of 1998, and slower consumer spending is likely to weaken growth in 1999.

Taxation

Under the Canadian taxation system individuals are taxed on a calendar year with returns due by 30 April in the following year.

Residents are taxed on their world-wide income, non-residents on income from Canadian sources. There is a double tax agreement between Canada and the UK.

For those in employment, a 'tax deduction at source' system operates for income tax and employers issue a T4 form by the end of February each year indicating the previous year's tax deductions, pension contributions and unemployment insurance. Taxation is levied at both Federal and Provincial level. Income tax at Federal level ranges from 17 per cent up to an income of $29,590; 26

per cent from $29,591 to $59,180 and 29 per cent over $59,180. These figures operate after each individual's personal allowance has been taken into account.

Tax deductions are also granted for charitable donations, tuition, medical expenses, childcare expenses, union dues, old age, disability, dependents and married status.

There is a capital gains tax, but not normally on the sale of a principal residence. There are no wealth, inheritance, gift, estate or succession taxes. Provincial taxes vary from one area to another.

Exchange rate

Canadian dollars (C$) 2.30 = £1.

Exchange control

There are no restrictions on the export or import of currency from or into Canada.

Language

The existence of two major linguistic groups is one of the features that helps to give Canada its unique character. English and French are both official languages and enjoy equal status, and the latest statistics show that nationally over 16 per cent of the population are fluent in both languages. Owing to the increased number of Asian immigrants, Chinese is the country's third most used language.

Expatriate community

The population consists of people from a variety of cultures and traditions but many Canadians trace their origins back to French and Anglo-Saxon ancestors. Integration is encouraged but cultural traditions are still strong.

Security

Canada is rightly regarded as being free of any major internal problems that threaten security. In any case, the military and the police force are well trained and equipped. Therefore, apart from such common 20th-century problems as are experienced throughout the Western world, Canada can be said to be secure.

Residence permits

The World Bank lists Canada as among the top five countries in the world taking into account natural resources, infrastructure, physical capital and human resources. It is not surprising, therefore, that there is a considerable demand for immigration and residence permits from inhabitants of less fortunate countries.

For many years Canada has had an on-going immigration policy and this is likely to continue. Indeed The Minister of Citizenship & Immigration, Lucienne Robillard, stated recently: 'Immigration has always been a source of economic and social strength for Canada. It will continue to be vital to the future of our country. In addition to their hopes and dreams, immigrants bring with them rich human experience, expertise and initiative, as well as willingness to help us build a stronger Canada, for ourselves and our children.' The plan for 1998 was to admit up to about 225,000 newcomers, which is about 1 per cent of the population. The three main categories for newcomers were:

1. Independent immigrants, who are mainly skilled workers likely to contribute to the country's economy and migrants with sufficient funds to establish a successful business. The target was about 140,000 in this category.
2. The family reunification class (about 55,000 in 1998), comprising people sponsored by a close family relative.
3. Refugees or others who can prove a fear of persecution in their native country. The target here was about 30,000 immigrants.

For those wishing to work, a points system is operated and an Occupations list is regularly published by the Government showing the number of points currently available for each type of job. Points are also awarded for age, education, vocational training, ability to speak good English or French. Good character and good health are also important. It is necessary to produce evidence that the applicant has no criminal history and a medical examination must be passed. All applications must be submitted for consideration by the Office of the Canadian High Commission in the applicant's home country.

Work permits

People who wish to work in Canada must obtain authorisation from a Canadian immigration office.

Personal effects

Provided they are kept for a minimum of one year after arrival, most personal effects may be imported into Canada without incurring any duty.

Housing

Migrants frequently lease houses or apartments when they first arrive and there is usually a reasonable availability in this category. Condominiums (flats or terraced houses) are popular for renting, but community charges also have to be paid each month. Many homes have below-ground basements for storage and are generally two storeys high.

The costs of average size family homes vary very much in this vast country. Prices are lower in the more rural provinces and peak in the major cities. A survey of house prices by Royal Le Page disclosed the following price comparisons: Toronto £94,000; Hamilton £68,000; Ottawa £70,000; Montreal £53,000; Calgary £61,300; Edmonton £51,000; Winnipeg £41,000; Regina £34,700 and Vancouver £145,300.

For most larger cities, information is readily available through real estate agents and periodicals. In Toronto for example a free-distribution magazine entitled *New Homes and Condos For Sale* contains many pages of new housing developments in and around the city. It divides southern Ontario into four regions for listing purposes and includes useful maps. All prices quoted are approximate due to fluctuating exchange rates. Mortgage interest rates are around 7 per cent. Maximum advances are generally 90 per cent of the purchase price and these generally require payment of an insurance premium of up to 2.5 per cent of the amount borrowed, which is added to the loan. Advances of 75 per cent or less do not require payment of the premium.

There are no restrictions on migrants buying residential property.

Education

There is no single national system as each province is responsible for its own arrangements. The main difference between the UK and Canadian system is that each student accumulates credits in a grading system which remains with them throughout their school career. Basic education is mainly co-educational, and is compulsory from ages 6 to 16 years and free in public elementary and secondary schools. Some pre-school facilities are available for 4- and 5-year-olds. There are alternative forms of higher education to the university system at the age of 18 plus.

Buying property

Legal fees charged by lawyers range from 0.75 to 1 per cent of the purchase price, but some lawyers who specialise in house conveyancing charge a flat fee of around £150, plus disbursements for title searches and other expenses, amounting to about 1.5 per cent.

A local transfer tax is assessed in most provinces when a property changes hands. This is usually less than 1 per cent of the purchase price.

Mortgages are generally arranged through banks, trust or insurance companies and credit unions. They normally require an up-to-date survey report on the property to be submitted with applications for home loans.

Where to live

The British will probably prefer the milder coastal climates. The bitterly cold winters in the middle of the country make first-floor access to houses essential because of the deep snow. Therefore Vancouver is very popular in the west, together with Montreal and Toronto in the east. In the national parks ownership of residential property is restricted to those in essential local employment.

Communications
Air

In such a vast country, effective air communications are vital. Therefore, the 61 airports in Canada are kept very busy by international flights, internal passenger flights and other varied services such as crop dusting, forest fire patrol, pipeline inspection and aerial surveying. Over 8 million people travel every year on international air services and over 20 million on domestic flights.

Rail

The railways have played an important role in the development of Canada. Today, two continent-wide lines, Canadian National and Canadian Pacific, span the country. They are used especially for the transportation of large quantities of goods. Smaller railway operations run on a provincial basis.

Road

About 14 million vehicles use Canada's excellent road network.

Water

As Canada has some of the world's largest lakes and is dominated in the east by the St Lawrence Seaway, communications on the water form an integral part of Canada's transport network.

Telecommunications

The Canadian telecommunications network is vast and is regarded as being one of the most efficient in the world.

Recreation

Canadians spend about 20 per cent of their income on leisure activities, so recreation obviously forms an important part of their life.

With four distinct seasons, the choice of outdoor activity is wide. In winter, there are opportunities for ice hockey, skating, tobogganing and skiing. The summer months can be occupied by playing tennis, swimming, golf, cycling and jogging. Spectator sports include hockey, ice hockey and baseball.

Canada's major cities have theatres, cinemas and concert halls. Smaller communities participate in amateur theatricals, annual fairs, folk music and handicraft exhibitions. In terms of history Canada does not have many monuments to a glorious past, but the Indian cultures and 'gold rush' memorabilia provide a source of great interest.

The greatest single asset in Canada is the stunning environment. The vast countryside provides an idyllic setting for pursuits such as walking, cycling, hunting, fishing, canoeing and camping.

Driving

Driving is on the right.

Health service

Responsibility for health and welfare is distributed between federal and provincial governments, who administer the services, which are paid for by National Insurance contributions. The cost of medical and hospital treatment is high, but a government-sponsored insurance plan is available (details vary from province to province). However, dental and drug prescriptions are not normally covered by the schemes. Private health insurance is an option and is tax deductible.

A wide range of social services and benefits is available (family allowance and pensions) and details of rights as an immigrant can be obtained from the DSS (pamphlet SA20).

Climate

Being such a vast country it is impossible to categorise the climate; it varies greatly, from tundra to cool temperate, from snow-covered peaks to windy dry prairies, from climates that vary little during the year to those susceptible to great extremes without warning. Between November and April the temperature can fall as low as minus 30°C.

Average mid-summer temperatures (°C)

Quebec City (Quebec)	18.1–25.8
Ottawa (Ontario)	12.6–25.3
Vancouver (BC)	20.9–22.5
Montreal (Quebec)	20.9–26.4
Toronto (Ontario)	23.6–28.1
Calgary (Alberta)	19.8–25.8

NEW ZEALAND

General information

Status

Commonwealth nation

Capital

Wellington

Area

269,800 sq km (103,736 sq miles)

Population

3,435,000, comprising 2,553,000 in North Island and 882,000 in South Island

Location

Latitude 35°S to 46°S; longitude 167°E to 178°E, New Zealand is located in the southern Pacific across the Tasman Sea from Australia, which is about 2,200km to the east. It comprises two main islands (North and South), which differ considerably, in character, geology, vegetation and climate, and a number of smaller islands scattered over a wide area. Approximately 75 per cent of the inhabitants reside in the North Island, especially along the fertile coast and on the plains. The major cities are on the North Island and include the ever expanding Auckland, which is built around two harbours and has a population of around one million people. The capital is Wellington, which is also built around a fine harbour and is known as 'the windy city' (population about 330,000). It is located at the opposite end of the North Island. The largest inland city is Hamilton (population 153,000) which is in the centre of the North Island. Adjoining one of the richest pastoral regions in the world, Hamilton is bisected by the Waikato, the country's longest river, and there are excellent residential and recreational facilities in the area. Other major towns include Palmerston North, New Plymouth, Gisborne, Napier and Hastings. Rotorua is well known for thermal activities and as a Maori tourist centre.

The South Island is much more mountainous with the Southern Alps including soaring Mt Cook, Fiordland National Park and the Kaikoura Range. On the southern side of the island are the Canterbury Plains, centre of extensive sheep farming, and nearby is the garden city of Christchurch (population 307,000) which is claimed to be the most English municipality in the whole of New Zealand. Other towns of importance include Dunedin (over 100,000 inhabitants) a centre of education, Nelson, Invercargill and Queenstown.

In many ways New Zealand has much in common with Britain, but with a more temperate climate, perhaps better scenery, and plenty of space for living and enjoyment. The much more relaxed and casual way of life, and all the outdoor sports facilities, make New Zealand a wonderful country in which to raise a family.

Political stability

New Zealand has a long history of political stability. The National Party (currently in coalition with the minority New Zealand First Party) was led by Jim Bolger for nine years until the end of 1997, when Mrs Jenny Shipley became the country's first woman Prime Minister, after having served as Social Welfare Minister.

New Zealand is a non-nuclear nation.

Economy

The economy of New Zealand was badly affected when the UK entered the European Community and ceased to be a major market for agricultural exports. New markets had to be found in Australia, the Far East and America. This has been successfully achieved to a large extent and export diversification covering manufactured goods, forestry products, fishing and horticulture have helped to solve some of the problems. The fall in the exchange rate of the New Zealand dollar against the pound sterling and certain other currencies is encouraging overseas tourists from Europe and the Far East who find the vast range of natural attributes very attractive.

Unemployment figures for last year were around 7 per cent. Inflation is just under one per cent.

Taxation

Income is taxed under a Pay as you Earn (PAYE) system at rates ranging from 21.5 per cent to 33 per cent, after certain tax free allowances. A double taxation agreement exists between New Zealand and the UK. Non-residents are only assessable for New Zealand tax on income with a source in New Zealand.

A Goods and Services Tax (GST) at 12.5 per cent is levied on all purchases, including new housing.

Cost of living

New Zealand is not considered an expensive country to reside in, and food and material goods are competitively priced. Numerous households have at least one car and many city dwellers have a second home in the country or by the sea. The rate of inflation is low and may fall still further, while the exchange rate of the New Zealand dollar against the pound sterling is predicted to begin to improve. Retail sales are rising.

Exchange rate

New Zealand dollars (NZ$) 2.95 = £1.

Exchange control

No restrictions on the import or export of money.

Language

English and Maori are the official languages. The Maori people were the original settlers and now form about 12 per cent of the total population.

Expatriate community

The vast majority of the population have family origins elsewhere, mainly Britain, but there are small groups from Holland and the Far East.

Security

New Zealand is located well away from known trouble spots.

Residence and work permits

The Government is actively seeking enterprising and skilled migrants who will help with the growth of the country. British qualified teachers are also urgently required.

Migrants wishing to settle permanently in New Zealand will find that the emphasis is on the skills they possess, their experience in their trade or profession, their ability to speak the English language and the likelihood of successful settlement in New Zealand. A points system is operated, with highest allocations going to those with excellent qualifications, substantial work experience, ages between 18 and 34 years, and an offer of employment. Substantial fees are payable with applications. The pass mark for the points system is calculated weekly and can be found on the New Zealand immigration service Web site: http://www.immigration.govt.nz. Business people who can provide an active contribution to the country with investment, experience, useful skills and are able to play an active role in setting up new enterprises, are encouraged under the migration policy. Points are granted on a sliding scale for substantial funds brought to New Zealand; business experience in and out of New Zealand; and their qualifications. Age is also taken into account with highest points granted to those between 25 and 34 years. Those over 65 years are not eligible.

The current annual migration programme is likely to be increased during 1999. Visas are not required by British Passport Holders for stays up to six months, for they are granted a visitor permit valid for six months on arrival. Stays may be extended to a maximum of nine months.

There is also a Working Holiday Scheme for young people aged between 18 and 30. Two thousand, two hundred and fifty of these visas are available each year for a fee of £65 each. Applicants can undertake casual or part-time work to help them with holiday expenses, for up to 12 months. On arrival in New Zealand they have to produce proof that they have a return travel ticket and a minimum of NZ$1,000 in funds per month for living expenses.

Personal effects

Goods that have been owned for at least 12 months can be imported as personal effects, without paying any duty.

Housing

A high proportion of families are buying or have bought their own home. Single storey houses (bungalows as we know them) are often on quite large plots and are often constructed of timber and brick. Terraced houses and low-rise flats are rarely found except in heavily populated cities such as Auckland. The demand for property is good and the average price for a family dwelling throughout New Zealand is around £50,000, ranging from about £80,000 in Auckland to about £31,000 in Dunedin. Mortgages can be arranged with various banks. Interest rates dropped during the last quarter of 1998 but are now around 6.5 per cent for floating rate loans and may increase by up to 1 per cent during 1999.

Where to live

The major cities of Auckland, Wellington and Hamilton have excellent residential facilities and schools. The rural and marine locations on the Coromandel Peninsula and the Bay of Islands area in the extreme north are among the many attractive locations in the North Island. In the South Island, Christchurch, the major centre of habitation, is close to sheep farming country, and there are also attractive towns at Invercargill, Dunedin and Nelson. Tourists, both local and international, are attracted to the Southern Alps, Mount Cook, the Glaciers and Milford Sound.

Average house prices in Greater Auckland are about £92,360. In Greater Wellington the figure is £63,000; in Hamilton it is £60,000 and in Christchurch it is around £56,600.

Education

Kindergarten or pre-school facilities are available in many locations for those of 3–5 years. At 6 years, children of New Zealand and Australian residents are entitled to free Primary School education. At 11 years they enter Intermediate classes. Secondary classes cater for ages 13 to 18 years. There are also fee-paying private schools and seven state-funded universities.

Communications

Air New Zealand and Qantas provide regular services to New Zealand via the USA, with a journey time of about 25 hours, plus the 'lost day' on crossing the international date line. Air New Zealand also offer a service via some South Pacific islands and another route is via Japan with Japanese Airlines. Britannia Airways offer reasonably priced charter flights and there are some attractive offers with 'Round the World' tickets. Internal domestic flights are available to many locations and road and rail services are good.

Recreation

Outdoor life is very attractive to New Zealanders who often spend their summer weekends and vacations by the sea or in the country. Sailing, fishing, horse-racing, hiking, cycling, cricket, rugby and golf are all enjoyed. Skiing and skating particularly in the South

Island are popular in winter. Clubs form an important part of the social life and there are theatres and cinemas (including open-air ones in the summer) in the larger townships. Barbecues provide a popular form of socialising. Television is popular, particularly local and international 'soaps'.

Driving

Short-term visitors can drive on their British licence or International Driving Permit. Permanent residents need to take a New Zealand driving test.

Health services

Good medical services are provided, but there are often long waiting lists at some hospitals. The public health system now imposes part charges for services, based in the main on income levels. A large proportion of the population is now covered to a certain extent by private health insurance.

Climate

A temperate climate prevails, which is warmer in the North Island, as it is nearer to the Equator. The South Island features glaciers and ice fields around the Southern Alps and tends to be cooler and has more rain. Strong winds are not uncommon. Average January temperature in Auckland is 23°, while the average in July is 15°.

SOUTH AFRICA

General information

Status

Republic

Capital

Pretoria (administrative)
Cape Town (legislative)

Area

1,184,825 sq km (457,345 sq miles)

Population

Approximately 30 million

Location

As the second largest country in southern Africa, South Africa occupies the southern tip of this continent, and is about five times larger than the UK. The long coast line borders both the Indian Ocean to the south and east and the Atlantic to the south west.

There is a wide variety of landscapes and geographical regions, including mountains over 8,000 feet high, and many attractive lakes and rivers.

Political stability

After years in the political wilderness because of worldwide resentment against apartheid, changes in political opinions have taken place and a new constitution has evolved that provides for a parliament accommodating whites, coloureds and Indians.

By 1991 all discriminatory legislation was officially abandoned and shortly afterwards South Africa was re-admitted to the Commonwealth and the Olympic Games following many years of exile.

After a general election held in April 1994, the Government of National Unity was set up with Nelson Mandela of the African National Congress as President. The other parties in the legislature include the National Party, the Pan Africanist Congress, Inkartha Freedom Party, the African Christian Democratic Party and the Freedom Front.

President Mandela retires during 1999 and the world waits with interest (and perhaps anxiety) to see how his successor, Thabo Mbeki, will handle the many problems that will confront him.

Security is still a problem in some areas, particularly where unemployment is high, but the authorities are trying hard to improve the situation.

Economy

South Africa is endowed with a wealth of natural resources with many minerals and some of the world's largest deposits of gold, diamonds and platinum. Vast areas of grassland and pasture support a thriving agricultural industry which ensures that the country is self-sufficient in food and there are large areas of forest which are commercially exploited. Manufacturing, too, is important, providing over 20 per cent of the gross domestic product, and vital export earnings. Tourism is another source of income and this is growing.

Unemployment is high, particularly among blacks. The cost of living is quite reasonable for people from Europe as the rand is still falling in value against international currencies.

Taxation

Those in employment pay income tax on a PAYE system. This is levied on a sliding scale, rising to a maximum of 45 per cent on incomes exceeding 100,000 rand per annum. Value Added Tax is payable on most goods and services apart from some basic food-stuffs. There is no capital gains tax. A donations tax is payable on property donated by South African individuals or companies at the rate of 25 per cent. On death an estate duty is payable amounting to 25 per cent of the dutiable amount of an estate, after allowing for an abatement of one million rand.

Exchange rate

Rand (R) 9.81 = £1.

Exchange control

South African exchange control does allow money brought into the country to be repatriated.

Language

English and Afrikaans are the official languages.

Expatriate community

Originally there were many white settlers from Holland, Germany and France. At a later stage numerous British settlers arrived followed by other people from Europe, including Belgium, Greece, Italy, Portugal, Scandinavia and Switzerland. Thus there is a wide variety of nationalities among the expatriate community.

Security

It is wise to take precautions in the home against theft, by installing suitable security systems. In some holiday resorts and big cities mugging and street crime are a problem. Vigorous steps are being taken by the authorities to reduce the level of crime.

Residence and work permits

All visitors must be in possession of a valid passport on entering South Africa, but British passport holders do not require a visa for temporary residence of up to three months. Thereafter they can apply for permission to stay for a further period to the Office of the Director General for Home Affairs.

Those who wish to work in South Africa can only be considered if they have a firm offer of employment compatible with their experience and qualifications.

The current immigration policy is felt to be too restrictive and consideration is being given to introducing a scheme, similar to that in Canada, which will select migrants by assessing the attributes they would bring to South Africa.

The 'Family Reunion Scheme' requires that the resident family members are either citizens of South Africa or permanent residents, and they also have to commit themselves to support the applicant(s) financially during their stay, or until they have secured employment. Retirees need to produce financial proof that they have sufficient pension and/or income from abroad to support themselves. Financially independent persons can apply for permanent residence if they can transfer to South Africa at least 1,500,000 rand, of which 700,000 rand has to be invested locally. Self-employed persons who wish to start their own businesses are also considered if they can prove that they have sufficient funds to support themselves and their family and transfer a sum of money prescribed by the Immigrants Selection Board as being sufficient to establish their business. Fees are charged to successful applicants for permanent residence and applications may take many weeks to process. The address of the South African Embassy in London is Trafalgar Square, WC2.

Where to live

South Africa is divided into nine provinces, namely Western Cape (main city Cape Town); Northern Cape (main towns Upington and Port Noloth); Eastern Cape (main cities Port Elizabeth and East London); Free State (main city Bloemfontein); North West (main town Kuruman); Kwazulu/Natal (main city Durban); Gauteng, where Pretoria and Johannesburg are situated; Eastern Transvaal (main town Middelburg) and Northern Province (main town Pietersburg).

Cape Town, the legislative capital is a city with a population of about 168,000. It stands against the backdrop of magnificent Table Mountain and has some fine examples of Cape Dutch architecture. The port is of great importance and there is a variety of modern shopping malls.

East London has a similarly sized population to Cape Town and is adjacent to long stretches of attractive coastline where many watersports can be enjoyed all the year round. There are some major industries and a variety of residential amenities.

Also in Eastern Cape is Port Elizabeth, with a population of over half a million people. Again, there are some fine beaches and leisure facilities. Major industries include car manufacture, footwear, food and confectionery.

Durban has a population of around 450,000 and is famed for its summer carnivals and beach activities. An abundance of hotels attract holiday visitors, and local industries include ship repairing; motor component manufacture and assembly; textiles; chemicals; and food.

Johannesburg is South Africa's largest city, with over one and a half million inhabitants. This inland city stands 6,000 feet above sea level and owes its origins to the discovery of gold. Laid out on a grid pattern, there are many high-rise office blocks and buildings set among parks and gardens and a multiplicity of entertainments and shops. The international Jan Smuts airport is 30 km from the city centre.

The administrative capital of Pretoria (population 823,000) lies 50 km north of Johannesburg. Easily accessible from Pretoria's commercial centre are rolling hills and much attractive countryside and there are several nature reserves in the vicinity. Residents and visitors have a choice of excellent shopping centres and many cultural pursuits.

Housing

As a result of the very favourable rate of exchange, the price of homes are generally well below those in the UK. For example, in a suburb of Cape Town three-bedroom houses with private garden, have been on the market at under £90,000; luxury three-bedroom flats with sea and mountain views, in a prime security block could be purchased for about £80,000 and in Eastern Cape, two- and four-bedroom apartments with patio and excellent views start at approximately £53,000. At Port Zimbali in the KwaZulu-Natal Province there are a series of new projects, while a family home in a good location at Berea, in the same Province, has been offered at just over £80,000. Mortgage interest rates are high. The residential market was sluggish in 1998 and average prices in some areas declined in real terms.

How to buy

Estate agents in South Africa are required by law to be registered with the Estate Agents Board and to take examinations. If you are seeking a home through an estate agent check if the firm is a member of a professional body, such as the Institute of Estate Agents of South Africa (address PO Box 315, Johannesburg 2000).

The purchase procedure involves payment of a deposit (generally 10 per cent of the purchase price) to the vendors estate agent, which is held in the agency's trust account, pending finalisation of the written deed of sale. This deed contains the contractual obligations of the buyer and the seller and takes about 8 to 12 weeks to finalise. Most property in South Africa has a freehold title and verbal agreements are not recognised. When the deed is signed by both parties it is submitted by the Conveyancing attorney to The Registrar of Deeds for recording. Transfer duty for a property purchased in an individual's name amounts to 1 per cent on the first 60,000 rand of the purchase price, plus 5 per cent on any amount between 60,001 and 250,000 rand and 8 per cent on amounts above the latter figure. Transfer costs amount to just under 1 per cent and have to be paid to the vendor's conveyancer.

As usual it is advisable to have the property surveyed (known as 'inspection' in South Africa) and this costs from about £50. Mortgage loans, usually known as 'bonds', are available through commercial banks and building societies, but interest rates are high at present, so if possible it is better to raise a loan in the UK.

Education

Education is compulsory between the ages of 6 and 18 years and standards are high in state schools, where education is free, although parents are normally expected to make voluntary contributions to school funds towards further recreational and other facilities. There are also some good private schools.

Communications

Most European airlines fly to South Africa, but the main carrier is South African Airways, who provide a daily flight from London and services from other airports. Charter flights are also available at discounted fares.

There are inland coach and rail services including the luxurious Blue Train which connects Pretoria and Cape Town. This is claimed to be a five-star hotel on wheels.

Driving

Driving is on the left-hand side of the road and standard international signs are used.

An international driving licence is acceptable, but migrants must obtain a South African driving licence within six months of taking up permanent residency.

Petrol costs approximately 35p per litre.

Health services

Standards of health care and facilities are good, but patients are expected to pay for consultations or treatment themselves. Thus health insurance is essential. BUPA, PPP, and Exeter Friendly Society all provide cover for members living in or visiting South Africa.

Recreation

There are plenty of opportunities and facilities for outdoor sports and the climate allows for year-round enjoyment of cricket, tennis, golf, swimming, football, athletics and other activities. There are opportunities for mountaineering, fishing, motor racing and scuba diving and there are a variety of national parks well worth exploring.

Timeshare property

The purchase of timesharing property is popular in South Africa and there are many interesting developments in various parts of the country. Buying a fortnight or a month of timeshare in one of these schemes might be quite an economic way of finding out

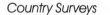

about living in the country from practical experience before committing the family to living there permanently.

Climate

Being located south of the equator, the seasons are, of course, the reverse of those in Europe. The climate is temperate and subtropical and the coastal belt normally enjoys warmer weather than the high veld.

THE UNITED STATES OF AMERICA (FLORIDA)

General information (USA)

Status

Federal Republic

Capital

Washington DC

Area

9,399,300 sq km (3,615,125 sq miles)

Population

250 million (approx)

General information (Florida)

Status

State

Capital

Tallahassee

Area

151,670 sq km (58,560 sq miles)

Population

13,000,000

Political stability

The USA is the richest and most powerful country in the world and is also regarded as the leader of the Western Alliance. Since the US is a federation, Florida is run with a certain degree of autonomy with regard to local issues. At national level, Florida is represented in both the House of Representatives and the Senate.

Economy

Cost of living

The cost of living is higher in the US than in the UK, but this is compensated for by much higher wages. Thus, when all factors are taken into account, living costs in real terms are reasonable.

Exchange rate

US dollars (US$) 1.59 = £1.

Location

Latitude 24°N; longitude 80°W.

The Sunshine State of Florida forms the south-east peninsula of mainland USA, separating the Atlantic Ocean from the Gulf of Mexico. Florida is on the same latitude as the Sahara. Winters are mild and generally dry, summers are hot and humid – with average temperatures above 80°F – and subject to short, sharp torrential storms. There is also a risk of hurricanes in the late summer and early autumn, but their paths are watched closely and there is a well-practised alert system.

Florida is one of the world's fastest-growing tourist destinations, and the resident population of 13 million is boosted each year by more than 43 million visitors, about a million of whom are from Britain.

Communications are excellent – flights from the UK are frequent and competitive, with a good choice of first-class, economy, excursion and discount fares.

The state is also developing quickly as a desirable area for international property purchase. The standard of living is high and housing represents good value for money. Land and property may be expensive near the fashionable coastal resorts and central-state attractions, but prices remain very attractive in less-developed areas.

In the 1960s, the Florida authorities granted permission for the Disney corporation to develop a 27,000-acre site near Orlando – 42 square miles, twice the size of Manhattan. Since the construction of Disney World, there has been an explosion of tourist attractions and theme parks unmatched anywhere else. Today there are more than 50 entertainments in addition to the Disney complexes themselves, which also include the EPCOT Centre, Disney-MGM and its latest attraction, Animal Kingdom. Universal Studios plan to double in size by the year 2000.

Like Orlando, southern Florida and the central Gulf coast have shared in the tourism and development boom. These areas, too, are expanding fast, particularly around Miami, the affluent cities of Palm Beach and Fort Lauderdale and the popular destinations of St Petersburg and Clearwater with their magnificent sands. Tampa is one of the largest ports in the USA and developers have been laying claim to the coastal strip north from this metropolitan bay to New Port Richey and south to Fort Myers and Naples.

Celebrated beaches and extravagant man-made amusements are by no means the only reasons for Florida's popularity. Nature has been kind here. There is extensive forest, as well as concrete jungle. Vegetation is lush and there are thousands of lakes, mangrove swamps and marshes. South and west of Miami are the fabulous Everglades, a national park of almost one-and-a-half million acres.

The Everglades are not a swamp, but a vast, shallow river, only inches deep, which rises and falls during the rainy and dry seasons and flows from Lake Okeechobee to the sea. There are hundreds of species of birds, mammals and fish and varieties of tropical and temperate plants and grasses. The ecological balance of the Everglades has been upset by the construction of canals and dykes, which have impeded the natural flow and water levels of the so-called 'River of Grass'. Conservationists fear that the delicate environment which took millions of years to evolve could soon cease to exist unless the balance is restored.

The coral and limestone islands of the Florida Keys derive their name from the Spanish word *cayo*. They stretch for 320 km into the Gulf of Mexico, many of them linked by the 42 bridges of the overseas highway. Diving is a popular activity, and conditions are superb, particularly off Key Largo, where there is a prolific coral reef.

Florida's natural beauty has become even more important in the campaign to repair an international reputation seriously damaged by attacks on tourists. Several overseas visitors have been murdered, and in a single year there were more than 12,000 crimes against tourists in greater Miami, mostly thefts from cars and muggings. The State has adopted a more aggressive policy on fighting crime and reported an increase in the number of tourists in 1996 to more than 43 million. The British Foreign Office has issued guidelines for visitors to Florida.

While emphasising that most people encounter no difficulties, the Foreign Office reminds visitors to be vigilant about their personal security and advises:

☐ Avoid walking in obviously run-down areas.
☐ Do not wear ostentatious jewellery.
☐ If arriving at night, take a taxi to your hotel and collect your hire car the next day.
☐ Drive on main highways and use well-lit car-parks.
☐ Don't stop if your car is bumped from behind. Instead, indicate to the other driver to follow you to the nearest public area and call for police assistance.
☐ Don't sleep in your car, on the roadside or in rest areas.

The Florida authorities provide advice on routes to take and the locations of guarded rest areas – freephone 1 800 342 7768. The

Foreign Office travel information service can be contacted on 0171 270 4129. Hire cars in Florida are no longer allowed to carry any mark, sticker, or other feature to show that they are rental vehicles.

Buying a property

Property transactions in Florida, and the professionals involved in them, are subject to state laws and the code of practice of the Florida Real Estate Commission. Procedures are very different from those in the UK and careful planning is required to ensure a satisfactory purchase.

Basic rules

The following principles should be rigorously applied. Building standards are high in Florida and most builders, developers and agents are thoroughly reputable, but check their credentials and make sure they are licensed.

Do not buy a property unseen. Visit the house or development personally. When building work is finished, make sure all is in order and to specification.

Refuse to sign a contract before you and your legal and financial advisers have studied it carefully. Do not rush your decision. Once signed, the contract is binding on both parties, so ensure it contains all the protection you need.

Do not hand over any money directly to a vendor, builder or developer. Instead, pay your deposit into a secure escrow (third-party) account, usually with a lawyer or title company. Shop around for finance. Interest rates and deposits required can vary from lender to lender.

Identify the total cost, including the fees and taxes payable on completion. Negotiate which of these 'closing costs' will be paid by the vendor and which will be your responsibility. Confirm what is included in the price – furniture and fittings, swimming pool, for example.

If you intend to rent out your Florida property – and strict immigration laws could limit the time you spend there yourself – check existing and imminent regulations on short-term lets, which are prohibited or severely restricted in many parts of the state.

If you are buying a business in conjunction with a visa application, make sure before you commit yourself that the enterprise fulfils immigration requirements.

The real estate broker

Real estate brokers in Florida must be licensed by the state and can lose their licence if they contravene the regulations. The Florida Real Estate Commission administers a compensation fund for buyers who suffer losses from unprofessionalism by licensed brokers. If you agree to do without a broker in return for a discount on the purchase price, you will be forfeiting this protection.

Although brokers are legally obliged to act fairly to all parties, remember that when they are employed by the vendor, they are expected to obtain the highest price possible. You may choose to hire a separate buyer's broker to look after your interests and to secure the best price and terms available. In this case you will pay his or her commission. Brokers must disclose in writing which party they are representing.

Florida law relating to brokers was amended in October, 1997. The changes defined four types of brokers and abolished the legal status of the _dual agent broker_, who had previously been able to work for both the buyer and the seller.

The _single agent_ represents the buyer or the seller, but cannot represent both in the same transaction. The single agent's responsibilities are:

- [ ] honest and fair dealing;
- [ ] loyalty;
- [ ] confidentiality;
- [ ] obedience;
- [ ] full disclosure;
- [ ] accounting for all funds;
- [ ] skill, care and diligence;
- [ ] presenting all offers and counter offers in a timely manner.

The _transaction broker_ offers limited representation to a buyer, a seller or both in a real estate transaction, but does not act as a single agent or trustee. The responsibilities include:

☐ honest and fair dealing;
☐ limited confidentiality, unless waived in writing;
☐ accounting for all funds;
☐ skill, care and diligence;
☐ disclosure of all known facts that materially affect the value of residential property;
☐ presenting all offers and counter offers in a timely manner, unless previously directed otherwise in writing;
☐ any additional duties entered into by written agreement.

The *single agent with authority to transition to transaction broker*. If agreed by the buyer and the seller, a single agent may act as a transaction broker to sell an in-house property. An agreement must be signed or initialed.

The *non-representative* broker has a duty of honesty and fair dealing and the duty to use skill, care and diligence in a transaction. A non-representative licensee does not represent the buyer or the seller in a transaction.

Insist that the broker or agent shows you a selection of houses and developments. There is a wide choice in Florida, with no shortage of new property. Compare prices and quality and check what other development plans exist in the neighbourhood.

The broker should assist you throughout the transaction, keeping an eye on the progress of building work, inspecting the property when it is finished, attending the closing meeting with you or on your behalf, and helping with your mortgage, insurance, taxation, visas and even the connection of electricity and water supplies.

The contract

The contract sets out the details and conditions of the purchase. Have it checked by a lawyer who is experienced in Florida property transactions and make sure you understand it fully before you sign. It will state the purchase price, terms for payment, known restrictions and easements affecting the use and enjoyment of the property and the closing date when deeds and money will be exchanged.

The contract will also state how the closing costs are to be divided between the buyer and seller. This is subject to negotiation and there are no fixed rules. For example, you can negotiate that the vendor will pay for the title search. Other financial matters to be agreed include an adjustment for annual bills, such as property tax and insurance.

It is important that the contract contains all the conditions and clauses to guarantee your full protection. In particular, you should make sure you will have clear title to the property and the right to a refund of your deposit if your mortgage application – or the mortgage terms you require – are refused. These details, therefore, must all be included in the contract.

You should be similarly protected if the vendor fails to fulfil any condition of the contract or if further restrictions become known (regarding short-term lets, for example). The contract should clearly state what land, buildings, fittings and furniture are included and whether the purchase depends on other matters, such as the successful sale of another property or the structural soundness of the house and its freedom from termite infestation. The Florida Bar, which regulates lawyers, and the Florida Association of Realtors, have an approved set of residential and commercial real estate contracts for your use.

Finance

Banks in Florida are becoming increasingly cautious, particularly about loans to non-resident aliens, and often require deposits of 30 per cent or more. You will have to make an initial down payment, known as earnest money, when you sign the contract and pay the balance of the deposit when the purchase is completed.

In deciding how much you can afford to pay for your property, also allow for your closing costs, including legal and mortgage fees, and your regular expenses – monthly mortgage repayments, property taxes, insurance, management fees, utilities and mainte-nance costs. Repayments on property loans (including any in the UK) should not exceed 28 per cent of your gross monthly income.

The bank will employ an agency to check your credit worthiness. Enquiries will be exhaustive. You will need to prove your financial status by showing evidence of your current and last two years' salaries, or balance sheets and tax returns if self-employed, and your prospects of future employment. The bank will want to see recent credit card and UK bank statements and will require evidence that you have fulfilled your mortgage and other loan commitments in Britain and can meet the costs of purchase.

Shop around to compare the loans, interest rates and loan terms on offer. There are variable and fixed rates, and a mortgage broker will advise you on your particular requirements and circumstances. Find out if there are prepayment penalties or limitations of your right to sell without the lender's consent.

You can choose to pay 'loan discount points' – a point being equal to 1 per cent of the sum you are borrowing. This one-off payment will serve to bring down the overall rate of interest and you need to calculate the long-term saving it affords.

Lenders vary in the fees they charge and the services they require in making the loan, services for which you will have to pay. Lenders will want mortgage insurance against payment default, life and disability insurance and hazard insurance against events such as fire and storms.

US law entitles property buyers to receive a 'good faith estimate' when they apply for a loan. It lists the likely costs of obtaining a mortgage and closing the transaction. These expenses (some of which may be met by the vendor) will include:

- [ ] administration and legal fees;
- [ ] brokers' commission;
- [ ] lender's fees;
- [ ] loan discount points;
- [ ] fee for your credit report;
- [ ] mortgage and hazard insurance;
- [ ] property valuation (not a structural survey);
- [ ] termite inspection;
- [ ] survey of boundaries;
- [ ] title examination and insurance;
- [ ] the closing fee;
- [ ] fees for recording the deed and mortgage;
- [ ] local, county and state taxes;
- [ ] balance of the deposit;
- [ ] initial mortgage repayment.

The lender must make it clear if he or she requires a particular attorney, title company, title insurance company or other closing agency.

Before deciding on your loan, therefore, shop around not only for the mortgage itself but also for the most competitive closing services and costs. Since you must pay these fees on the day of closing, negotiate well in advance with the vendor, the lender and other agencies involved.

Bank accounts

You should open a US bank account and deposit enough money to meet the closing costs. Allow plenty of time for the transfer of the funds. The closing costs will also include a sum to be deposited in an escrow account to cover property taxes and insurance. From then on, you will pay in a monthly amount for these with your mortgage repayments.

To protect your credit rating, make sure your mortgage and other bills are paid on time and keep enough in the account to meet unforeseen expenses. Your homeowner's insurance should cover the building and outbuildings, contents and third-party liability and should provide cover even when the property is unoccupied.

Some bills already paid by the vendor will overlap into the period when he or she is no longer the owner. Similarly, some of the bills you are going to receive will apply to the time before you took possession. The amount you owe each other will be worked out proportionately and settled at completion.

Property taxes, for example, are usually paid annually. Statements are sent out on 1 November, based on the value of the property the previous January. There is a small discount for prompt payment.

Condominiums

The condominium is a special legal concept, similar to the French system of *co-propriété*. The development is divided into individual apartments or houses. Buyers own their unit outright as well as a share of the buildings and land, and receive a recordable deed as proof of ownership.

The construction and management of condominiums and the conditions for their use and enjoyment are strictly controlled. They are managed by an association of owners, with an elected board, and each owner contributes towards the annual maintenance budget. Under Florida law, a document outlining the terms must be presented to the buyer before completion. This is called a prospectus.

This method of purchase has a number of advantages. If you are unable to occupy your Florida property permanently there are obvious benefits in terms of security and maintenance, and you may be able to let your unit. The development could have its own leisure facilities, such as a swimming pool and tennis courts. On the other hand, you will not have complete control over the running of the property; the board of management may reach decisions with which you disagree; and there could be restrictions on your use and enjoyment of the property.

New property

When a new house has been finished, you or your representative will be required to make a thorough examination of it to check the work has been carried out exactly as you wished. You should note everything you would like the builder to make good.

Make sure all the building costs have been paid, and that the contract relating to your individual construction and purchase has been approved by your lawyer. When you are satisfied that everything is in order, completion can take place. Failure to obtain a contractor's final affidavit of no liens could result in double payments for construction costs.

Title

Title search in Florida is done by a title company or an attorney, who will examine the public records or the 'abstract' (legal documents relating to the property) to confirm that the seller is the legal owner and there are no title defects, restrictions or easements.

Your lender will insist you buy title insurance as protection against any future claim on the title from a third party. This insurance will protect only the lender, however, and you should also take out an *owner's* title insurance policy.

Closing

The completion of the transaction – known as closing or settlement – will be co-ordinated by the title company, the lending institution, your mortgage broker, real estate broker and lawyer. You may ask for your lawyer to accompany you to check all the details. When clear title has been established, you can assume ownership of the property and pay the closing costs. If you cannot attend the closing meeting in person, you may be represented by your lawyer or broker. In this case, you will be sent the documents to study, sign and return, and you should consult a lawyer with specialist knowledge and experience.

In addition to the earlier good-faith estimate, you are entitled, one day before closing, to see the settlement statement, which lists the services you are receiving, their costs and the money to be exchanged between buyer and seller.

The statement is explained at the closing meeting and your deed and mortgage will be recorded at the county courthouse. The documents can then be handed over to you and the vendor and other parties involved can receive the money and fees they are due. The deal is complete.

Rental

If you wish to let your property, especially on a short-term basis, make sure before you sign the initial purchase contract that you will be allowed to do so. Many local authorities in Florida limit or prohibit property rentals for periods of less than one or even three months.

You must have a licence and a licence number as well as a US taxpayer identification number (or Social Security number if you qualify for one). You must charge your guests a sales tax on every short-term rental. This has to be paid monthly to the state and, in some areas, to the county as well. It applies even if the rental is paid overseas. If you fail to charge and pay the tax you could face harsh penalties.

Tax

British nationals who spend 183 days or more in a calendar year or 122 days in each of three consecutive years in Florida may be deemed resident in the USA for tax purposes. Otherwise, they are classed as non-resident aliens and will be taxed on income arising in the USA, including income from the rental of property. There is also a personal property tax, called a tangible tax, which is based on the value of furniture and household goods in rental properties.

The US tax year is from 1 January to 31 December. Annual income must be declared by 15 June of the following year. You may apply annually for a reduction in tax payable by offsetting various expenses against your rental income. These include mortgage interest, the costs of maintenance and repairs, management fees, property taxes, insurance and an allowance for depreciation. If your allowances and deductions are greater than your income, you can carry forward the difference to offset future income.

A husband and wife must complete separate tax returns, entering on each form 50 per cent of the rental income from a jointly owned property and 50 per cent of the appropriate allowances.

A double tax treaty exists between the UK and the USA. Tax paid by non-resident aliens on US property rentals may be credited against their British tax liability.

Non-resident aliens selling property in Florida will be taxed on their profit. The buyer must withhold 10 per cent of the purchase price and pay it to the US Revenue. If the gain being made is less than 10 per cent, application can be made for a smaller sum to be withheld.

Gift and inheritance tax

If you buy your Florida property in joint ownership, you should take specialist legal advice on the gift and inheritance tax consequences. Tax on the gifting of property is charged at gradual rates after an exemption allowance and inheritance taxes are also liable on property owned by non-resident aliens in the USA.

Visas and residence

The USA has strict immigration laws and you should ensure you are eligible for the visa you require before committing yourself to buying a property or business in Florida. Immigration experts such as Ira Levy, a former US consular officer and now a visa consultant based in London, and James R LaVigne, a US attorney and member of the American Immigration Lawyers' Association, can help you to select and apply for the most appropriate visa.

In particular, you must confirm that the business you are buying fulfils immigration requirements. Purchase funds for a business can be put into an escrow account with a firm of lawyers while you wait for your visa to be approved. This will protect money on deposit, should the US Embassy fail to approve an investment as qualification for a visa. Laws passed in 1996 have introduced tighter controls on the entry and departure of aliens, and new penalties on people who overstay their visas.

Permanent residence

Permanent residence (the 'green card' or immigration visa) can be obtained through the sponsorship of a close family member who is a US citizen or permanent resident. However, in many cases there are long waiting periods.

It is also possible to secure the green card through an offer of employment. The US employer must file a petition with the immigration authorities and will normally need a 'Labor Certification' indicating that no American worker was available to fill the position.

Professionals with a further degree or exceptional ability in the arts, science or business are eligible, and the 'Labor Certification' and job offer requirements may be waived in the national interest.

The 'Labor Certification' is not required for certain priority workers – individuals with 'extraordinary ability' in science, the arts, education, business or athletics, 'outstanding' professors and researchers and executives and managers of international companies. Various other professional, skilled and non-skilled workers might also qualify for employment-based permanent residence.

The green card may be acquired through an investment of at least $1 million in a new business ($500,000 in a rural or high unemployment area). The enterprise must provide at least 10 full-time jobs for American workers. It can be newly created, or can involve the reorganisation or expansion of an existing business or the rescue of an ailing enterprise. Green cards may also be available for intra-company transferees.

Temporary residence

British visitors wishing to spend up to 90 days in the USA do not need a visa. The *B-2 visa* (B-1 for business trips) will permit stays of up to six months at a time. Holders must have enough money to fund their visit, and their permanent residence must remain outside the USA. This can be a relative's or a friend's house and not necessarily one they own themselves. The B-2 visa is for pleasure only, and the holder is not allowed to work in the USA.

The B-2 visa should not be used for regular visits of six months with only a brief absence from the USA in between. Unless there is a substantial interval between visits, immigration officials could refuse admission or extension of the visa on the grounds that the holder has abandoned overseas residence.

There are, however, a number of temporary (non-immigrant) work visas which permit extended stays in the USA.

E-1 (Treaty Trader) and E-2 (Treaty Investor) visas

These visas require the establishment or purchase of a business in the USA and are available to citizens of countries which have a trade or investment treaty with the USA. These citizens can be the owners of the business, or executives, managers or other essentially skilled employees.

The E-1 and E-2 visas are often appropriate for small- and medium-sized enterprises. With extensions, there is no maximum limit on the overall stay in the USA.

In the case of the E-1 visa, 'substantial and frequent trade' in goods or services must exist between the US company and the applicant's own country before the visa application is made.

The E-2 visa requires an investment in a new or existing business in the USA, creating jobs for Americans. The investment must meet a number of stringent tests. No minimum investment is specified, although in practice most are of $100,000 or more. The investor should own at least 50 per cent of the business and be involved in its development and direction – even if there is a partner or manager. On this basis, visas can be renewed as long as the business continues.

Because of the treaty between the United States and the United Kingdom, only British passport holders who are inhabitants of the British Isles and Europe may qualify for an E-1 or E-2 visa. The Embassy no longer registers companies, but requires that a complete visa package be submitted to determine if the company and the individual visa applicant qualify for an E visa. It is taking between two and four weeks to adjudicate initial E-1 or E-2 company registrations and qualifications.

L-1 (Intracompany Transferee) and H-1B (Temporary Worker) visas

The L-1 and H-1B visas require a job offer, and the Immigration and Naturalisation Service must approve a petition filed by the US employer. Unlike the E-visas, the L-1 and H-1B do not depend on the nationality of the applicant.

The L-1 visa is available to executives, managers or employees with 'specialised knowledge', who are employed by foreign companies with a parent, subsidiary, branch or affiliate in the USA. The applicant must have been employed by the company outside the USA for one of the previous three years.

The L-1 visa permits a maximum stay of seven years for executives and managers and five years for employees with 'specialised knowledge'. As an alternative to an L-1 visa, a foreign company which has had a US subsidiary for more than one year may elect to transfer the employee to the US under the employment based-1 category (EB-1). This can then be the basis for an application for permanent residence (green card). The H-1B visa is for university graduates and other professionally qualified employees being posted to a job in the USA. The one-year previous employment rule does not apply. The maximum stay for an H-1B visa is six years.

New legislation

In September 1996, the United States Congress passed, and the President signed, an Immigration Reform Act which relates to the inspection, apprehension, detention, adjudication and removal of inadmissible and deportable aliens. It also provided new penalties for two categories of aliens who are, or have been, unlawfully present in the United States.

Although the 1996 amendments did not make any substantial changes to non-immigrant work visas and employment-based visas, they did impose new penalties and deportation for people who overstay their visas. The 1996 Immigration Reform Law provides for a more stringent record of the entry and departure of every alien. Under the terms of the Act, people who overstay their visa may be barred from returning to the United States for three years. In certain circumstances an overstay of more than 180 days may result in a 10-year ban. Offenders may not be eligible to extend their stay or to change their status, and may be unable to obtain a new visa except in their country of nationality.

Part Five:

Appendices

1 Telephoning Around the World

In many countries around the world it is possible to dial direct to any number in another country. The necessary codes for dialling from and to some of the most popular overseas locations are listed below. The time differences, plus or minus GMT, are also given to help you avoid phoning friends at inappropriate day or night hours! BT (British Telecom) operates a useful Chargecard Service, which makes it possible to make cashless calls throughout the UK and to ring UK numbers from over 120 countries abroad. A statement of BT Chargecard calls made is rendered with the quarterly bill, showing the time, date, duration, cost and number dialled for each call. Each cardholder has an individual PIN number for security. Furthermore, it is possible to dial direct to a British Telecom international operator, thus avoiding any possible language problems. For more BT information telephone 0800 345 144 or visit their Web site at www.bt.com/services.

There are other card service organisations but costs are high compared with the pre-payment organisations. Numerous schemes of this type have been established recently and huge savings on phone costs can be achieved by using their services. These generally require a deposit of between £20 and £50 towards the cost of future calls. Each subscriber has a Freephone number and a personal PIN number that gives access to the service. On initiating a call the client is advised of the amount currently standing to their credit and after completing the call it is possible to ascertain immediately the cost of the call.

Many of the telephone services in the larger countries such as the United States, Australia and New Zealand have telephone organisations that make occasional special offers for overseas call in off-peak periods, such as only £10 for a call of any time-length, so it is well worth watching out for these, which are often advertised in local papers.

Mobile phones are of course another method of keeping in touch with friends, family and business and the distances now available with these machines are impressive.

	Code for UK	Code from UK	Time difference Hours +/– GMT
Andorra	00 44	00 376	+ 1
Australia	001 144	00 61	+ 8 to 10
Austria	00 44	00 43	+ 1
Canada	011 44	00 1	– 3 to –8
Cyprus	00 44	00 357	+ 2
France	00 44	00 33	+ 1
Germany	00 44	00 49	+ 1
Gibraltar	00 44	00 350	+ 1
Greece	00 44	00 30	+ 2
Ireland	00 44	00 353	Nil
Israel	00 44	00 972	+ 2
Italy	00 44	00 39	+ 1
Madeira	00 44	00 35191	Nil
Malta	0 44	00 356	+ 1
New Zealand	00 09	00 64	+ 12
Portugal	00 44	00 351	+1, –1
South Africa	09 44	00 27	+ 2
Spain	07* 44	00 34	+ 1
Switzerland	00 44	00 41	+ 1
Turkey	9* 944	00 90	+ 2
United States	011 44	00 1	– 5 to –10

* Wait for the second dialling tone.

2 Radio and Television

Many of those living abroad will find the programmes provided by the BBC a great help in keeping in touch with events at home, and indeed in many other parts of the world. The BBC World Service has been established for many years and is renowned as a source of reliable information transmitted 24 hours a day throughout the year.

The very useful monthly publication *On Air* is the Corporation's international programme guide for the World Service. It can be obtained by postal subscription at £24 a year from BBC World Service, PO Box 765, Bush House, Strand, London WC2B 4PH. Copies are also often available for reading at British Consulates abroad.

The radio programmes include hourly news bulletins, as well as covering current affairs, arts, business and finance, classical music, development and environment, drama and reading. In addition there are educational programmes, which offer data on a wide range of subjects. Programmes produced in many of the 44 languages are also broadcast by the BBC.

BBC Prime Television in Europe is a 24-hour TV entertainment channel for viewers across Europe. It features drama, films, documentaries and children's programmes. It is widely available via cable and distributed in Europe by selected organisations.

The BBC Learning Zone transmits educational TV programmes overnight and includes a new Learning English programme to assist children and adults to learn the language in a stimulating manner.

BBC World Television combines news reporting with premier current affairs programmes and documentaries. A 24-hour international news and information channel is another feature.

Local cable operators or distributors may be able to supply these programmes. For more information about the BBC overseas contact the Web site: www.bbcworld.com.

It is possible to listen to the World Service via the Internet. The World Service home page is on <http://www.bbc.co.uk/world-service/> and the short wave frequency pages are on <http://www.bbc.co.uk/world service/freq>.

In much of Western Europe it may be possible to hear the BBC World Service on medium wave (648 kHz), or BBC Radio 4 on long wave (198 kHz). In south-eastern Europe and the Middle East the World Service is also broadcast on medium wave 1323 kHz.

Another source of English language programmes is Voice of America. This station can be received on a number of frequencies and broadcasts news and feature programmes with a US bias. Frequency charts and programmes can be obtained from Voice of America, on the Internet.

Watching foreign television can also be a considerable aid to learning a local language. Constant repetition of certain words in programmes or advertisements can finally lodge vocabulary in the memory of the most hopeless linguist.

3 International Lawyers

There are a number of lawyers with experience in handling the sale of overseas properties who have offices in London and other cities. They can help to ensure that a proper, unencumbered title is obtained to villas and apartments purchased overseas, and help with foreign legal matters generally.

Their fees tend to be higher than for similar transactions in the UK, because of the technical work involved, but are normally a worthwhile expenditure.

A selection of these firms is given below:

Amhurst Brown Colombotti, 2 Duke Street, St James's, London SW1Y 6BJ (tel: 0171 930 2366; fax: 0171 930 2250).
(Specialists in Spain, Italy, France and Poland)

Baily Gibson, 5 Station Parade, Beaconsfield, Buckinghamshire HP9 2PG (tel: 01494 672661; fax: 01494 678493).
(Specialists in Spain)

Bennett & Co, 39a London Road, Alderley Edge, Cheshire SK9 7JT (tel: 01625 586937) and at 19/20 Grosvenor Street, London W1X 9FD.
(Specialists in Spain, France, Portugal, Greece, Cyprus, USA, Caribbean and Turkey)

Brooker Grindrod, Suite 3, Dudley House, High Street, Bracknell, Berkshire RG12 1LL (tel: 01344 56565).
(Specialists in Spain)

Carter Slater & Co, 41 Harborough Road, Kingsthorpe, Northampton NN2 7SH (tel: 01604 717505).
(Specialists in Spain, France, Cyprus and Portugal)

Cornish & Co, 1–7 Hainault Street, Ilford, Essex IG1 4EL (tel: 0181 478 3300).
(Specialists in Spain, Portugal, France, Cyprus, Italy, Gibraltar Malta, Greece and timeshares)

De Pinna, 35 Piccadilly, London W1V 0PJ (tel: 0171 208 2900; fax: 0171 208 0066).
(Specialists in France, Spain, Germany, Italy and Portugal)

Glaisyers Glickman, 559 Barlow Moor Road, Chorlton Cum Hardy, Manchester M21 8AN (tel: 0161 881 5371).
(Specialists in Spain)

Hedleys, 15 St Helen's Place, Bishopsgate, London EC3A 6DJ (tel: 0171 638 1001; fax: 0171 588 7547).
(Specialists in Portugal, Spain, Germany and France)

John Howell & Co, 17 Maiden Lane, Covent Garden, London WC2E 7NA (tel: 0171 420 0404; fax: 0171 836 3626).
(Specialists in Spain, France and Portugal) also European property centre, and estate agency for all Europe

Lavigne & Lane, PA, Attorneys at Law, 150 Minories, London EC3N 1LS (tel: 0171 264 2110).
(Specialists in Florida)

Leathes Prior, Solicitors & Notaries, 74 The Close, Norwich NR1 4DR (tel: 01603 610911; fax: 01603 610088).
(Specialists in France, Holland, Portugal, Spain and Italy; also timeshare. Notaries able to prepare foreign powers of attorney.)

Lita Gale, 43/5 Gower Street, London WC1E 6HH (tel: 0171 580 2066).
(Specialist in Spain and Portugal)

Neville de Rougemont, Suite C4, City Cloisters, 188–194 Old Street, London EC1V 9FR (tel: 0171 490 4656; fax: 0171 490 4417).
(Specialists in Portugal)

Sean O'Connor & Co, 4 River Walk, Tonbridge, Kent TN9 1DT (tel: 01732 365378; fax: 01732 360144).
(Specialists in France)

Justin Ryan William Oddy & Co, Rua 5 de Outubro 174, 8135 Almancil, Portugal (tel: 351 089-395556).
(Specialists in Portugal)

Pannone and Partners, 123 Deansgate, Manchester M3 2BU (tel: 0161 909 3000; fax: 0161 834 2067).
(Specialists in France and Spain)

Dr G Pazzi-Axworthy, Llys Eira, Birklands Lane, St Albans,
Hertfordshire AL1 1EQ (tel: 01727 823186).
(Specialist in Italian law)

Penningtons, Dashwood House, 69 Old Broad Street, London
EC2M 1PE (tel: 0171 457 3000).
(Specialist connections in Italy, France, Denmark, Holland, Germany,
Russian Federation/CIS, South Africa and Hong Kong)

Prettys, 25 Elm Street, Ipswich, Suffolk IP1 2AD (tel: 01473 232121).

Pritchard Englefield, 14 New Street, London EC2M 4TR
(tel: 0171 972 9720).
(Specialists in France and Germany)

Taylors Solicitors and Notaries Public, The Red Brick House,
28–32 Trippet Lane, Sheffield S1 4EL (tel: 0114 276 6767).
(Specialists in France)

Turkish Law Office, 93 Westway, London W12 0PU (tel: 0181 740 5581).

M Florez Valcarcel, 130 King Street, London W6 0QU (tel: 0181 741 4867;
fax: 0181 741 4867).
(Spanish Lawyer and Notary Public specialist in Spain)

John Venn & Sons, 95 Aldwych, London WC2B 4JF (tel: 0171 395 4300;
fax: 0171 395 4310).
(Specialists in Spain, Portugal, Italy, France and Switzerland)

4 **Further Reading**

A good selection of specialised books and magazines is now available and some of these are listed below.

GENERAL

Buying a Home Abroad by David Hampshire, 1998. Survival Books.

Finding Work Overseas by Mathew Cunningham. How to Books Ltd.

Good Non Retirement Guide by Rosemary Brown. Published annually. Kogan Page, London.

How to Get a Job in Europe by Mark Hempshell, 1998. How to Books Ltd.

How to Retire Abroad by Roger Jones, 1996. How to Books Ltd, Plymouth.

Living and Working in Europe by Cobbe & MacCarthaigh. Gill and Macmillan.

Private Villa Guide (homes to rent for vacations), published 6 times a year from 6th Floor, Berwick House, 35 Livery Street, Birmingham B3 2PB.

Sun, Sand and Cement by Cheryl Taylor. Rosters, 1 Hall Road, London NW8 9PN.

Working Abroad, the Daily Telegraph Guide by Godfrey Golzen. Published annually. Kogan Page, London.

AUSTRALIA

How to Live and Work in Australia by Laura Veltman, 6th edition 1997. How to Books Ltd.

Live and Work in Australia and New Zealand by Pybus. Vacation-Work.

Living and Working in Australia by Hampshire, 1998. Survival Books.

CANADA

Finding a Job in Canada by V Gerrard, 1996. How to Books Ltd.

Live and Work in Canada by Harper, 1992. Dawson.

Migrating to Canada by M J Bjarnason. How to Books Ltd.

FRANCE

At Home in France by Jane Hawking. Allegretto Publications.

Buying a Home in France by David Hampshire, 1996. Survival Books.

Buying and Selling Your Home in France by Henry Dyson. Longman, London.

Chez Nous – Privately Owned Holiday Accommodation in France. Annual. Chez Nous Advertising Services, Bridge Mills, Huddersfield Road, Holmfirth HD7 2TW, W Yorks.

French Leave '99. Private holiday homes to rent in France. French Leave, 2a Lambton Road, London SW20 0LR.

How to Rent and Buy Property in France by Clive Kristen. How to Books Ltd.

Kelly's Guide to Buying and Renovating a Property in France. Staveley & Kelly, London.

Live and Work in France by Pybus, 1998. Vocation Work.

Living and Working in France by Alan Hart, 1998. How to Books Ltd.

Living in France by Philip Holland. Robert Hale.

Setting Up in France by Laetitia de Warren and Catherine Nollet. Merehurst Ltd.

GERMANY

How to Live and Work in Germany by Christine Hall, 2nd edition. How to Books Ltd.

Live and Work in Germany by Pybus. Vacation-Work.

GREECE

How to Live and Work in Greece by P. Reynolds. How to Books Ltd.

IRELAND

Buying and Selling in Ireland – Guide to Your Home. Editor David Coylin. Published by B F Fox & Co.

ITALY

Buying a Home in Italy by Pybus and Robinson, 1998. Survival Books.

How to Live and Work in Italy by A Hinton. How to Books Ltd.

Living and Working in Italy by David Hampshire, 1999. Survival Books.

Rent and Buy Property in Italy by A Hinton. How to Books Ltd.

MALTA

Malta Fact File published by Cassar & Cooper (Real Estate) Ltd, PO Box 36, Tigne Sea Front, Sliema, Malta.

NEW ZEALAND

Finding a Job in New Zealand by Joy Muirhead. How to Books Ltd.

Live and Work in New Zealand by Harper, 1994. C Dawson.

Living and Working in New Zealand by Joy Muirhead, 1997. How to Books Ltd.

PORTUGAL

Buying Property in Portugal, Portuguese Chamber of Commerce, London.

How to Live and Work in Portugal by Sue Tyson-Ward. How to Books Ltd.

SPAIN

Buying a Home in Spain by David Hampshire. Survival Books.

Complete Guide to Buying a Property in Spain, 3rd edition. Property Search Spain, Sherraton House, Castle Park, Cambridge CB3 0AX.

Live and Work in Spain and Portugal by Pybus and Robinson, 1998. Vocation Work.

Living and Working in Spain by RAC Richards. How to Books.

Spanish Property Owners' Community Handbook by David Searl. Lookout Publications, Centro Idea, Ctra Mijas, km.3,6, 29650 Mijas, Malaga, Spain.

SWITZERLAND

Living and Working in Switzerland by David Hampshire, 1997. Survival Books.

UNITED STATES OF AMERICA

Buying a Home in Florida by David Hampshire. Survival Books.

Live and work in USA and Canada by Pybus. Vacation-Work.

Living and Working in America by David Hampshire. Survival Books.

TIMESHARING

Time Share – All You Need to Know by Mason. Robert Hale, London.

PERIODICALS

The American, a newspaper published in Britain for Americans living in the UK. Fortnightly, *The American*, 114–115 West Street, Farnham, Surrey.

Belle Cose, a quarterly magazine for Italian property. Brian A French Associates, 6 Fleet Road, Hampstead, London NW3 2QS.

Costa Blanca News, a weekly newspaper in English; Apartado 95, Benidorm, Alicante, Spain.

Costa del Sol News, weekly newspaper in English, 100 pesetas.

Cyprus Daily and *Cyprus Weekly*, English language newspapers. PO Box 1992, Nicosia, Cyprus.

Emigrate, a magazine for those planning to quit Great Britain. Published annually by Outbound Newspapers, 1 Commercial Road, Eastbourne BN21 3XQ.

Entertainer, the English language weekly in two editions for Andalucia and the Costa del Sol. Apartado 414, 04630 Garrucha, Almeira, Spain.

European Magazine East, monthly. Ctra Cadiz Rm 179, Ofc.7, Urb Casablanca, 29600 Marbella, Malaga, Spain.

Focus on France, quarterly magazine with properties for sale in France. Outbound Publishing, 1 Commercial Road, Eastbourne BN21 3XQ.

France Review, English language newspaper reporting on France. BP03, 47120 Villeneuve de Duras, France.

French Property News, monthly. 2a Lambton Road, London SW20 0LR. Web site: http://www.french-property-news.com.

Homes Overseas, a bi-monthly magazine in colour devoted to homes in Europe and further afield. Published by Blendon Communications Ltd, 46 Oxford Street, London W1N 9FJ.

Iberian Daily Sun, an English language daily newspaper; San Felia 25, Palma, Majorca, Spain.

International Express, a 64 page weekly newspaper containing articles and reports from the Daily Express and Express on Sunday. Sold from newstands in many parts of the world.

International Herald Tribune, an English language edition is produced in Paris and is available in many European countries, mainly at airports or railway bookshops. It tends to relate an American version of world news.

Island Sun, fortnightly newspaper for the Canary Islands. Eurocentre, 40/41 Playa del Ingles, Grand Canary.

Lookout, a general interest English language monthly magazine with regular features on property and procedures for living in Spain. Publisher's address: Centro Idea, Ctra de Mijas, km 3.6, 29650, Mijas, Málaga, Spain.

Mallorca Daily Bulletin, address as for *Iberian Daily Sun.*

Malta Property News, local information and details of property available for sale in Malta and Gozo. Published quarterly by Frank Salt Ltd, 2 Paceville Avenue, Paceville, Malta.

On Air, a monthly guide to BBC World Service radio and TV programmes Annual subscription £24. BBC World Service, Bush House, Strand, London WC2B 4PH.

The Reporter, monthly magazine in English for expatriates in Spain. Avenida de Suel 23, Pueblo Lopez, 29640 Fuengirola, Málaga, Spain.

Resident Abroad, a monthly illustrated magazine published by *Financial Times.* Of interest to all planning to work or retire overseas. Published monthly and obtainable from PO Box 461, Bromley, Kent BR2 9WP.

Sur in English, tabloid English language weekly newspaper serving Andalucia. Details from Avda Dr Maranon 48, 29009 Málaga, Spain. Web site: http://www.surinenglish.com.

Villas & ..., monthly glossy magazine for Spanish Costa del Sol properties. Centro Commercial Diana, Local 1–22, 29680 Estepona, Málaga, Spain.

Weekly Telegraph, a newspaper for expatriates which summarises news and features from the *Daily* and *Sunday Telegraph.* Subscription Services, PO Box 14, Romford RM3 8EQ.

World of Property Magazine. Published quarterly with editorial and classified property advertisements for nearly 20 countries. Outbound Publishing, 1 Commercial Road, Eastbourne BN21 3XQ.

5 Useful Addresses

American Embassy
Grosvenor Square, London W1A 2JB (tel: 0171 499 9000)
Andorran Delegation
63 Westover Road, London SW18 2RF (tel: 0181 874 4806)
Anglo-Portuguese Society
Canning House, 2 Belgrave Square, London SW1X 8PJ (tel: 0171 245 9738)
Association of Estate Agents in Malta
The Whispers, Ross Street, Sliema, Malta
Australian High Commission
Australia House, Strand, London WC2B 4LA (tel: 0171 887 5118)
Austrian Embassy and Consular Section
18 Belgrave Mews West, London SW1X 8PX (tel: 0171 235 3731)
Bank of England
Threadneedle Street, London EC2R 8AH
Blackstone Franks
Barbican House, 26–34 Old Street, London EC1V 9HL (tel: 0171 336 1000)
British Association of Removers Overseas
3 Churchill Court, 58 Station Road, North Harrow HA2 7SA
(tel: 0181 861 3331)
British Embassy in France
35 Rue du Faubourg St Honoré, 75383 Paris
British Embassy in Portugal
Rua S Domingos à Lapa 35–37, Lisbon, Portugal
British Embassy in Spain
Fernando El Santo 16, Madrid 4, Spain
BUPA International
Equity & Law House, 102 Queens Road, Brighton BN1 3XT
Canada Immigration & Visa Enquiries
38 Grosvenor Street, London W1X 0AA (no telephone enquiries)
Channel Islands
Guernsey States Office, St Peter Port, Guernsey; Jersey States Office,
Royal Square, St Helier, Jersey

Conti Financial Services (specialists in arranging overseas finance)
204 Church Road, Hove, Sussex BN3 2DJ
Corona Worldwide (The Women's Corona Society)
c/o Commonwealth Institute, Kensington High Street, London W8 6NQ
Cyprus High Commission
93 Park Street, London W1Y 4ET (tel: 0171 499 8272)
Cyprus Real Estate Agents Association
PO Box 1455, Nicosia, Cyprus
Department of Social Security
Information Division, Leaflets Unit, Block 4, Government Building,
Honeypot Lane, Stanmore HA7 1AY
Department of Social Security
Overseas Branch, Benton Park Road,
Newcastle upon Tyne NE98 1YX (tel: 0191 213 5000)
Europea – IMG Ltd
Provender Mill, Mill Bay Lane, Horsham, West Sussex RH12 1TQ
(tel: 01403 51884)
Exeter Friendly Society
Beach Hill House, Walnut Gardens, Exeter EX4 4DE
**Federation of Overseas Property Developers, Agents and Consultants
(FOPDAC)**
3rd Floor, 95 Aldwych, London WC2B 4JF
First National Trustee Co (FNTC)
International House, Castle Hill, Victoria Road, Douglas, Isle of Man
IM2 4RB (tel: 01624 630630)
French Chamber of Commerce in Great Britain
197 Knightsbridge, London SW7 (tel: 0171 304 4040)
French Embassy
58 Knightsbridge, London SW1X 7JT (tel: 0171 201 1000)
German Embassy
23 Belgrave Square, London SW1X 8PZ (tel: 0171 824 1300)
Gibraltar Information Bureau
4 Arundel Great Court, 179 Strand, London WC2R 3DT (tel: 0171 836 0777)
Goodhealth Worldwide Ltd
Millbay Lane, Horsham, West Sussex RH12 1TQ
Greek Consulate General
1a Holland Park, London W11 3TP (tel: 0171 221 6467)
Inland Revenue
For booklets: Public Enquiry Room, Inland Revenue, West Wing,
Somerset House, London WC2R 1LB

Inland Revenue
For payments of pensions or dividends overseas: Inspector of Foreign Dividends, Inland Revenue, Lynwood Road, Thames Ditton, Surrey KT7 0DP (tel: 0181 398 4242)
Interpares
Calle Olmos 19, Cerrado de Calderón, 29018 Málaga, Spain
Interval International
Coombe Hill House, Beverley Way, London SW20 0AR (tel: 0181 336 9300)
Irish Auctioneers and Valuers Institute
38 Merrion Square, Dublin 2, Eire (tel: 00353 1661 1794)
Irish Embassy
17 Grosvenor Place, London SW1X 7HR (tel: 0171 235 2171)
Isle of Man Government
Government House, Bucks Road, Douglas, Isle of Man
Israel, Embassy
2 Palace Green, London W8 (tel: 0171 957 9575)
Italian Consulate
38 Eaton Place, London SW1X 8AL (tel: 0171 235 9371)
Law Society
113 Chancery Lane, London WC2A 1PZ (tel: 0171 242 1222)
Ira H Levy, US Visa Consultants
27 York Street, London W1H 1PY (tel: 0171 224 3629)
McCarthy & Stone Overseas Ltd
26–32 Oxford Road, Bournemouth BH8 8EZ
Malta High Commission
36 Piccadilly, London W1 (tel: 0171 292 4800)
New Zealand High Commission
New Zealand House, Haymarket, London SW1Y 4TQ (tel: 0171 930 8422)
Portugal, Association of Foreign Property Owners in
Details from AFPOP, Apartado 728, 8500 Portimao, Portugal (tel: 010 351 82 458509)
Portuguese Consulate General
62 Brompton Road, London SW3 1BJ (tel: 0171 581 8722)
Private Patients Plan
PPP House, Upperton Road, Eastbourne BN21 1LH
Property Owners Club
Brittany Ferries, Plymouth (tel: 0990 143555)
Resort Condominiums Europe Ltd
Kettering Parkway, Kettering, Northamptonshire NN15 6EY (tel: 01536 310101)
Royal Institution of Chartered Surveyors
12 Great George Street, London SW1P 3AE (tel: 0171 222 7000)

South Africa, Institute of Estate Agents in
PO Box 315, Johannesburg 2000, Republic of South Africa
South African Embassy
South Africa House, Trafalgar Square, London WC2N (tel: 0171 930 4488)
Spanish Embassy
22 Manchester Square, London W1M 5AP (tel: 0171 486 8077)
Spanish National Tourist Office
57 St James's Street, London SW1A 1LD (tel: 0171 499 0901)
Swiss Embassy
16–18 Montagu Place, London W1H 2BQ (tel: 0171 723 0701)
Timeshare Council
23 Buckingham Gate, London SW1E 6LB (tel: 0171 821 8845)
Turkish Consulate General
Rutland Lodge, Rutland Gardens, London SW7 1BW (tel: 0171 589 0949)
Turkish Embassy
43 Belgrave Square, London SW1X 8PA (tel: 0171 393 0202)
Villa Owners Club Ltd
HPB House, Old Station Road, Newmarket CB8 8EH
Women's Corona Society
c/o Commonwealth Institute, High Street, London W8 (tel: 0171 610 4407).
Runs one-day courses for emigrants; has overseas branches in many
countries and provides a welcome link for newcomers.
WPA Health Insurance
Rivergate House, Blackbrook Park, Taunton, Somerset TA1 2PE
(tel: 01823 623330)

Index

Index of Advertisers

Visit Kogan Page on-line

Comprehensive information on
Kogan Page titles

Features include

- complete catalogue listings,
  including book reviews and
  descriptions

- special monthly promotions

- information on NEW titles and
  BESTSELLING titles

- a secure shopping basket facility
  for on-line ordering

PLUS everything you need to know about
KOGAN PAGE

http://www.kogan-page.co.uk